revisions: gender and sexuality in late modernity

revisions: gender and sexuality in late modernity

Lisa Adkins

Open University Press
Buckingham • Philadelphia

Open University Press
Celtic Court
22 Ballmoor
Buckingham
MK18 1XW

email: enquiries@openup.co.uk
world wide web: www.openup.co.uk

and
325 Chestnut Street
Philadelphia, PA 19106, USA

First Published 2002

A catalogue record of this book is available from the British Library

ISBN   0 335 20522 4 (pb)   0 335 20523 2 (hb)

Library of Congress Cataloging-in-Publication Data
Adkins, Lisa, 1966–
   Revisions : towards a sociology of gender and sexuality in late modernity / Lisa
   Adkins.
      p. cm.
   Includes bibliographical references and index.
   ISBN 0-335-20523-2 – ISBN 0-335-20522-4 (pbk.)
   1. Sex role.   2. Social mobility.   3. Feminism.   4. Sex role in the work
environment.   I. Title.

HQ1075 A24 2002
305.3–dc21

                                                                    2001056012

Typeset by Graphicraft Limited, Hong Kong
Printed in Great Britain by Biddles Limited, Guildford and King's Lynn

contents

acknowledgements

A number of people have been generous enough either to read through and provide comments on the different chapters in this book or to listen to various aspects of the ideas presented here at seminars and conferences. Of these I would particularly like to thank Alison Bashford, Anni Dugdale, Catherine Casey, Mary Evans, Brian Heaphy, Rosemary Hennessy, Margaret Jolly, Helen Keane, Scott Lash, Celia Lury, Katy Richmond, Brigid Rooney, Miri Song, Beverley Skeggs, Catherine Waldby, Valerie Walkerdine and Julian Wood for their enthusiastic engagement, encouragement and critical commentary on various aspects of my analysis.

Most of the writing for this book was completed while I was employed at the Australian National University and I would like to thank Frank Jones, formerly of the Sociology Program, at the Research School of Social Sciences, for his support of this project during my time there. The writing was completed in my new post in the Sociology Department at the University of Manchester and I would like to thank my new colleagues and especially Nikos Papastergiadis, Mike Savage and Beverley Skeggs (again) for their tremendous encouragement and support during this period and for making Manchester such a stimulating and exciting work environment. Thanks also to the Comings and Goings reading group for their amazing generosity.

A huge thanks also goes to Kirsten Farrell, Lyndal Kennedy, Helen Keane (again), Daniel Stoljar, Kim Curry, Rachelle Higgins, Susan Robertson, Kate Burton, Antonella Magnavacca, Nigel Carleton, Andy Bonny, Beverley Skeggs (once again), Mariam Fraser, Jeffrey Bruce, Antonietta, Marianne and Vince Vitellone for soccer, beers, laughs and friendship. I would also like to thank my parents – Doreen and Bob – and Ian and Isa for their ongoing support. Finally, my biggest thanks goes to Nicole Vitellone for her continuous engagement over a number of years with the ideas presented here and for her belief that I could see the project through to the end in the context of huge upheavals to our lives.

Parts of the material in this book have been published elsewhere and due thanks go to both The University of Chicago Press and Sage Publications Ltd for use of copyright material.

Parts of Chapter 3 'Feminization, Mobility and Cultural Economy' were originally published in *Signs: Journal of Women in Culture and Society* (2001) 26(3): 31–57 as 'Cultural Feminization: "Money, Sex and Power" for Women', Lisa Adkins, © 2001 by The University of Chicago. All rights reserved. Reprinted by permission of The University of Chicago Press.

The original version of Chapter 4 'Reflexivity and the Politics of Knowledge' was first published in Tim May (ed.) *Qualitative Research: Issues in International Practice* (2002) as 'Reflexivity and the Politics of Qualitative Research', Lisa Adkins, © Sage 2002, reprinted by permission of the Editor and Sage Publications Ltd.

An earlier version of Chapter 5 'Reflexivity, Risk and the (Neo Liberal) Politics of Sexuality' first published in *Body and Society* (2001) 7(1): 35–56 as 'Risk Culture, Self-Reflexivity and the Making of Sexual Hierarchies', Lisa Adkins, © Sage 2001, reprinted by permission of Sage Publications Ltd.

introduction

The themes of movement, flexibility and mobility occupy centre stage in much recent social and cultural theory and more substantive work in the social sciences. To give just a few examples, we find reference for instance to mobile or 'liquid modernity' (Bauman 2000); flexible citizenship (Ong 1999); flexible bodies (Martin 1994, 1997, 2000); flexible accumulation (Harvey 1989); travelling cultures (Clifford 1992, 1997); mobile objects (Lury 1997); mobile desire (Adkins 2000a); and to ideas that 'good' research in the social sciences requires '*flexible* structure[s] of interpretation' (Alvesson and Skoldberg 2000: 9, emphasis added). Indeed, we find arguments that the 'social' is now characterized by flows and mobilities and more particularly that the social is materially reconstructing from the 'social as society' to the 'social as mobilities' (Urry 2000: 2). As a consequence it is suggested that the discipline which held society as its key methodological focus – sociology – needs to reformulate its methods (Urry 2000: 18–19). Thus rather than on order, structure and stasis, sociology should focus on movement, mobility and contingency; and rather than on societies, sociologists should focus on the post societal flows and mobilities of images, information, knowledge, capital, money and people.

We can point towards a number of important grounds which suggest that this call for a reformulation of the methods of sociology makes sense. This is especially so in the context of the reconfigurations of time-space coordinates associated with globalizing processes, reconfigurations which Harvey (1989) has famously characterized as involving 'time-space compression'. Literal increases in travel (evidenced in the huge expansion of international tourism), the (relatively) footloose nature of capital, the emergence of electronic communication networks which allow for speeded up and spatially stretched out flows and exchanges of capital, information and knowledge, as well as transnational corporations, global media and global brands (see e.g. Lash and Urry 1994; Featherstone 1995; Morley and Robins 1995; Castells 1998; Franklin *et al.* 2000; Urry 2000) attest to such a reconstruction of time-space coordinates and thus appear to confirm the urgency with which the discipline of sociology needs to reformulate its rules of method.

In addition a number of key intellectual precedents can be pointed towards in support of a reformulation of the rules of sociological method, and in particular the move away from a sociology where 'the social' is imagined as relatively homogenous, bounded and reproduced in time-space. These include James Clifford's (1992, 1997) work on culture-as-travel which challenged the view that cultures are spatially bounded and fixed, and emphasized the *routed* rather than the rooted aspects of culture (see also Hall 1997a). In so doing Clifford thus highlighted how culture needs to be seen as less of a site dwelling and more like 'a hotel lobby, urban café, ship or bus' (Clifford 1997: 25). The need, he argued, is to consider circuits, not single places (1997: 37) to be able to do justice to the transnational forces that criss-cross the globe which are deterritorializing culture. The groundbreaking work on hybridity and diaspora by Stuart Hall (1990, 1997a, 1997b), Homi Bhabha (1990) and Paul Gilroy (1993) focusing on issues of movement, connection, place and identity formation also forms a key backdrop to this move, particularly in its fore-grounding of the hybrid and translated character of culture, experience and subjectivities. Such work challenged absolutist and bounded notions of culture and thus problematized easy distinctions of inside and outside, centre and periphery, home and travel.

While the recent foregrounding of mobilities in social and cultural theory can be linked to such works, these analyses nevertheless warn against universalistic understandings of such processes. Indeed they stress the signific-ance of recognizing the incomplete, uneven and often unpredictable character of processes of mobility and flow. This point has been underlined, for example, by studies of global culture, which have stressed its non-homogenizing and particularizing logic (see e.g. Appadurai 1993; Perry 1998; Franklin *et al.* 2000). What such works suggest is that mobility is complex in character, and in par-ticular, even if characterizable as a series of cross-cutting flows, the modern world should not necessarily be conceptualized as emptied out of coordinates of time-space, constructions of place, and axes of identity formation. As Clifford makes clear in his discussion of travelling cultures, understanding culture as such does not mean that all there is to culture is travelling, and that there are no locales or no homes (Clifford 1997: 36). Rather such an understanding suggests that the latter are being reworked and require reconceptualization. Dwelling, therefore, is 'no longer simply the ground from which traveling departs and to which it returns' (1997: 44). Mobilities may, in other words, provide a ground for the very reconfiguration of time, space, belongings, places and identities (Ong 1999; Ahmed 2000).

This book is about such processes of reconfiguration and rework-ing, especially as they apply to questions of sexuality and gender. However it is concerned with this process of reconfiguration in a very specific way. In particular, it explores this reconfiguration in the context of a 'social' characterized by both increasing mobility and increasing reflexivity. That is, and very broadly put, it seeks to explore the refashioning of gender and sexuality in the context of the social reconstituting as mobilities and in a context in which there is increasing reflection on – even critical consciousness about – the rules, expectations and norms of 'social' life, including those relating to sexuality and gender.[1] This focus on both mobility and reflexivity may at first strike as odd. This is especially so given that debates concerning the two tend not to articulate with each other and moreover, that notions of mobility and reflexivity appear to be tied to very different propositions regarding late modern societies. In particular, while the sociology of mobilities tends to disconnect in many important respects from traditional sociological models of society, especially in its emphasis on the social post society (or more precisely mobilities post society), the sociology of reflexivity (including theories of reflexive modernity and as it sometimes termed the reflexive modernization thesis) relies in some important respects on such models. Thus in the sociology of mobilities as articulated by Urry there is an attempt to break with the idea of the social modelled on ideas of structure, while theories of reflexive modernity are articulated in more traditional terms, and in particular, draw heavily on the language of structure and agency.

Despite these epistemological and methodological differences, nevertheless the debates concerning reflexivity and mobility share something fundamental. This is a substantive thesis of social change. In short, in both (although how this is conceived is rather different) it is argued that there is a declining significance of social structure for the organization of 'social' life. In theories of reflexive modernization this is conceptualized as increasing powers of agency vis-à-vis structure (or as it is sometimes put, the 'freeing' of agency from structure). It is the increasing powers of agency vis-à-vis structure which, for example, allow for increasing reflexivity in regard to the rules and norms of 'social' life. In the sociology of mobilities the decline of social structure is conceptualized not as a reformulation of the powers of agency vis-à-vis structure however, but as the undercutting of nationally based social structures (and hence the usefulness of structure–agency schemes) via post societal processes of flow, movement and contingent ordering (Urry 2000: 18). It is this shared theme of the decline of the significance of social structure with which this book is concerned. In particular it is concerned with processes of the reconfiguration of gender and sexuality in the context of the decline of the significance of social structure for the organization of the 'social', and interrogates processes of reconfiguration in the context of increased reflexivity and mobility.

This immediately, and again, may strike as odd. After all, if we were to accept certain sociological models of the social, a decline in the significance of 'social structure' would mean not a reconfiguration of gender and sexuality but their dispersal. This is because in certain sociological understandings gender and sexuality (especially sociological understandings of gender) have been understood to be both primarily socio-structurally organized and to be so at the level of specific societies. Expressions of this understanding are found, for example, in empirically based studies which seek to pinpoint the specifics of such structures via detailed comparisons or the organization of gender between and within different nation states, for instance comparative projects of the organization of gender within and between the different member states of the European Union. On this kind of model where gender and sexuality are conceived as a matter of social structure, a decline in the significance of social structure for 'social' organization would presumably therefore imply a decline in the significance of gender and sexuality as specific organizers and regulators of the social. Indeed in the literature on reflexive modernity precisely this kind of reasoning is followed. Thus the 'freeing' of agency from structure is understood by some to involve an undoing of what are often termed as 'traditional' rules, expectations and forms of authority associated with modernity, including those organized along axes of gender, class and status. For instance Ulrich Beck has commented 'people are being released from the constraints of gender . . . men and women are released from tradi-tional forms and ascribed roles' (1992: 135). Thus theories of reflexive modernity propose a detraditionalization of the social and, as a consequence, increasing individualization where rather than being a matter of social deter-mination, class, gender, sexuality – even life and death – are now a matter of individual decisions (Beck and Beck-Gernsheim 1996: 29). Theories of reflex-ive modernity propose not a reconfiguration of gender and sexuality in the context of increasing reflexivity but their dissolution.

Similarly, in terms of the sociology of mobilities, the idea of a reconfiguration of gender and sexuality in the context of a social reconstruct-ing as mobilities may not appear to make immediate sense. Once again the dominant understanding of gender and sexuality within sociology as socio-structurally constituted at the level of the nation states implies that a social materially reconfiguring as flows and contingent orderings would entail an undercutting and dispersal of gender and sexuality as a key axes of organiza-tion and regulation vis-à-vis the 'social'. However in the sociology of mobilities as articulated by Urry, although there is no mention of sexuality, we do find claims that gender is not exactly dispersed via the reconstruction of the social as mobilities, but that mobilities and flows may provide new grounds for its constitution. So for example in a further new 'rule' of sociological method, and drawing on the language of Clifford, Urry notes that sociolo-gists should now examine how class, gender, ethnicity and nationhood are 'constituted through powerful and intersecting temporal regimes and modes of dwelling and travelling' (2000: 18). The problem in this respect however is that in his analysis of mobilities Urry does not follow through on his own new rule. For example while throughout his text we find mention of new sources of difference and inequalities as well as exclusions in the context of the newly reconfigured 'social', there is no analysis of how such differences, inequalities and exclusions are constituted in the context of mobilities and flows; indeed they tend analytically speaking simply to be mapped on to a scheme of different criss-crossing mobilities. In short, no account is given of how differences, exclusions and inequalities are constituted post social structure.

A similar problem is also found in the literature on reflexive modernization. For instance, on the one hand the progressive freeing of agency from structure is understood to release people from the socio-structural traditions of modernity, including those of class, gender and sexuality. On the other hand reference is made to the continuing relevance of these categories, for example, as bases of identification, in the development of social bonds, and as sources of conflict and inequality (see e.g. Beck 1992). Moreover, they are understood as 'particularistic' 'ascribed' characteristics: 'race, skin color, gender, ethnicity, age, homosexuality, physical disabilities' (Beck 1992: 101). Indeed for Lash (1994) such particularistic, ascribed characteristics may determine current class positions in the context of reflexive modernity. Commenting on the emergence of a new lower class or underclass, for example, Lash suggests 'the personnel filling these class positions are typically determined by more particularistic, "ascribed" characteristics – by race, country of origin and gender' (1994: 134). But while both Lash and Beck understand such 'ascribed' characteristics to form the basis of new inequalities, conflicts, class formations and identities, neither pays attention to processes of ascription in relation to reflexivity. That is to say neither interrogate the ways in which reflexive modernity and its attendant processes – increases in reflexivity, individualization and detraditionalization – may be constitutive of processes of ascription and particularization and how these relate to new forms of identification, conflict and inequalities. In short, and much like the sociology of mobilities, little systematic attention is given to how these processes are working in the context of the decline of social structure.

It is this latter problematic which I aim to address in this book, in particular in regard to gender and sexuality. I do so in relation to three substantive areas: cultural economy (Chapter 3), the politics of knowledge in social research (Chapter 4), and the politics of sexuality 'post post AIDS' (Chapter 5). In so doing I question the commonly found thesis that processes of mobility and reflexivity are linked to – as indicated above – a straightforward dispersal, breakdown or undoing of sexuality and gender. However I do not argue that gender and sexuality are seamlessly reproduced in this context, for what is suggested in the chapters that follow is that reflexivity and mobility are a crucial ground for the reconfiguration of gender and sexuality. They are thus not best conceived simply as processes which break down gender and sexuality, for they are also central to new articulations of gender and sexuality.

In Chapter 3 this is illustrated via an extended discussion of cultural economy and gender. The economy is important for discussion as it has been located as a privileged site of both reflexivity and detraditionalization in relation to gender. This chapter draws attention to the ways in which this privileging of the economy as a site of reflexivity and detraditionalization rests on a specific line of reasoning whereby a form of mobility, specifically the transposition of a feminine habitus into the economic sphere of action, is understood to be key for these features of the economy. (I term this line of reasoning the cultural feminization thesis.) This latter understanding is widely associated with an increasing stylization or aestheticization of work linked to what some writers have termed the de-differentiation of culture and economy (Du Gay 1993). Crucial here is the argument found in the cultural feminization thesis that workers – both women and men (particularly in the service sectors of the economy) – are increasingly performing the aesthetics of femininity. It is this latter which is understood to be constitutive of increasing reflexivity and detraditionalization in relation to gender. In particular, rather than being a disadvantage, femininity is now a labour market resource (for both women and men) which is understood to denaturalize gender at work and undo the binaries (abstract/embodied, rational/irrational) which have been so central to techniques of gendering in the economic sphere.

While endorsing the view that specific processes of the denaturalization and desocialization of gender are taking place at work, the chapter nevertheless challenges the understanding that the breakdown of the masculine/feminine binary concerns the end of gender in relation to the economy. Thus this chapter points both to the ways in which gender in cultural economies has been established as mobile, fluid and indeterminate, and to the ways in which this mobility has provided the very grounds for the making of new differences. What is at issue here is therefore not conceived of as a 'feminization' of work and workers, but rather as mobility vis-à-vis gender performance at work, a mobility from which certain workers are excluded. Indeed it is shown that such mobility in regard to gender styles is a privileged identity position in late modernity from which there are some significant exclusions. Many women workers for instance are excluded from this position via a naturalization of femininity, that is, may be excluded from this position when femininity is made immanent. In short, this chapter suggests that gender is not simply undone by mobility, but that such fluidity provides a ground for new articulations of gender. The latter do not concern social and/or natural forms of determination, but rather articulations of gender involving positions of mobility and immanence in respect to cultural styles.

The privileging of a mobile identity position in late modernity is also made visible in Chapter 4 where attention turns to the politics of reflexivity in relation to ways of knowing. What is of interest here is the ways in which reflexivity has been (and continues to be) recommended as a critical practice in relation to social research. More specifically in this chapter attention focuses on the ways in which reflexivity has been understood to provide a location from which subject–subject forms of knowledge can be produced which avoid the problems of universalism attributed to previous modes of knowing and knowledge practices associated with social science methodology. What this chapter shows however is that much like the reflexivity at issue in cultural economies discussed in Chapter 3, such reflexivity involves a mobile relation to identity. More specifically, this chapter highlights how reflexive social science concerns a speaking position involving an imagined mobile relation to identity on the side of the knower in relation to the known. This imagined mobile identity is investigated in regard to two forms of reflexivity currently at issue in discussions of the politics of knowledge in social science: self-reflexivity (or what is sometimes termed endogenous or meta-reflexivity) and 'in-the-world' reflexivity (or what is sometimes referred to as referential or infra-reflexivity (Latour 1991; May 1998). Moreover, this chapter shows that while claiming to redress problems of universalism, and in particular the problems related to the concealment of specific epistemological privileging via a breakdown of existing epistemological hierarchies, reflexivity enacted at the level of knowledge practices itself entails the inscription of a hierarchy of speaking positions. In particular, this chapter looks at how reflexivity in relation to knowledge practices inscribes a hierarchy of gendered speaking positions, since as this chapter illustrates, a mobile relation to identity on the side of the knower in relation to the known is a property which is more likely to be attributed to men than to women even as it appears to unsettle gender norms. This chapter therefore points towards significant exclusions from the vision of mobility that a reflexive speaking position assumes.

In Chapter 5 the politics of reflexivity are considered as they relate to sexuality. At issue here in particular are such politics in relation to the techniques and procedures associated with HIV testing, especially as they relate to Australia. HIV testing is an important issue for analysis in a book concerned with the 'social' post-structure as the techniques and procedures associated with testing have been linked to increasing reflexivity, and in particular have been understood to incite self-reflexivity. In addition, though the techniques and procedures of testing have also been understood to involve a detraditionalization of sexuality. Specifically, (on some accounts) they have been understood to challenge the heterosexual–homosexual binary via a responsibilization of heterosexuality in regard to HIV/AIDS. Thus, much like the sociology of reflexive modernization or reflexive modernity in general, certain analyses of HIV testing assume that reflexivity in regard to sexuality goes hand in hand with detraditionalization. What this chapter suggests however is that a reflexive attitude towards sexuality should not be read unproblematically. The techniques and procedures of HIV testing, for example, make self-reflexivity only fully available to the category of heterosexuality, and define other sexualities as in need of more external forms of monitoring. They therefore make responsibilization more available to the category of heterosexuality than to other sexualities. This chapter therefore highlights how rather than straightforwardly undoing the homosexual–heterosexual binary the techniques associated with HIV testing inscribe a hierarchy of sexual identities in terms of reflexivity, a hierarchy which is particularly pernicious in contexts of neo-liberal modes of regulation where the voluntary governance of the self increasingly defines 'good' citizenship (Higgs 1998; Vitellone 2000a). Indeed it is suggested here that the techniques and procedures of HIV testing are closely aligned to such modes of governance. Thus at issue in this chapter is the neo-liberal governance and politics of sexuality.

What all three substantive chapters in this book therefore illustrate are the ways in which mobility and (especially) reflexivity should not be simply understood as undoing gender and sexuality, but provide a new ground for forms of post-structural classification. In so doing it joins up with other recent work which has illustrated how reflexivity and mobility provide such a ground. Skeggs (2002), for example, has looked at how reflexivity in relation to the self (self-reflexivity) relies on specific techniques for knowing and telling the self (such as the technique of confession) which attribute knowledge and epistemological authority to the person in a manner in which such authority is made to seem like an innate property of that person. Moreover, she shows how such authority allows certain forms of experimentation in relation to the self, including experimentations (such as specific forms of telling the self) which may appear to decentre the self, that is, to attribute the property of mobility to the person. But Skeggs also shows how these properties (and techniques for knowing and telling) are more available to some than to others and in particular that such experimentations often rely on forms of appropriation, which dispossess certain 'selves' of such properties. For example, in sociology and anthropology telling stories of the subaltern has been a technique through which such appropriation and exclusion has taken place. Specifically, Skeggs shows how such techniques have both dispossessed the subaltern ('working classes', 'women') of properties of experimentation in relation to the self and classified them as such, while at the same time they have attributed storytellers with properties of authority and mobility. Skeggs therefore highlights how reflexivity does not disperse difference, but rather that reflexivity is a technique through which classification itself may take place.

This point is also highlighted in Cronin's (1999, 2000a, 2000b) study of European advertisements, and especially her analysis of the relations of gendered address of such advertisements. Here Cronin found an ironic and self-conscious, that is self-reflexive, form of address to be typically attributed to advertisements which are male-targeted. In contrast what Cronin terms a literal or non-reflexive form of address was found to be characteristic of female-targeted advertisements. Male (particularly young male) consumers are then increasingly addressed as self-reflexive while women are addressed in non-reflexive terms. Moreover, Cronin shows how an ironic visual address allows for an interpretative flexibility or reflexive form of engagement which provides a privileged position from which to contest cultural rights and belonging. This is a position from which women tend to be typically excluded. In short Cronin's study shows how reflexivity enacted in terms of the visual provides the grounds for gendered relations of privilege and exclusion in terms of the political rights associated with consumer citizenship.

This book therefore shares with studies such as Cronin's and Skeggs's an illustration of how both mobility and reflexivity are not simply dispersers of relations of authority, privilege and exclusion and foregrounds how the latter are being reworked in such contexts. It does so however not via interrogations of mobilities in terms of large-scale spatial processes (for instance global movements of people, commodities, money or knowledge), or of reflexivity at the level of social systems (see e.g. Alexander 1996). Rather the cases considered in this book are much more small-scale and situated. Considering these cases has allowed the politics of gender and sexuality post social structure to be addressed. Thus this book suggests that mobilities on small spatial scales, for instance of the sort talked about by Bourdieu (1977, 1990) across and within different fields of action, may be just as important for sociologists to study (in terms of both their consequences and their implications) as those on large spatial scales (see also Lash 1993a, 1993b, 1994; McNay 1999a, 1999b).

This book also has another methodological proposition. Specifically, it considers reconfigurations of gender and sexuality post social structure via a consideration of both the social and cultural (specifically the aesthetic) dimensions of reflexivity and mobility. Indeed it suggests that the relations between the cultural and the social (Lury 1995) are central to understanding such reconfigurations. As will be shown in Chapter 2 however, the question of what weight and analytic significance to give to the social and/or the cultural is a major point of contention in relation to theories of reflexive modernity (Lash 1994; Licthblau 1999; McNay 1999a, 1999b). For instance it has been suggested that theories of reflexive modernity or reflexive modernization are limited because of a generalized lack of consideration to the cultural dimensions of reflexivity. That is, it has been suggested that theories which are describing a fundamental reorganization and indeed even a decline or retreat of the social (and especially the socio-structural) ironically give over too much explanatory power to the social and hence such accounts are unable to account for whole dimensions of contemporary experience (Lash 1994; Licthblau 1999).

This last point is particularly important to a book which is seeking to address the reconfiguration of gender and sexuality in the context of mobilities and reflexivity. This is because recent debates around sexuality and gender have also been marked by some considerable tension around what emphasis to place on the cultural and/or the social (see e.g. Butler 1998a, Fraser 1998). For example, some (but certainly not all) analyses of gender and sexuality emanating from the social science disciplines, including certain strands of feminist sociology, insist that gender and sexuality are best understood as primarily social in character, and in particular as socio-structural. Moreover such arguments are often explicitly pitched against analyses of gender and sexuality which foreground (what is understood to be) their cultural constitution, especially analyses which foreground issues of linguistic and discursive practice as being of significance for the constitution of gender and sexuality. Thus in contemporary debates regarding sexuality and gender a very sharp division is often enacted in terms of the 'social' and the 'cultural', with the consequence that there are few analyses which attempt to breach this cleavage.

Current debates regarding reflexive modernity or the reflexive modernization thesis and gender and sexuality both therefore share a tension regarding the social and the cultural, and in particular a tension regarding what analytic weight to give to either and/or each. Indeed, while there are few analyses taking up aspects of the reflexive modernization thesis to consider the constitution of gender and sexuality in late modernity, those that have done so (unsurprisingly) find themselves squarely in this zone of contention. So for instance in an important analysis outlining the limits of reflexivity in relation to gender and sexuality, McNay (1999a) argues strongly against a cultural understanding of reflexivity and insists on its social character and in particular insists that reflexivity is the outcome of specific forms of social change. However against such claims, and those of certain sociological approaches to gender and sexuality more generally, the analysis I offer in this book suggests that it is not enough to examine processes of reflexivity and mobility in this register. More specifically, the analysis offered in this book suggests that reflexivity and mobility should not be understood as the effect or outcome of particular kinds of social change. This is because and as will be made clear, to do so is to (ironically) make invisible crucial uneven manifestations of reflexivity (including those related to the take-up of a reflexive stance towards gender in cultural economies, the enactment of reflexivity in relation to knowledge practices, and claims to possess a reflexive, 'responsibilized' attitude towards sexuality) central to new forms of classification and division in regard to sexuality and gender post social structure. In short, to insist that reflexivity and mobility are the effects of certain societal transformations is to make invisible precisely those issues which critics of an emphasis on cultural dimensions of contemporary life claim to be able to illuminate. Moreover, and as I hope the chapters that follow will serve to illustrate, to understand reflexivity in this manner is to negate the ways in which both the social *and* the cultural are being reworked and refashioned by reflexivity and mobility, that is are central to the constitution and ordering of the social and cultural fields post society or post social structure.

These issues are debated in Chapters 1 and 2. In Chapter 1 the major propositions of the reflexive modernization thesis are mapped out and explained. This thesis has had a wide-ranging impact in sociology and beyond, but surprisingly has had relatively little impact in relation to sociologies of gender and sexuality, including branches of feminist sociology. Instead, and as this chapter lays out, many sociologists of gender and sexuality have been locked in to the debates discussed above, that is those relating to the relative significance of the social and the cultural. What this chapter suggests however is that in the light of the sociology of mobilities and the reflexive modernization thesis, many of the defenders of the 'social' for the analysis of sexuality and gender may be seen to be working with taken-for-granted understandings of the social which may have limited purchase in the contemporary world. In addition however, and via a review of the debates regarding the social and/or the cultural in relation to feminist theory, especially the recent debates concerning the merits and relative significance of the methods of (what are often characterized as) historicization and deconstruction or destabilization, it is suggested that if the sociology of mobilities and the reflexive modernization thesis are to have some purchase in the analysis of sexuality and gender in late modernity then it is crucial that they do not separate out the social from the cultural. This is so, and as this chapter lays out, as not only are clear cut distinctions between the two in relation to sexuality and gender difficult to maintain, but also because maintaining this division makes some key aspects of gender and sexuality invisible.

As already mentioned above, a similar tension concerning the relative significance of the social and the cultural is also at issue in relation to the reflexive modernization thesis. This is the subject of discussion in Chapter 2. Particular attention is focused here on analyses which have considered the *limits* of reflexivity and (the few) analyses which have either explicitly or implicitly provided analyses of gender and/or sexuality via a take-up of aspects of the reflexive modernization thesis. What this chapter illustrates about the social/cultural tension in debates around reflexive modernization (as suggested in Chapter 1 in relation to recent feminist debates concerning gender and sexuality) is that to ignore the cultural (and specifically the aesthetic) dimensions of reflexivity is to make invisible specific uneven forms of reflexivity. More specifically, it is to render unintelligible specific uneven forms of reflexivity which are central to the reconfiguration of gender and sexuality post social structure. Indeed, as already alluded to, it will be suggested that to ignore such forms of reflexivity leads to a problematic assertion of a straightforward and unproblematic detraditionalization of gender and sexuality. That is to say, to ignore the aesthetic dimensions of reflexivity in relation to gender and sexuality and to insist on its entirely social character is ironically to make invisible precisely those issues which a social analysis of reflexivity claims to illuminate.

This chapter is also concerned with drawing out a further characteristic of these analyses of both the limits of reflexivity and of reflexivity, gender and sexuality. Specifically, it will highlight the ways in which these analyses of reflexivity assume that reflexivity is a consequence of movement, and in particular that reflexivity is constituted via mobility between and within (Bourdieuian) fields of action. Thus it will be shown, for example, how a reflexive stance towards gender is understood to be constituted via such mobility. As noted above, this mobility is different from that conceptualized by writers on mobility such as Urry. For these are movements which are embodied, embedded, situated, contested and moreover involve forms of reflexivity which cannot be unproblematically conceptualized in terms of the 'freeing' of agents from structure or agents reflecting on structure (Lash

1994). Such analyses therefore seem to provide an important ground for thinking through reconfigurations of sexuality and gender post social structure, and as will be made clear in this chapter, this ground proves to be crucial not only in terms of the articulation of the limits of reflexivity, but also for undoing the easy connections often made between reflexivity and individualization and reflexivity and detraditionalization. However while highlighting this common theme in these analyses of reflexivity, this chapter also shows how this idea regarding the significance of movement across and within fields of action for the constitution of reflexivity has been given a specific spin by sociologists of gender. Specifically, it has been argued that there is an increasing transposition of the feminine habitus into specific fields of action, a transposition which provides the grounds for the constitution of reflexivity in relation to gender and for detraditionalization. This then is the cultural feminization thesis discussed above, which is the basis of discussion and critique in Chapter 3. Before going on to discuss analyses of gender and sexuality that take up aspects of the reflexive modernization thesis and the cultural feminization thesis however, I turn to an exposition of the theory of reflexive modernization or reflexive modernity.

one

new sociological directions and feminist sociological controversies

introduction

One of the most influential (and controversial) sets of ideas in contemporary sociology is that connected with the reflexive modernization thesis. Associated most readily with the sociologists Ulrich Beck (1992, 1994, 1997, 1999) and Anthony Giddens (1991, 1992, 1994), and also with the social and cultural theorist Scott Lash (1993a, 1994, 1999), the impact of the theory of reflexive modernization or reflexive modernity is highly visible across a range of substantive areas in sociology as well as in contemporary debate in social and cultural theory. Thus the theory of reflexive modernization or reflexive modernity competes with and has been understood to provide an alternative to large-scale theories of contemporary social life, including theories of post-modernity, late modernity, disorganized capitalism and consumer culture. In addition a number of the key ideas and concepts associated with theories of reflexive modernity have been taken up, inform and have shaped contemporary debate in a range of subdisciplines within sociology. These include the sociologies of health (Lupton 1995; Peterson and Lupton 1996); sexuality (Weeks 1995, 1998; Hawkes 1996; Jackson and Scott 1997); intimacy (Illouz 1997; Heaphy et al. 1998; Jamieson 1998); economy (Lash 1994; Lash and Urry 1994; Martin 1998); social movements (Melucci 1996); youth (Jones and Wallace 1992); governance (Dean 1998; Higgs 1998); identity (Heaphy 1996; Melucci 1996); and the body (Lupton and Tulloch 1998). Within these different fields there is certainly no straightforward consensus regarding the exact meaning of reflexive modernity/modernization. Thus within and across them many of the key concepts associated with the reflexive modernization thesis tend to be mobilized and understood somewhat differently.[1] Indeed, even among the strongest advocates of reflexive modernity/modernization as a framework for understanding the features and experiences of contemporary life, there are some marked differences in approach and understanding and some central points of contention (see the explications of differences of approach in Beck *et al.* 1994, the discussions in Heelas *et al.* 1996 and my discussions in the following chapter). Despite these differences and points of contention however, I take the reflexive modernization thesis to turn around three interrelated theses regarding social life. First, that contemporary social life is characterized by increased capacities for reflexivity; second that this concerns a detraditionalization of the social in relation to the rules and traditions of modernity; and third that the decline of the certainties of industrial society has encouraged a process of individualization whereby people are now compelled to create themselves as individuals. Throughout this and subsequent chapters my use of the notion of the reflexive modernization thesis therefore refers to these three related propositions. I turn now to more detailed explications of these theses.

reflexivity

The theory of reflexive modernization has been characterized as suggesting that there is something new in the contemporary condition and this newness has something to do with an increased capacity for reflexivity (Alexander 1996). While there is some disagreement regarding the exact meaning of reflexivity (see e.g. Beck *et al.* 1994) nevertheless Lash (1994: 115–16) has usefully defined two forms of reflexivity generally at issue in analyses of reflexive modernity/modernization. First, there is structural reflexivity whereby agency reflects both on the rules and resources of social structure and on the conditions of existence of agency itself. Thus Beck has commented, 'the more societies are modernized, the more agents (subjects) acquire the ability to reflect on the social conditions of their existence and to change them accordingly' (1994: 174). Second, there is self-reflexivity in which agency reflects on itself and there is increasing *self-monitoring*. Hence for Giddens the context of late modernity means that the constitution of the self becomes an increasingly reflexive project: 'we are, not what we are, but what we make of ourselves' (Giddens 1991: 75).

In the reflexive modernization thesis such intensified capacities towards both structural and self-reflexivity are both understood to be linked to – and constituted by – a decline in the significance of structural forms of determination. As a consequence of the retrocession of the structural, agency is understood as being progressively 'freed' or unleashed from structure. Hence Lash has commented: 'reflexive modernization is a theory of the ever-increasing powers of social actors, or "agency" in regard to structure' (1994: 111), and it is this process which provides the conditions for increased reflexivity. Indeed, so thoroughgoing is this process that reflexivity is now understood to characterize a range of domains including the economic (Beck 1992; Lash 1994; Lash and Urry 1994), the political (Beck 1994, 1997, 1999), the aesthetic (Lash 1993a, 1994; Lichtblau 1999), the intimate, the personal and the sexual (Giddens 1992; Beck and Beck-Gernsheim 1995; Weeks 1995, 1998; Beck-Gernsheim 1998). Thus, in relation to identity, Melucci has commented: 'identity is in the process of being redefined as a pure reflexive capacity or self-awareness' (1996: 36), while Giddens (1992) has located self-reflexivity and especially the performance of a 'reflexive project of the self' where self-identity is constituted by a reflexive ordering of self-narratives, as key to participation in the contemporary affective practice of intimacy, especially achieving the 'pure relationship' involving emotional and intimate equality (see also Illouz 1997).

It is an understatement, however, to say that reflexivity is simply seen to characterize these different domains. What is at issue is a thoroughly new constitution of life forms and modes of interaction within late modernity with new types of bonds, ties, actions, contracts, communications and networks are all being formed in the face of reflexive modernization. For example, 'family' ties are now understood less in terms of obligations constituted by fixed 'ties of blood' and more in terms of negotiated commitments and bonds (Finch 1989; Giddens 1992; Beck and Beck-Gernsheim 1995; Beck-Gernsheim 1998; Heaphy *et al.* 1998); and labour market positions are constituted less by determinants such as class or gender location and more by self-design, self-creation and individual performances (Beck 1992; Martin 1998). Thus one reading of the reflexively organized social is 'what the social is and does has to be involved with individual decisions' (Beck 1992: 90). Many of modernity's key abstract collective categories of belonging, such as status and class are therefore now less a matter of external forms of determination and more a matter of individual decisions. Indeed, according to Beck and Beck Gernsheim (1996: 29)

> Life, death, gender, corporeality, identity, religion, marriage, parenthood, social ties – all are becoming decidable down to the small print; once fragmented into options, everything must be decided.

In short, reflexive modernity/modernization refers not simply to new forms of organization but rather to the constitution of a new form of sociality and the emergence of new life forms that have been created via the retrocession of structural forms of determination and the 'unleashing' of agency from structure.

detraditionalization and individualization

Two further sociological characteristics are also understood to flow from the conditions allowing for intensified capacities of reflexivity: detraditionalization and individualization. Indeed, in the reflexive modernization thesis detraditionalization and individualization are both understood to be products of reflexivity. Thus Beck (1992: 153) comments, individualization is conceptualized theoretically as the product of reflexivity, in which the process of modernization as protected by the welfare state detraditionalizes the ways of living built into industrial society.

Current reflexivity is seen, for example, by many to be inciting a process of detraditionalization. Hence the 'freeing' of agency from structure is often held to mean that 'traditional' forms of organization are disintegrating – that agents are increasingly free from the rules, expectations, and forms of authority associated with modernity. Discussing detraditionalization in relation to sexuality, Weeks (1998: 41), for instance, comments,

> The binary divide between homosexuality and heterosexuality, which was codified in the 19th century and has come to be regarded as the very definition of the natural in the 20th century, has been significantly challenged by the public emergence of vocal lesbian and gay movements and collective identities.

He sees this challenge as connected to a 'radical unsettling of traditional forms and values' (1998: 40). The broad idea called upon here – that traditional modes of life, interaction and organization are being challenged and destabilized – may be paralleled to the more general and classical view that the onward march of modernity is destructive or incites the collapse of tradition: 'the capitalistic market, with its "imperatives" of continuous expansion destroys tradition' (Giddens 1992: 197). But in the reflexive modernization thesis what is at issue is not the destruction of the pre-modern by the modern as in much classical social thought, but rather the collapse and undercutting of the traditions of modernity itself by a new modernity, another modernity.

This new modernity is also characterized by an increased role for the individual. With the disintegration of the modes of life and social forms of modernity, external forms of authority are understood as being replaced by the authority of the individual: 'individual subjects are themselves called upon to exercise authority in the face of . . . disorder and contingency' (Heelas 1996: 2). People therefore find 'themselves in the position where they have to . . . construct their own ways of life' (1996: 5). This emphasis on self-invention marks the second characteristic of contemporary life understood in the reflexive modernization thesis to flow from the conditions allowing for intensified reflexivity: an intensification of processes of individualization. Specifically, increased reflexivity is understood to incite processes whereby individuals are called upon not only to create and invent their certainties and forms of authority but also their own self-identities and themselves as individuals (Giddens 1991, 1992; Beck 1992, 1994). Thus the dissolution of the certainties of industrial society mean that individuals must now 'produce, stage and cobble together their biographies themselves' (Beck 1994: 13), that is, the standard biography becomes a chosen biography (1994: 15). Individuals are now therefore constantly compelled to constitute and create themselves as individuals: 'The individual himself or herself becomes the reproduction unit of the social in the lifeworld' (Beck 1992: 90). For instance, workers with standardized employment contracts are being replaced by 'do-it-yourself' workers who are compelled to stress the uniqueness, variety and individuality of their work (1992: 93). While in everyday family life whereas 'people used to be able to rely upon well-functioning rules and models . . . now an ever greater number of decisions are having to be taken' (Beck-Gernsheim 1998: 59). In the reflexive modernization thesis the freeing of people from social structure is thus understood to open up a more extended role for the individual in late modernity. As Bauman, has put it, human identity is being transformed from a given into a task, and actors are being charged 'with the responsibility for performing that task and for the consequences . . . of their performance' (2000: 31–2).

It is clear that the changes at issue in the reflexive modernization/ modernity thesis are far reaching. Indeed so profound are these changes that Beck has suggested sociology must reinvent itself in order to come to grips with these shifts; it must become 'a bit of art, a bit playful, in order to liberate itself from its own intellectual blockades' (1994: 24). And many sociologists have found in the reflexive modernization thesis precisely the kind of tools which allow this kind of creativity and movement away from some of the assumptions which have characterized the discipline. For example, in (aspects of) the reflexive modernization thesis Lash and Urry (1994: 3) find an important corrective to overly structuralist understandings of social process, commenting,

> One reason why so many analysts paint such a uniformly pessimistic scenario for the future is because of a reliance on an overly structuralist conception of social process . . . we will endeavor to correct this through focussing on upon subjectivity, and in particular on an increasingly significant reflexive subjectivity. We shall examine the causes and consequences of a subjectivity engaged in a process of 'reflexive modernization'.

Indeed, analyses of reflexive modernization have been located as marking a turning point in sociological analyses and as reinvigorating the discipline (Lash 1994). Not only do they appear to have immediate analytic and empirical purchase, but have had, and are continuing to have a wide-ranging impact well beyond the formally academic (Lichtblau 1999). Indeed so powerful is this impact that,

> After more than a decade in which literary critics, art and architecture writers and philosophers have dominated the 'theory scene' . . . it is gratifying that sociology can address the same major problems of the contemporary era with such political purchase and analytic power.

(Lash 1994: 118)

Although the theory of reflexive modernization or modernity has marked a turning point in sociological analyses, and has had a major impact on a range of fields, nonetheless to date it has had relatively little impact in the sociologies of gender and sexuality and especially feminist sociologies of gender and sexuality (although see McNay 1999a, 1999b and my discussions in the following chapter). In some senses this is surprising, for as is well documented there has been a general move away from the social science disciplines within feminism. Thus while at one time a substantial part of the feminist project seemed to centre on the excavation of key analyses at the heart of the social science disciplines, especially on analyses concerned with the character of modernity (see for example Sydie 1987; Marshall 1994) there is now relatively little feminist engagement with analyses emanating from the social sciences. Thus the most influential feminist works produced since the mid-1980s have tended to take place outside of a social science frame and instead have been produced in the arts and humanities. This shift has been described as a shift in focus in feminist analyses from things to words (Barrett 1990) or from the social to the cultural (Adkins and Lury 1996) and connects to the much broader movement within contemporary social and cultural theory alluded to by Lash above, in which the social sciences have been found wanting by a range of writers on a number of counts. Thus Barrett discusses the influence of poststructuralism in terms of this movement, especially its devastating critiques of many of the key assumptions of the social sciences in the following terms,

> In social science generally, such unexceptional concepts such as 'social structure', 'role', 'individual' or 'labour market' have become contentious in terms of what they assume about a social totality or infrastructure, or the presumed characteristics of social actors.
> (1992: 202)

In terms of feminist analyses such critiques have meant that socio-structural analyses of gender focused on, for instance, state or economic relations, have generally lost their purchase and in some quarters their legitimacy. In this context we may therefore ask if the theory of reflexive modernization offers feminist sociologies of gender and sexuality the kind of revitalized analytic and empirical purchase and new political salience which it has offered sociology more generally. If the theory of reflexive modernization can revitalize sociology in general in this context via new forms of empirical purchase and political salience, can this also be the case for feminist sociology?

feminist sociological controversies:
historicization vs deconstruction

In the context of the general shift from 'things to words' however such questions have tended not to be asked with many (although certainly not all) feminist sociologists focusing attention instead on the significance of a more familiar socio-historical analysis in relation to gender and sexuality. This has been particularly visible in recent debates which have asked whether or not recent analyses of gender and sexuality are able to take account of matters of history, the social and the economic. For example, a more familiar socio-historical analysis has been at issue in relation to critiques of recent analyses of gender and sexuality which, following Judith Butler, stress their performative constitution. Broadly stated, the latter involves the proposition that gender and sexuality are constituted via the linguistic repetition of discursive conventions, where the transgression of such norms is understood to be made possible via a reappropriation and citation of signifiers of difference, for instance, through practices such as drag (see Butler 1990, 1993). What has concerned some feminist sociologists and social scientists more generally regarding this understanding is that it is held by many to bypass the social and the historical. Thus, in a recent high profile exchange between Nancy Fraser and Judith Butler in *Social Text* and reprinted in *New Left Review*, Fraser argues that Butler's theory of performativity is 'abstract' and 'transhistorical' and is unable account for 'the actual contradictory character of specific social relations' (1998: 149). Rather than what she terms 'destabilization or deconstruction' (1998: 149), Fraser argues that historicization is a favourable approach to social theory, since historicization allows us to appreciate the 'specific character of contemporary societies' (1998: 149).

This claim – that an analysis of performativity somehow bypasses the historical and the social – has been made widely by sociologists working in the areas of sexuality and gender. Stevi Jackson (1998), for example, has argued that while Butler 'seems to be reaching towards some notion of a socially ordered world . . . the social eludes her grasp' (Jackson 1998: 138), while in a discussion of Butler's *Gender Trouble* (1990), Tim Edwards (1998: 477) has argued that despite hinting at 'social and structural mechanisms . . . the thrust of . . . [Butler's] analysis is that gender primarily exists at the level of discourse therefore tending to discount its significance as an institutionalized social practice'. Steven Seidman (1995, 1997) too has argued that 'Queer theory has largely abandoned institutional analysis' (1995: 134) and instead surrendered to what he terms a 'narrow culturalism or textualism' where the ' "social" is often narrowed into categories of knowledge and culture where the latter is . . . often reduced to linguistic, discursive binary figures' (1995: 139). So too he suggests that queer theory neglects the historical. Specifically, he suggests that the ' "historical" is . . . reduced to an undifferentiated space' for example, 'the modern West or the period 1880–1980' (1995: 139).

What stands out from these kinds of arguments however is that the primacy of the social and indeed what the social consists in are more or less assumed. For example, while it is argued that the social has primacy over 'the cultural', such writings generally do not articulate analyses of the social and the cultural and of the relations between the social and cultural to enable such claims to be assessed. We are told that the social consists of societies, social and structural mechanisms, institutions and institutionalized practices, but are not given an account as to how or why such social formations, processes, mechanisms and practices should take primacy in analyses of sexuality and gender. Instead this tends to be taken for granted.

Yet as my discussions so far in this book illustrate, recent analyses of the 'social', including those which focus on mobilities and on reflexive modernization suggest that these sociological critiques may be working with a less than contemporary understanding of the social to think through the relations between 'historicization' and 'destabilization'. For instance, following the sociology of mobilities and reflexivity, we may question the idea that an analysis of the social is tied to societies and social structures as well as the view that the latter have the power to reproduce themselves in time-space. Indeed, instead of reproducing such a model of the social it may be more constructive to ask questions regarding the relations between, for example, a sociology of mobilities and an analysis of gender and sexuality as performatively constituted, or a sociology of reflexivity and an analysis of performativity.

While many analyses which emphasize the primacy of the social and historical over the cultural in relation to sexuality and gender rest on such taken-for-granted understandings, nevertheless other analyses which have questioned the idea that sexuality and gender are best understood as performatively constituted have attempted to develop a more detailed analysis of the social and its relations with the cultural. This is the case in Rosemary Hennessy's extended analysis of queer theory and activism. Here, Hennessy also reads Butler's analysis of sexuality and gender as '*only* discursive' (1995: 148, emphasis in original) which reduces 'the social to discourses' (1995: 149) or, as she sees it, presumes 'that the social is equivalent to the cultural' (1995: 148). This assumption, Hennessy claims, is visible in Butler's approach to identity which she argues presupposes 'that identity is only a matter of representation, of the discourses by which subjects come to be established' (1995: 148). She argues this presumption is also visible in Butler's analysis of materialization in *Bodies that Matter* (1993) where, she suggests, Butler reduces 'materiality to discourse alone' (Hennessy 1995: 149) and thus 'conflates the materiality of the social into culture' (1995: 149). This she says is evident in the way Butler refers to heterosexuality as both an institution and as a norm. But, Hennessy asks, are institutions and normative discourses one and the same? She writes,

> Do institutions like the family, the military, or schools organize and rely on more than discourses: aspects of life like labor and wealth, or social resources like health and health care, the distribution of food and shelter?
>
> (1995: 149)

All of these aspects of life Hennessy concedes are 'discursively mediated and regulated', but, she argues, 'at the same time their materiality is not simply discursive' (Hennessy 1995: 149). Indeed, she suggests that reducing materiality to discourse alone obscures much social life, and to illustrate how social life may exceed the discursive she offers the example of the proposal to lift the ban on gays in the US military. Such a proposal, it is suggested, has only become possible under certain historical conditions. Amongst the latter Hennessy includes changes in the place of the United States in global politics after the Cold War and in the sexual division of labour which she suggests 'has enabled a more flexible patriarchal gender ideology in multinational capitalist economies' (1995: 149).

As this suggests, Hennessy, like Nancy Fraser, sees that Butler's analysis of performativity – especially its 'reduction' of the social to the cultural – as unable to attend to matters of history, and especially the crucial matter of historicization. Indeed, Hennessy contends Butler understands history in 'very local, limited terms' (1995: 149). Thus, while she notes that in her early work Butler discusses the ways in which the subversive potential of performances of gender parody depends on issues of context and reception, Hennessy argues that considering historical context is a different matter from historicizing, which she suggests would involve linking such performances 'to the social relations which make it possible', including the 'larger frame of late capitalism's geopolitics and multinational economy' (Hennessy 1995: 150). She suggests that a social practice such as drag, for example, needs to be analysed at several levels, including the conjuctural situation and the global relations to which the situation is tied.

historicizing queer: the aestheticization of everyday life

In suggesting, however, that an analysis of performatively constituted identities and the politics of the performative needs to be supplemented with analyses of 'the relation between identity and symbolic politics and the sociohistorical conditions which make queer subjects and visibility possible' (Nicholson and Seidman 1995: 19); Hennessy (1995: 153) argues further that such a procedure would make visible that the option of the practice of parodies of gender such as drag,

> depends on the availability not only of certain discourses of sexuality, aesthetics, style, and glamor but also of a circuit of commodity production, exchange, and consumption specific to industrialized economies.

In short, for Hennessy such a procedure would bring into view the ways in which a performative relation to sexual identities, queer identities and queer visibility are made possible by the specific socio-historical conditions of consumer capitalism, especially the 'general aestheticization of everyday life in consumer capitalism' (1995: 164) involving,

> the intensified integration of cultural and commodity production
> ... by way of the rapid flow of images and signs that saturate
> myriad everyday activities, continuously working and reworking
> desires by inviting them to take the form dictated by the com-
> modity market.
>
> (Hennessy 1995: 165)[2]

For Hennessy, the failure of theorists such as Butler to register or
elaborate on such sociohistorical conditions is to fail to recognize the close
connection between the notion of identities as performative and the figuring
of identities as self-fashioned 'lifestyles' in consumer culture. In particular, it
is to fail to register the association between the idea of performatively constituted identities and the emphasis in consumer culture on a self-conscious
'stylized construction of almost every aspect of one's life: one's body, clothes,
speech, leisure activities, eating, drinking, and sexual preferences' (Hennessy
1995: 165). Along with other commentators (see e.g. Featherstone 1991)
Hennessy notes that in consumer culture such a stylization or self-fashioning
increasingly constitutes individuality, and is figured as achievable through
the purchase of consumer goods. Moreover, she notes that consumer practices
in late capitalism promise a 'de-centering of identity' or 'promote a way of
thinking about identity as malleable' (Hennessy 1995: 166), since rather than
by moral codes or rules, identity is shaped through more and more consumer choices. It is this notion of identity – as self-fashioned, stylized and
malleable – which Hennessy suggests resonates with the understanding of
identity found in much queer theory and activism. For example, she suggests
'queer theory and activism's conception of identities as performative signi-
fications anchored in individual psychic histories is not very far from [a]
notion of identity as self-fashioning' (1995: 166). In particular, for Hennessy,
what queer and consumer culture's 'life-stylism' have in common is a separation of identity from the social and historical conditions relations which
enable it. Thus while queer theorists such as Butler ignore the historical
specificities of consumer capitalism, and therefore the conditions which make
possible a performative relation to identity, in consumer culture intensified
commodity fetishism ensures that,

> the social relations on which cultural production depends are even
> further mystified. The aestheticization of everyday life encourages
> the pursuit of new tastes and sensations as pleasures in them-
> selves while concealing or backgrounding the labor that has gone
> into making them possible.
>
> (Hennessy 1995: 165)

In this sense Hennessy suggests that so strong are the resonances
between queer and consumer capitalism's 'life-stylism', that queer theory
itself must be understood as participating in the aestheticization of everyday
life. Indeed, it must be recognized that queer identities and visibility are

themselves enabled by the social relations of consumer capitalism, and in particular are enabled through the reconfiguration of identity as stylized, self-fashioning and malleable in consumer culture.

One serious consequence of this participation in the aestheticization of everyday life, Hennessy contends, is that analyses such as Butler's speak only to 'the new bourgeois professional class' (1995: 150). She notes, for example, that the aestheticization of everyday life, and in particular the 'capacity for hyperconsumption promoted by appeals to lifestyle as well as the constituent features of various "lifestyles" [is] class specific' (1995: 166). Thus she discusses what she terms a 'class boundness of stylization' (Hennessy 1995: 166), especially the ways in which a self-fashioned, stylized, flexible consumer orientated identity is only fully available to the new urban middle classes of industrialized economies. Hennessy's point, therefore, is that because queer fails to recognize that queer identities and visibility are themselves made possible by the social relations of consumer capitalism (indeed, that queer itself is a fetishized consumer 'lifestyle' identity), and because a consumer orientated identity is specific to the new urban middle classes of industrialized economies, queer is an identity which is only fully available to urban middle-class lesbians and gay men. Analyses such as Butler's, therefore, only make visible middle-class queers, and make invisible not only the social relations – such as relations of labour – which make such visibility possible, but also non-middle-class lesbians, gays and queers.[3] Thus Hennessy (1995: 176) suggests projects which attempt to redress gay invisibility by

> promoting images of a seamlessly middle-class gay consumer or by inviting us to see queer identities only in terms of style, textuality, or performative play helps produce imaginary gay/queer subjects that keep invisible the divisions of wealth and labor that these images and knowledges depend on. These commodified perspectives blot from view lesbians, gays, queers who are manual workers, sex workers, unemployed, and imprisoned.

In this sense, Hennessy suggests, it must be recognized that queer theory and activism risks promoting 'an updated, postmodern, reinscription of the bourgeois subject's fetishized identity' (1995: 153).

In a slightly different register, similar problems with the notion of performatively constituted identities are also raised by Moya Lloyd (1999), who has argued that one of the weaknesses of the concept of performativity is that it is comprehensible primarily as an account of individuation.[4] She argues that while parody may be transgressive 'from the perspective of the specific linear history of practices that constitute a particular individuated subject' (Lloyd 1999: 208), there is no guarantee that such a performance will be read as parodic in the context of others. By only making visible the individuated subject, an analysis of the performative constitution of identities does not therefore 'forefront sufficiently the lateral relations between bodies and subjectivities within determinate historical contexts' (Lloyd 1999: 208;

see also McNay 1999b). While Lloyd does not comment on the notion of individuation more broadly, nevertheless the close connections between individuation, that is of subjects who can claim to be the author or in possession of their own identities – for example subjects who can claim a specific historicity – and class formation has long been acknowledged (see e.g. Featherstone 1991; Skeggs 1997). In particular, a number of writers have stressed that in consumer culture, individuation is central to middle-class formation. Moreover, a number of writers appear to have read performativity precisely in this vein, suggesting that the performative is linked to an intensification of individualization. For example, in analyses of contemporary economy, it is suggested that a recent privileging of the performative aspects of labour, particularly in service based economies, has amounted to an intensified individualization of work and workers (Crang 1997; McDowell 1997). Thus in suggesting that the notion of performativity seems to work best as an account of individuation, Lloyd's analysis appears to endorse the view that a theory of the performative in relation to sexuality only makes visible particular kinds of subjects, in particular individualized subjects.

What is interesting regarding the analyses of Hennessy and Lloyd is that not only do they offer more detailed accounts of how a consideration of the social and the historical may be brought into conversation with analyses of gender and sexuality as performatively constituted, but their analyses are also suggestive of some important ways in which the sociologies of mobility and reflexivity may be of significance for analyses of sexuality and gender. Thus while Hennessy and Lloyd are certainly not working with or explicitly drawing upon the ideas which together constitute the reflexive modernization thesis or the sociology of mobilities, nevertheless in opening up the question of how to understand the historical and social in relation to analyses of performativity – that is, by not assuming in advance what the social is – their analyses point to a number of ways in which notions of mobility, individualization, detraditionalization and reflexivity may have the kind of purchase and analytic power for 'sociological' analyses of gender and sexuality that they have offered sociology in general.

Hennessy's analysis, for example, suggests that the notion of mobility may be important in this respect. This is found in her suggestion that (certain) subjects occupy increasingly mobile, flexible or malleable positions in relation to sexuality and gender in the context of consumer lifestylization. Indeed she comments,

> the once-rigid links between sex, gender, and sexual desire that the invisible heterosexual matrix so firmly secured in bourgeois culture have become more *flexible* as the gendered divisions of labor among the middle class in industrialized countries have shifted. While these more accommodating gender codes are not pervasive, they have begun to take hold among the urban middle class particularly.
> (Hennessy 1995: 169; emphasis added)

Thus Hennessy's analysis suggests that alongside the mobilities located by Urry in his 'mobilities for the twenty-first century', those of gender, sex and sexuality may also be important to consider in the rewriting of the sociological project 'post society', particularly in regard to analyses of consumer culture. More than this, however, Hennessy implicitly links the emergence of mobile gender and sexual identities to detraditionalization and individualization. Thus for Hennessy consumer culture is understood as a detraditionalizing of identity, in that rather than by moral codes or rules identity is increasingly a matter of consumer choice. Moreover, the 'detraditionalized' socio-historical conditions of consumer capitalism, which make queer and other self-fashioned, mobile identities possible, are located as involving processes of individualization. Thus Hennessy understands consumer culture, not only as detraditionalizing but also individualizing. In particular, the consumption of consumer goods is understood to be constitutive of individuality. In Lloyd's critique of Butler the idea of individualization is also at issue, in this case an analysis of performativity in relation to sexuality and gender is read as only making visible individualized subjects, a point it seems with which Hennessy would strongly agree. From the analyses of Lloyd and Hennessy it seems therefore that some of the concepts found in the reflexive modernization thesis and the sociology of mobilities may offer some important tools for analyses of sexuality and gender for sociologists, particularly for thinking through the contested relations between 'historicization' and 'deconstruction'.

the limits of visibility

While this may be the case, it appears it will only be so for those who accept that there is a fairly neat divide and indeed division of issues which are a matter of sociohistorical analysis, and those which are a matter of 'deconstruction and destabilization'. Thus from Hennessy's analysis it would appear that class is only ever a matter of historicization which should not and can not be analysed as a matter of performativity. This issue has been highlighted by Mariam Fraser (1999) in an analysis of the politics of the performative. Discussing Hennessy's analysis, Fraser warns against a simple elision of queer theory and activism with the self-fashioned, stylized, malleable identities of consumer culture since, as she points out, analyses of the performative – especially Butler's – are careful to avoid a notion of individual intentionality.[5] Nevertheless she argues that the contexts in which queer and lifestylization are situated may mean that 'their political intentions and effects cannot be distinguished' (Fraser 1999: 117). In particular, Fraser suggests that because both queer and lifestylization are based around a theatre of identity, and both tend to be concentrated within the field of visibility, 'an equivalence may be forced between them' (1999: 117). Despite some important points of clarification, she therefore takes seriously the claim that there may be important points of connection between queer and the aestheticization of everyday life, and especially the more general point inferred from analyses such as Hennessy's, that the privileging of representation and, relatedly, performativity as the site of political contestation requires a far more thoroughgoing analysis, particularly in regard to questions of class.

Unlike Hennessy, however, whose analysis appears to imply that issues of class and socioeconomics can be separated out from the performative, and drawing on the recent work of Skeggs (1997), Lawler (1999) and (as she says ironically) Butler (1997) herself, Fraser draws attention to the ways in which class identities are not always invisible (as Hennessy seems to imply) and, in particular, that struggles around class are also struggles around representation. She goes on, however, to question the unproblematic privileging of the visible in the politics of queer by drawing further on the work of Skeggs, especially her extended ethnography of young white working-class British women (Skeggs 1997). In particular Fraser draws on one of the central themes of Skeggs's analysis, namely that rather than being recognized, young white-working class British women are often keen not to be recognized as working-class, that is they disidentify with working-class identities. Fraser extends Skeggs's observation that recognition has to occur for identifications to be made to the politics of queer, suggesting that recognition also 'has to occur for re-identifications to be made' (1999: 122). In so doing, she questions the assumption found, for example, in Butler's discussions of a politics of theatricality, that there will necessarily be a take-up or citation of the terms of discursive bases of opposition (such as homophobia). That is, Fraser questions the assumption that there will be an unproblematic reappropriation and citation of the signifiers of difference, which, in miming discursive conventions, reverse them. In particular, Fraser suggests that such a politics of theatricality is problematized in the ways that Skeggs's analysis of class disidentification points to a non-take-up or citation of the terms of discursive conventions. Fraser's point here is not, as she makes clear, to suggest that those who disidentify with class identities somehow fail to be political, but rather that Skeggs's analysis points to certain limits to the politics of the performative. In particular, for Fraser, Skeggs's work suggests that it may be a privileging of a reappropriation of the signifiers of identity which is 'potentially schismatic in much contemporary identity politics' (Fraser 1999: 124), especially since such a politics would seem to exclude those who choose not to be made visible, who do not want to be recognized, and who disidentify with categories of identification.

Fraser's analysis of the limits of the politics of performativity (via the extension of Skegg's analysis) is of importance for the debates I have considered in this chapter on a number of counts. First, while drawing attention to certain limits of the theory and politics of performativity, it also puts in question many of the terms of critique of queer forwarded by its 'social' critics. For example, it questions the rigid distinction put in place by such critics between the social and the cultural, especially the view that matters of the social, including wide scale social injustices such as those of class, are somehow separate from what is understood to be the 'cultural' matter of performativity. Thus her analysis points to the ways in which matters of social inequality and injustice and issues of identity are not quite so sharply differentiated and bounded as such critics proclaim. But in so doing, Fraser also questions another logic often at issue in such 'social' or 'materialist' critiques, namely the tendency found in analyses such as Hennessy's to understand the social as pertaining only to issues of class, and to understand the cultural as both separate from the socio-economic and issues of class and as concerning issues of sexuality, gender and 'race'.[6] As Fraser herself makes clear, she has no interest in reinforcing the distinction between class identities and analyses of socio-economic conditions and identities of 'race', sexuality and gender and a politics of performativity (Fraser 1999: 128 n23).

destabilizing historicization: 'merely cultural'

This logic has recently been made visible by Butler (1998a) in her reply to Nancy Fraser (1997) in the aforementioned *Social Text/New Left Review* debate in which Butler critiques aspects of Fraser's analysis of contemporary justice. The latter has proved to be particularly influential in discussions of contemporary politics, so before turning to Butler's critique, I will briefly outline some of its key themes. Broadly stated, Fraser's central claim is that in contemporary political life, the struggle for recognition is fast becoming 'the paradigmatic form of political conflict in the late twentieth century' (Fraser 1997: 11). She links the rise of the struggle for recognition to the decentring of class and to the rise of diverse social movements 'mobilized around cross-cutting axes of difference' (1997: 13). While such movements contest a range of injustices, and demand both cultural and economic change, nevertheless as prospects for redistribution appear to recede, increasingly identity-based claims predominate. According to Fraser, it is cultural domination rather than exploitation which is therefore understood as the fundamental injustice of contemporary life, injustices which are to be remedied not through socio-economic redistribution, but through cultural recognition.

To highlight the distinctive logics of recognition claims, Fraser contrasts ideal typical instances of injustices of socio-economic distribution rooted in political economy, and of cultural or symbolic injustices 'rooted in social patterns of representation, interpretation and communication' (1997: 15). As a paradigmatic case or ideal type of socio-economic injustice Fraser offers the Marxist conception of the exploited class. The injustices experienced by this class, she suggests, are a matter of distribution because 'the proletariat receives an unjustly large share of the burdens and an unjustly small share of the rewards' (1997: 17). The remedy for this injustice is therefore redistribution involving a restructuring of political economy. As an ideal type of cultural or symbolic injustice Fraser considers the case of what she terms a 'despised sexuality' (1997: 18). In particular she considers homosexuals whose 'mode of collectivity is that of a despised sexuality, rooted in the cultural–valuational structure of society' (1997: 18). Fraser (1997: 18) suggests therefore that the injustices gays and lesbians experience are denials of recognition:

> Gays and lesbians suffer from heterosexism: the authoritative construction of norms that privilege heterosexuality. Along with this goes homophobia: the cultural devaluation of homosexuality. Their sexuality thus disparaged, homosexuals are subject to shaming, harassment, discrimination, and violence, while being denied legal rights and equal protections – all fundamentally denials of recognition.

Thus, rather than through a logic of redistribution, struggles and remedies for injustices of heterosexism will need to be cultural. In particular, according to Fraser, a deconstructive cultural politics involving a deconstruction of the homosexual/heterosexual binary will remedy such injustices.

While Fraser notes the contemporary political imaginary is increasingly defined by notions of identity, difference and recognition rather than by notions of exploitation and socio-economic redistribution, nevertheless she argues that contemporary justice requires both redistribution and recognition. This she says is the case not least because struggles for recognition are taking place in the context of a world of exacerbated inequality related to income and property ownership, and access to paid work, education and health care. Fraser therefore proposes a strategy of socialism and deconstruction to redress contemporary injustices, that is, of meeting the requirements of justice for all in the contemporary age. In making such a proposal and integrating redistribution and recognition Fraser understands her analysis as bringing together 'two political problematics which are currently dissociated from one another' (1997: 12).

Yet although Fraser's heuristic modelling is used to highlight what she sees as 'some of the central political dilemmas of our age' (1997: 13), in the *Social Text/New Left Review* exchange Butler has argued that the redistribution/recognition framework may be seen as an example of the broad tendency found in much left thinking to locate certain oppressions as part of political economy and others as exclusively cultural, and in particular of the tendency to position lesbian and gay struggles at the cultural end of the political spectrum. Moreover, Butler links such a move to the related tendency to view such 'cultural' struggles as trivial compared to the more serious political matters of socio-economic conditions, distribution and political economy.[7] In short, Fraser's framework positions lesbian and gay issues as 'merely cultural'. As a foil to this view, and in particular to destabilize the redistribution–class/recognition–sexuality framework and with it the socio-economic/cultural distinction, Butler outlines aspects of a political economy of sexuality. To do so she turns to early socialist feminist arguments regarding the reproduction of labour, especially the argument that the regulation of sexuality, especially normative heterosexuality (and more specifically still the organization of heterosexuality in the form of the heterosexual family) is central to the workings of political economy, indeed is central to the workings of the mode of production. In highlighting aspects of the political economy of sexuality, Butler therefore intends to put in doubt the view that sexuality is 'merely cultural' and to unsettle the stability of the very distinction that makes this line of reasoning possible.

Part of Fraser's response to this critique, quite right in my view, is to suggest that in revisiting early socialist feminist arguments, Butler has reproduced much of the functionalism characteristic of these accounts, indeed has resurrected an 'overtotalized view of capitalist society as a monolithic "system" of interlocking structures of oppression that seamlessly reinforce one another' (Fraser 1998: 285–6). Moreover, I would add that while Butler's political economy of sexuality clearly questions the view that issues of sexuality are 'merely cultural' and separate from injustices of distribution, such an approach does not address Nancy Fraser's central problem with analyses of performatively constituted identities. In particular, it does not address Fraser's concern that the notion of performativity is abstract and transhistorical and unable to come to grips with the character of specific social relations. In this respect Mariam Fraser's analysis, bringing together a consideration of performativity with historically specific class identities, and looking at the ways in which questions of socio-economic conditions and questions of subjectivity and identity cannot be divided, clearly does a great deal more work to address this central issue of contention than Butler's move of outlining a political economy of sexuality.

But if 'historicization' and 'deconstruction' so firmly separate out the 'social' from the 'cultural' – for instance issues of class from issues of sexuality – in ways which Mariam Fraser shows to be so limiting for understandings of identity and schismatic for contemporary politics, particularly the politics of identity, then this clearly has important implications for the reflexive modernization thesis outlined at the beginning of this chapter and the sociology of mobilities discussed in the introduction to this book. For instance if the reflexive modernization thesis is to have the kind of analytical and political purchase for feminist sociology that it has offered sociology in general, then it would seem vital that it does not separate out and analyse some issues such as sexuality as 'merely cultural' and position others as 'socio-historical' and as carrying more analytical and political significance. As I will show in the following chapter, however, the relations between the 'social' and the 'cultural' mark a key point of contention in relation to the theory of reflexive modernity. Thus while for some the problem with the framework of reflexive modernization as articulated by writers such as Beck and Giddens is that it lacks a cultural dimension at all, for others to develop a cultural understanding of reflexivity is to negate its social basis. In short, while the relations between social and cultural fields are a central area of contention in contemporary feminist debate on how best to go about the task of analysing gender and sexuality in late modernity, this is also the case in relation to debates surrounding how best to understand reflexivity.

two

reflexivity and mobility in social theory

introduction

In the previous chapter I outlined some of the central tenets of the reflexive modernization thesis as well as some key areas of contention in contemporary feminist debate. In so doing I suggested that within some strands of feminist sociology there has been a tendency to rely on a taken-for-granted under-standing of the social, where both the 'obviousness' and primacy of the social are often assumed. This was illustrated with reference to the challenges to traditional understandings of the social found in accounts of reflexive modernization and in relation to recent debates within feminism concerning the relations between the social and cultural fields or, as they are also some-times termed, the relations between historicization and deconstruction. I also argued that if the reflexive modernization thesis is to have the same kind of analytic and political purchase for feminist sociology that it has had for sociology in general, then it is crucial that it does not separate out certain issues (such as sexuality) as 'merely cultural' and locate others (such as broad scale inequalities) as socio-historical, and moreover assume that these carry more analytical and political weight. In addition though, at the end of the last chapter, I mentioned that the debates around the reflexive modernization thesis may be characterized as involving a similar tension found in recent feminist debate. Specifically, in debates around the reflexive modernization thesis the relations between the social and the cultural are a point of some considerable contestation.

In this chapter I map out this tension with particular reference to the analyses of reflexivity by Lash (1994), Dean (1996, 1997) and McNay (1999a, 1999b). I focus on these analyses on a number of counts. First, they take up aspects of the reflexive modernization thesis to offer important analyses of contemporary cultural and social formations, including the information economy and new forms of community, as well as to consider the politics of such formations particularly as they relate to issues of class and gender. These analyses highlight just how important the concepts of reflexivity, detraditionalization and individualization may be for analyses of the contemporary age. This chapter therefore draws attention to the significance of these concepts for contemporary social and cultural theory.

Second, I focus on these analyses as in their discussions of reflexive modernity they either implicitly (Lash) or explicitly (McNay) pay attention to issues of gender and also (although to a much lesser degree) sexuality. Thus via the reflexive modernization thesis these writers offer analyses of gender and sexuality. They therefore provide a ground for addressing the question posed in the previous chapter, namely, can the reflexive modernization thesis offer a revitalized empirical, analytic and political purchase for sociological (and especially feminist sociological) analyses of gender and sexuality. This chapter therefore pays close attention to either the implicit or explicit analyses of gender and sexuality offered in these analyses in order to address this question.

Third, attention is focused on these analyses as they point to some important *limits* of the reflexive modernization thesis (especially Lash's and McNay's). For Lash this amounts to an overly cognitive understanding of reflexivity in the accounts of Beck and Giddens, while for McNay this involves a tendency towards voluntarism in regard to questions of identity transformation which she highlights with particular reference to gender and sexuality. Interestingly to illuminate these limits, both turn to the social theory of Bourdieu, and in particular Bourdieu's notions of differentiated fields, habitus, and 'a feel for the game'. In so doing however, these analyses either implicitly or explicitly draw on an assumption that reflexivity is constituted via *mobility* between and within social–cultural fields. Thus this chapter will draw attention to this common assumption in these analyses, but it will also highlight that although these analyses share this assumption, in certain crucial respects they appear to pull against each other. In particular these analyses appear to pull against each other in respect to the question of whether or not reflexivity should be understood as social and/or cultural. McNay for instance argues that reflexivity should be understood as a thoroughly social phenomenon while Lash insists that a theory of reflexive modernization is not complete without the articulation of a cultural or aesthetic dimension. Here then the tensions surrounding what weight to give to the social and/or the cultural and the relations between the two in debates on the reflexive modernization thesis are made visible.

While highlighting these tensions this chapter will crucially ask what difference a social and/or cultural approach to reflexivity makes in terms of understandings of gender and sexuality in late modernity. As I will show, a focus on the aesthetic dimensions of reflexivity (in Lash's analysis) makes reflexivity almost exclusively masculinist, while a focus on the social dimensions of reflexivity (in McNay's analysis) suggests that (in certain important respects) gender and sexuality are detraditionalizing. I argue in this chapter that the implications of these different analyses is that reflexivity should not be regarded as social *or* cultural, but that in terms of understanding gender and sexuality post social structure it is important that the relations between the two are explored. I begin this chapter with a detailed exposition of Lash's analysis of the limits of reflexivity, his critique of the reflexive modernization thesis as articulated by Beck and Giddens, and his arguments regarding aesthetic or what he also terms hermeneutic reflexivity. I spend some time on this analysis as Lash's arguments are made with particular reference to the economic sphere, which is the subject of analysis in Chapter 3.

the limits of reflexivity

There have been a number of critiques of some of the central ideas which together constitute the reflexive modernization thesis; in particular several authors have highlighted some important limits to reflexivity. There has been, for example, a questioning of the idea that there is an ongoing, straightforward retrocession of 'the structural', with a number of writers arguing for a recognition of the emergence of new structural conditions (Lash 1994; Adam 1996; Alexander 1996). Discussing detraditionalization and individualization, and especially the view that traditional external forms of authority are giving way to the authority of the individual, Adam, for example, talks of the emergence of new and different external authorities in which she includes 'experts who hold authoritative knowledge (including social theorists), the media in its multiple guises and even money' (1996: 139).[1] In a similar vein Lash discusses the need to address the structural conditions of reflexivity. This is the case he suggests, particularly in relation to change in economic life, where the freeing of agency from structure 'is perhaps most powerfully instatiated' (Lash 1994: 119), especially in the development of what he terms 'reflexive accumulation', that is, a new framework for economic growth which is usually understood as 'flexible specialization', or what he sometimes refers to as 'cultural economy' (Lash 1993b). In this framework, economic growth takes place by the freeing of agency from structure, or rather, Lash writes, 'capital accumulation is possible only on the condition that agency can free itself from rule-bound "fordist" structures' (1994: 119). Specifically, demands for increasingly specialized consumption and the flexible production that this entails mean that firms and workers must innovate quickly. Fast innovation means that far more work must go into the design of products, with the consequence that production is better characterized as a knowledge-intensive design process than as a material 'labour process'. This knowledge intensity, Lash suggests, necessarily involves reflexivity. First it involves self-reflexivity in that the monitoring of workers by external rules is replaced by self-monitoring. Second, it involves 'structural reflexivity' (Lash 1994: 119) in that the rules and resources of workplaces no longer control workers but become the object of reflection for agency. That is, workers can reformulate and use such rules and resources in order to innovate.

In these ways Lash suggests the reflexive modernization thesis seems to have some considerable explanatory potential regarding the flexibilization of production. But, he asks, why do we find reflexivity in some places and not in others? Why in some economic sectors and not in others? And why do Giddens and Beck not pay attention to these questions, or indeed why do they not even register within their frameworks? To highlight the significance of this point Lash contrasts on the one hand the massive increases in the number of reflexive producers, in, for example, business services, the software sector and computer production, and on the other the post-Fordist creation of millions of 'junk jobs', that is of downgraded manufacturing jobs, the creation of a 'McDonald's proletariat' in the service sector, and the creation of large armies of unemployed. All of these new labour market positions, Lash argues, make it clear that alongside what he terms 'reflexivity winners' there are millions of 'reflexivity losers'. With this in mind he asks,

> Just how 'reflexive' is it possible for a single mother in an urban ghetto to be? . . . Beck and . . . Giddens write with insight on the self-construction of life narratives. But just how much freedom from the 'necessity' of 'structure' and structural poverty does this ghetto mother have to construct her own 'life narratives'?
>
> (1994: 120)

Lash's point in all of this is to suggest that to be able to account for such systematic inequalities it is urgent to consider the 'structural conditions of reflexivity' (1994: 120). Yet herein, as Lash himself makes clear, lies an apparent tension. If reflexivity – as he agrees – involves the freeing of agency from structure, indeed the retreat of social structure, how can inequality have a structural explanation (1994: 120)? The structures to which Lash refers are however not *social* structures, for instance the familiar social structures of Marxism – economic, political and ideological – but these are new non-social *cultural* information and communication structures, 'an articulated web of global and local networks of information and communication structures' (Lash 1994: 120–1). For Lash, in reflexive modernity, life chances depend not on place in and access to the mode of production, but rather place in and access to the mode of information. Moreover, to ignore these new information and communication structures is to be unable to account for 'systematic inequalities in our globalized informational capitalism, as well as the systematic inequalities between core and peripheral nations' (Lash 1994: 120).

Lash not only draws attention to the unevenness of reflexivity, and in particular to a politics of class pertaining to reflexivity which is invisible in the accounts of Beck and Giddens, he also questions the assumption found in these accounts that reflexivity arises in the context of both individualization and detraditionalization. He points, for example, to the significance of community, or what at times he terms pre-modern relations for reflexive accumulation. Thus he argues,

> pre-modern and communal–traditional forms . . . can be conducive to information flow and acquisition which are the structural conditions of reflexive production . . . communal regulation is optimal for the scope and power of information and communication structures.

(Lash 1994: 127)

Here then traditional communal forms are seen not as outmoded for workers or for economies, or as being destroyed by the processes of late modernity, but rather as conducive to and incited by new forms of production. Moreover, Lash suggests these new traditional communal forms are being constituted as agency is freed from structure. Lash looks to Germany and Japan for examples of reflexive production and in particular to demonstrate the significance of 'pre-modern', traditional forms in these regimes. He shows that promotion incentives in large firms in Japan are often tightly linked to the acquisition of knowledge or information, and that flows of information are optimized through personalized trust relations. Thus employment contracting is often 'relational' where exchange relationships involve not only straightforwardly cash–nexus exchanges but also symbolic exchanges, for example, of shared identities. All such forms are key to reflexive accumulation, they all optimize information flow. This emphasis on the significance of communal exchanges for reflexive production is also stressed in relation to the German case. Here, inclusive information structures and highly reflexive production are achieved through the corporate governance of production systems, for instance through the technical college and apprenticeship systems. In both cases Lash stresses that what is at issue is an ethics of commitment and obligation not to the self but to a community, 'this community being the firm in the Japanese case and the Beruf in the German case' (1994: 126). Practices in such communities are not simply a matter of the acquisition of money, power or status but are motivated towards 'workmanship [sic] or the good of the firm' (Lash 1994: 126). The freeing of agency from structure for Lash is therefore not a simple matter of progressive individualization but rather is constitutive of new communal forms. It is in the largest and most modern firms in Germany and Japan where it is suggested that such communal forms are to be found, structures which Anglo-Saxon firms until recently were attempting to develop.

In discussing these traditional–communal forms of reflexive production however, Lash points to a further contour of the politics of reflexive accumulation. Specifically he points to 'the systemic exclusion of women from the I&C structures' (1994: 133). Thus he comments on the tendencies towards an exclusion of women from places in and access to the mode of information, including access to knowledge and information intensive occupations and to informational, knowledge and communication goods outside of worklife in the household. He comments,

> In countries like Germany this exclusion of women (and minorities) is exacerbated by the corporatist institutions of the apprenticeship, the welfare state and the education system, in which women perform welfare services, not in firms operating through the market, not by working in jobs in the welfare state, but (as excluded from labour markets) in the home. Hence the very low labour-force participation rate of women in Germany.
>
> (Lash 1994: 133)

Moreover, outside of corporatist forms of governance this exclusion is also at issue. In neo-liberal labour markets such as those of the UK and the US women 'are shunted away from the information intensive end of the labour force and disproportionately into the new lower class positions' (Lash 1994: 133). While for the Japanese case, although women's employment rates are relatively high, 'a substantial portion of women's economic activity has been outside the large companies – especially in small companies or in family enterprises including farms' (Saso 1990: 7). In addition, a high proportion of women work in manufacturing as production workers and 'long serving women are usually found in small companies where wages are considerably lower than in larger companies' (Saso 1990: 69). In short, in the Japanese case women are excluded from precisely those spaces which Lash argues are those of reflexive production: large companies with emphases on information and knowledge flow and acquisition (Adkins 1999).

Reflecting on this exclusion from the new reflexive classes Lash suggests that women may be part of a new lower class or underclass. But although this for Lash is a new class category, as noted in the Introduction, he suggests 'the personnel filling these class positions are typically determined by more particularistic, "ascribed" characteristics – by race, country of origin and gender' (1994: 134, see also Beck 1992: 101). Lash does not attend to the processes of ascription, however – he simply assumes that in terms of reflexive accumulation these 'ascribed characteristics' are already formed. Therefore he does not consider if there is a relationship between reflexive accumulation and such processes, nor does he interrogate the nature of women's exclusion from reflexive occupations. Indeed we might ask how this exclusion works and how the process of ascription relates to the new structural conditions of reflexivity. How is it that many women end up being 'reflexivity losers'?

reflexivity 'in' the subject or in the world?

While Lash certainly does not answer this question directly, nevertheless we can surmise that the answer must have something to do with his critique of

Beck and Giddens's overly cognitive or rationalistic understanding of the late modern self and human action, and in particular the downplaying of what he terms hermeneutic or aesthetic reflexivity (see also Lichtblau 1999; Pellizzoni 1999). For Lash's point regarding the kinds of post-traditional forms of community he describes is not to say that the reflexive modernization thesis as proposed by Beck and Giddens is somehow wrong because the contemporary world comprises 'traditional' communities. This is because for Lash while these forms he describes are communal, nevertheless they are post-traditional because they are reflexive. But the kind of reflexivity at issue in these kinds of post-traditional communalization does not involve subject–object forms of knowledge which constitute reflexivity in the accounts of Beck and Giddens. What is at issue is not monitoring, calculating subjects reflecting on the world in an objective or realist way. Rather, Lash suggests the kind of reflexivity at issue in such post-traditional communities is the kind talked of by Bourdieu (Bourdieu 1990; Bourdieu and Wacquant 1992) where 'knowing' is situated in the life world, where reflexivity concerns the reflection on the unthought and unconscious categories of our thought (Wacquant 1992).

For Lash the important point regarding Bourdieu's sociology for conceptualizing reflexivity is that it breaks with the objectivism of Beck and Giddens, who presume a subject who exists outside of a world and for whom the world is conceptually mediated. Instead of bracketing off the lifeworld to arrive at individualized, subject–object forms of knowledge, Bourdieu's re-flexive sociology involves 'bracketing subject–object knowledge and situating knowers in their life-world' (Lash 1994: 156). Moreover, it is this kind of understanding, and indeed this kind of reflexivity, which is at issue in terms of the post-traditional communal forms Lash describes. In such communities everyday activities are about the routine achievement of meaning, that is the production of substantive goods 'guided by an understanding of more gener-ally what is regarded as substantively good by that community' (Lash 1994: 157), but the substantively good is not experienced as an imperative which is divorced from the everyday. Rather it is already present in the world of meanings and practices which are learned, but become 'unconscious as if inscribed on the body' (Lash 1994: 157). Reflexivity in such post-traditional communities is therefore not 'in' the subject or 'in' the self, but is in shared background practices, in something akin to Bourdieu's 'habitus', that is, in the durable yet transposable set of dispositions and competencies which (unconsciously) shape perceptions and actions.

On this understanding reflexivity is not about agents reflecting on social structures (as in Beck and Giddens). In fact, and as Lash makes clear, reflexivity is not about structures and agents at all but the uncovering of unthought categories which are themselves preconditions of our more self-conscious practices. Reflexivity is thus not a subject–object monitoring relation, but is a hermeneutic relation where unthought categories are not simple causes of reflexivity but are to be hermeneutically interpreted. More than this, however, as Bourdieu and Wacquant (1992) highlight, these un-thought categories are classificatory categories of our most immediate habits and practices. Bourdieu's reflexivity is therefore a reflexivity of 'our unthought, though bodily inscribed, categories. It is in short a sociology of the ontological foundations – in categories of habit – of conscious action' (Lash 1994: 155; Crossley 2001), which include bodily predispositions and orientations, that is learned, yet unthought, techniques of the body.

But Lash extends Bourdieu's sociology further to understand reflexive communities as delimited *fields* in which shared meanings, practices and obligations are at play. That is, and following Bourdieu, Lash conceives reflexive communities as comprising distinct fields of action.[2] Still more, Lash is suggesting that Bourdieu's 'field' is increasingly becoming the same thing as the informational and communication (or cultural) field (Lash 1993b, 1994), indeed that the contemporary world has become increasingly like Bourdieu's theoretical world. Thus he is suggesting that within the informa-tional and communication field new forms of cultural community have developed which are vastly different from traditional communities, and which in turn offer possibilities of even more intensified reflexivity. In short they entail reflexivity and understanding of the unthought categories, of the shared meanings that are the basis of community, that is they involve hermeneutic reflexivity. Manchester United supporters and the core membership of the ecological community are offered as further examples of such communities. According to Lash, such post-traditional communities (or post-traditional Gemeinshaft) are reflexive in four ways. First, one is not born or thrown into them but throws oneself into them (membership is a matter of choice). Second, they may be stretched over abstract space. Third, they consciously pose themselves the problem of their own creation and constant reinvention; indeed, 'members of the new communities are typically quite aware of the symbols central to the creation of their new identities' (Lash 1993b: 205). Fourth, their tools and products tend not to be material but abstract and cultural.

In forwarding this hermeneutic – or what elsewhere he terms aesthetic reflexivity (1993b) – Lash may be understood to be making a number of important moves. Perhaps the most significant of these is via the idea of hermeneutic reflexivity, he is able to account for how a 'we' exists or how the creation of collective identities takes place in the context of the retrocession of the social. Thus unlike Beck and Giddens, whose accounts foreground radical individualization (I am I), Lash provides a framework through which reflexivity is unhinged from individualization. In addition, in emphasizing the non-cognitive and interpretative elements of identity and reflexivity, this understanding breaks with the scientism of Beck and Giddens. Alexander (1996) has praised Lash's account on these grounds, but nonethe-less Alexander is not convinced that Lash's analysis adequately accounts for reflexivity; indeed he asks where does this account leave reflexivity? The problem as Alexander sees it is that looking to other sources of reflexivity via writers such as Bourdieu leads Lash into a theoretical dead end. In particular Alexander suggests this move cannot get at 'the kind of critical reflexivity that differentiates contemporary democratic, multicultural and civil societies from earlier more authoritarian, homogeneous and anti-individualistic regimes' (1996: 137). Alexander suggests that to be able to account for this kind of critical reflexivity requires connecting ideas about community situated ethics to the idea that critical thinking depends on the existence of more abstract, universalistic systems of reference. Such a move cannot, he suggests, be made via the social theory of Bourdieu, as this is precisely what it does not insist on since it embeds meaning-making in historically delimited institutional fields and geographically particular communities. In short, Alexander is suggesting that Lash's analysis cannot account for the kind of reflexivity which characterizes the contemporary condition. Beck and Giddens, he argues, are at least aware that there is something in the contemporary condition that is different and new, and that this newness has something to do with an increased capacity for reflexivity.[3]

I want to leave this issue aside for a moment (I will return to it in the conclusion), and instead return to the question I posed earlier. Specifically, to the question of how is it that so many women are reflexivity losers? Only now, following Lash's understanding of hermeneutic or aesthetic reflexivity, I want to refine this question and ask how does Lash's 'we' of reflexive modernity end up excluding many 'women'. If, as Lash suggests, the information and communication or cultural field can be increasingly likened to a Bourdieuian delimited field, and reflexivity in the era of the mode of communication is a hermeneutic reflexivity – a reflexivity of unthought categories, of shared meanings which form the basis of post-traditional community – what is it about this field, about this habitus of reflexive communities, whether they be the reflexive communities of the workplace or of Manchester United supporters, which is so exclusionary for women? Put another way, how is it that Lash's account – even though it offers such an important corrective to the scientism of Beck and Giddens – ends up making reflexivity so masculinist? Does contemporary social theory exclude women from the field of reflexivity as classical sociology excluded women from the field of the social? Should we now talk not of natural women and social men as feminist sociologists did in their parodies of classical sociology (see e.g. Marshall 1994; Sydie 1987) but of social women and reflexive men?[4]

reflexivity as feminist solidarity

In other accounts of reflexivity, however, women are not so excluded from reflexivity. In Jodi Dean's (1996, 1997) analysis, for example, reflexivity is not only inclusive of women, but reflexivity is understood as a basis for feminist solidarity. To use Lash's terms Dean retrieves a conception of a 'we' for contemporary feminism after identity politics via reflexivity. So we might

then ask what is it about Dean's understanding of reflexivity which is inclusive of women? Can this help us get at why Lash's reflexivity is exclusionary?
Dean's starting point for her retrieval of the 'we' for contemporary feminism
is the schismatic nature of identity politics, and in particular how, as she sees
it, identity politics has led to a rigidification of group identities. While the
politics of identity is so often understood as revealing the idea of solidarity
for women to be problematic – assuming as it does a sameness of all women
– Dean argues that the problems of essentialism and exclusion which have
been attached to the idea of solidarity do not stem from the goal of solidarity
itself. Rather, she says, these problems are related to a rigidification of group
identities. They arise, Dean argues, from a

> mistaken emphasis on 'ascribed' identities, an emphasis on what
> is culturally and biologically given 'to be' an identity as '*a woman*',
> on what the term already signifies, and on a presumption that
> getting the proper 'ascription' is all that is necessary for solidarity.
> (1997: 245, emphasis in original)

Such an emphasis on ascribed identities, Dean suggests, prevents
a focus on the theoretical and material conditions for a more inclusive
feminist solidarity. By solidarity Dean (1997: 245) is therefore not talking
of a solidarity of identity – sameness – rather she understands solidarity to
designate a relationship, 'a mutual expectation of a responsible orientation
to relationships'. But how might such solidarity be constituted? Dean (1997)
argues that a feminist solidarity of difference depends on self-reflection, that
is on self-reflexivity. One of the ways to develop such a capacity for reflexivity she suggests is through movements within and throughout different
groups. Experiences in one group may enable reflection on the norms and
expectations of other groups 'helping us to find a way to navigate through
difference' (Dean 1997: 225). Dean calls on the work of Kathy Ferguson
(1993) and Trinh T. Minh-ha (1990) to highlight the ways in which such a
capacity for reflection may be developed. Ferguson's notion of 'mobile
subjectivities', that is, subjectivities which rely on the spaces and relationships created in disagreements and discussions is, for example, understood
by Dean to both replace the comfort of the idea that there can be an easy
synthesis of differing feminist perspectives and to illustrate how such reflection
may be constituted. Trinh T. Minh-ha's description of movement among
groups as an intervention which undercuts the inside/outside opposition
is also understood to concern the kind of reflection in which Dean is interested. Thus she suggests 'Ferguson and Trinh are not only elaborating new
approaches to understanding subjectivity, but they are also telling us how
we acquire or develop the capacity for reflection' (Dean 1997: 256).

A number of points stand out as important in this account of
reflexivity. First, like Lash, Dean does not tie reflexivity to individualization
(I am I) or to self–other relations and instead aims at retrieving a 'we' in late
modernity – in this case for contemporary feminism. Second, and also like

Lash, in Dean's analysis of reflexivity there is an emphasis not on the person or on the self but on background practices. In particular, much like Lash's reflexivity, Dean understands reflexivity to be constituted via reflection on and a denaturalization of background practices and assumptions, or as Probyn (1993) has put in the context of a discussion of Paul Rabinow's work on reflexive ethnography, Dean's reflexivity is about 'making the familiar strange'. Thus for Dean reflexivity involves a questioning of 'the norms and practices of our common endeavours' (1997: 250). In this sense Dean's analysis makes feminist communities clear contenders to be understood as the sort of reflexive communities defined by Lash: one is not born into them but throws oneself into them; they may be stretched over abstract space; they consciously pose themselves the problem of their own creation and constant reinvention; and their tools and products tend not to be material but abstract and cultural. Crucially, however, in Dean's analysis the sort of reflexivity that will retrieve a 'we' for contemporary feminism – a 'we' which is not about exclusion or the rigidification of identities – is constituted by *mobility* between, through and within groups. Thus it is mobility which enables the kind of critical reflection and questioning which disrupts self–other relations and allows the emergence of a hybrid 'we' or what Dean (1997: 257) refers to as the perspective of the situated third. On such mobility Dean (1997: 256) writes,

> As we take over the norms and expectations of a group, as we are socialized as insiders, we acquire a particular self-understanding. Once we step 'outside' this group and 'into' another one, we gain a greater sense of our individual specificity. We have distanced ourselves from the first group and acquired the capacity to reflect on our identity as a member of this group.

Thus it is mobility that is crucial for the kind of reflexivity which Dean suggests may form a basis of a feminist solidarity of difference. Such reflexivity allows a 'move away from a reified and oppositional approach to difference, one that anchors difference in the roles of "self" and "other", to remind us of our ability to see from a variety of perspectives' (Dean 1997: 256). Indeed, for Dean, such forms of reflexivity – that is, taking the perspective of the situated third in relation to 'ourselves and our interactions' and realizing that no difference is absolute and relationships are fluid rather than fixed – will transform differences such as those of race, sexuality and class from barriers into 'resources for connections among feminists' (1997: 260). Mobility is therefore not only central to the constitution of reflexivity, but also to the making of resources – in this instance resources for a feminist solidarity of difference. Thus Dean's analysis implies that the disputes and points of contention in contemporary feminist debate discussed in the previous chapter may be redressed via a politics of reflexivity.

So despite the fact that Dean's and Lash's analyses share a number of important affinities, in Lash's analysis while many women are excluded from the field of reflexivity, in Dean's, reflexivity is the basis for feminist solidarity.[5] But Dean's notion of reflexivity differs from Lash's in one crucial respect. In particular it explicitly rests on the idea of mobility. Indeed such mobility is precisely what is constitutive of reflexivity. So we may now return to Lash's analysis and ask, following Dean, if Lash's reflexivity is exclusionary because his account somehow denies mobility to women? Or to pose the question another way does Dean's analysis not exclude women from the field of reflexivity because she attributes mobility to women?

Interestingly, Lash too talks (briefly) of a reflexivity which is connected to mobility, but here he is talking about a kind of reflexive community that he suggests cannot be understood in terms of Bourdieuian fields. Here he is speaking of diasporic communities which he argues maintain a collective 'being in the world'. While such communities, Lash argues, are not reflexive in the sense that one does not choose to join them but is thrown into them, they are reflexive in two senses. First, he suggests, as diasporic, there is a 'sort of "mobile" being in the world, which lends to it a certain mediation in regard to the "original" ethnie in country of origin' (Lash 1994: 162). Second, such community is reflexive in that the diasporic self is aware of heterodoxy, but decides not to move into the position of subject as opposed to object, but to remain in his or her ethnie's being in the world. The diasporic self is, Lash suggests, a bit like the reflexive anthropologist, 'whose classificatory habits clash and mesh and to a certain extent inter-translate with those of the foreign other' (1994: 162). So too he argues is this the case for the 'diaspora-by-night' (1994: 162) of the gay community, whose habits clash and intertranslate with those of the heterosexual other. But, and as already mentioned, Lash differentiates the reflexivity constituted via the mobility of such diasporic communities from the reflexivity of post-traditional communities – such as Manchester United supporters or the communities of reflexive production – which he suggests are akin to Bourdieu's delimited fields. Thus Lash's analysis assumes that the kind of reflexivity constituted by a mobile being in the world and a more Bourdieuian notion of reflexivity are quite separate.

In other analyses of reflexivity which draw on the work of Bourdieu however, mobility – especially mobility across and within fields – is understood as central to the constitution of reflexivity. Thus a distinction between a reflexivity connected to mobility and a reflexivity of unthought categories and meanings is not so tightly drawn. In the following section I discuss one such analysis, that of Lois McNay. I will spend some time on this analysis on a number of counts. First, McNay has provided one of the few accounts which seriously and quite systematically considers both the possibilities and limits of the reflexive modernization thesis for understanding transformations of both gender and (although to a lesser degree) sexual identity in late modernity. Second, I draw on McNay's account to illustrate how in a further analysis of reflexivity, mobility is assumed to be central to the constitution of reflexivity. Third, McNay's analysis is of interest here as it offers a way of addressing one of the main questions posed so far in this chapter, namely how it is that in Lash's analyses women are excluded from the field of reflexivity. McNay's analysis suggests that this is an issue of certain aspects of gender identity not being particularly amenable to reflexivity, a point which Lash's analysis may be said to negate. Finally, I spend some time on McNay's analysis to draw attention to a further assumption in her analysis of identity transformations in late modernity, namely that reflexivity is not only constituted by mobility but also by a general process of the *feminization* of social fields. As I will make clear in the following chapter this is an assumption that underlies many recent analyses of identity transformation in late modernity and this is particularly so in analyses of transformations of gender identity.

gender, embodiment and reflexivity

Discussing theories of reflexive modernity broadly, but especially the work of Giddens, McNay has argued that theories of reflexive identity – especially the idea that identity is an issue of reflexive self-transformation – fail to fully consider issues connected to gender identity, a failure which leads to an overemphasis on the expressive possibilities thrown up by processes of detraditionalization. She suggests that a more sustained examination of questions related to gender, embodiment and sexuality reveals aspects of identity that render it less amenable to emancipatory processes of refashioning. This is not to say, as McNay points out, that identity is somehow immutable, but she argues that in ignoring more embedded aspects of identity, certain theories of reflexive modernity run the risk of reinstating the disembodied and disembedded subject of masculinist thought.

This overemphasis on the potential for the transformation of social identities in theories of reflexive modernity, McNay suggests, can be linked to the influence of Foucault's work (1978, 1985). She suggests that Foucault's work provides both the backdrop and sets certain limits to the idea of self-consciously constituted identities found in theories of reflexive modernity. More specifically, McNay argues that the tension between the docile bodies of Foucault's early work on discipline (1978), and the emphasis in his later work on practices of the self and the aesthetics of existence (1985) where, she argues 'the impression is given that identity, particularly sexual identity, is fully amenable to a process of self-stylization' (1999a: 97), is reproduced in understandings of reflexively constituted identities. In particular, McNay is concerned that the reproduction of this tension produces a lack of attention to embodied aspects of identity. Thus while Foucault's early work assumes a passive, blank body on to which power relations are mapped (see also Lash 1990), in his later work 'the materiality of the body remains unthought in so far as it is conceived as the non-problematic backdrop to practices of the self' (McNay 1999a: 97). For McNay what both Foucault's early and later work share is therefore a lack of attention to issues of embodiment and it is this legacy which she suggests is reproduced in theories of reflexively constituted identity. Specifically, in the latter there is little if any interest in issues of embodiment. McNay singles out Giddens's work on reflexivity and the transformation of intimacy in this regard, but the lack of attention to and interest in issues of embodiment can be equally discerned in, for example, Beck and Beck-Gernsheim's work on love. The problem regarding this lack of focus on embodied and embedded aspects of identity, and especially to 'relatively involuntary, pre-reflexive and entrenched elements in identity' (McNay 1999a: 98) is that it leads, McNay argues, to a tendency towards voluntarism. Thus in theories of reflexively constituted identity there is an overemphasis on the possibilities of a self-fashioning of identity in late capitalism.

To highlight the ways in which certain theories of reflexivity ignore the more embedded aspects of identity McNay turns to the work of Bourdieu. Like some other contemporary feminist sociologists and cultural theorists (Skeggs 1997; Fraser 1999; Lawler 2000), McNay argues Bourdieu's work has important implications for feminist theories of gender identity. In particular she points to the ways in which for Bourdieu large scale social inequalities are not understood in terms of a distant institutional oppression or domination, but through a subtle, everyday inculcation of power relations 'upon the bodies and dispositions of individuals' (McNay 1999a: 99). For McNay it is this recognition of the incorporation of the social into the corporeal which is understood to do the critical work of opening up the issue of the more embodied and embedded aspects of identity and makes Bourdieu's work important for feminist understandings of identity. Moreover, McNay understands Bourdieu's work to act as a corrective to the view found in theories of reflexive modernization that identity is increasingly a matter of reflexive self-transformation. It is the notion of habitus which is crucial here. As I drew attention to in my discussion of Lash's analysis, in Bourdieu's work the incorporation of the socio-cultural into the corporeal is captured by the notion of habitus, that is, a 'system of lasting, transposable dispositions which, integrating past experiences, functions at every moment as a matrix of perceptions, appreciations, and actions' (Bourdieu 1977: 83).[6] Thus, and as McNay puts it, the notion of habitus refers to embodied rituals of everydayness by which a given culture produces its own 'obviousness'. As noted earlier, it is the habitus, for example, which allows institutions to attain authority since institutions only become viable if they are objectified in bodies in the form of durable dispositions that 'recognize and comply with the specific demands of institutional activity' (McNay 1999a: 99).

Much like for Lash in his critique of the reflexive modernization thesis, what is important for McNay about Bourdieu's notion of habitus is that here identity is not simply understood as an issue of predetermination, but nor is it conceived as a conscious, reflexive matter of self-transformation. The habitus works within certain limits (the field), but within these limits the habitus engenders a range of practices – modes of behaviour, thoughts, expressions, perceptions – which are both relatively unpredictable and limited in their diversity.[7] Thus rather than a determining structure, within certain limits, the habitus is generative and productive which 'establishes an active and creative relation . . . between subject and the world' (McNay 1999a: 100). But as I also drew attention to in my earlier discussion of Lash's analysis, in Bourdieu's conception practice is understood not to be fully *consciously* organized. Specifically, habitus is realized in a manner devoid of reflexive control through a 'feel for the game' (Bourdieu and Waquant 1992). That is, although not completely arbitrary, social practice often works outside of conscious control and reflection through a pre-reflexive level of practical mastery. As Williams (1995: 581) has put it, 'Most of us, most of the time take ourselves and the social world around us for granted; we do not think about what we do because, quite simply, we do not have to'. The 'feel for the game' is therefore a pre-reflexive, non-cognitive form of knowledge which 'is learnt by the body but cannot be explicitly articulated' (McNay 1999a: 101). We can think of driving a car as an example of such knowledge. It is something that is practised and learned but which becomes for most parts instinctual, pre-reflexive and non-cognitive. Bourdieu therefore,

> underscores the place of the body, its gestures, its stylistics, its unconscious 'knowingness' as the site for the reconstitution of a practical sense without which social reality would not be constituted as such.
>
> (Butler 1999: 114)

What is crucial for McNay regarding the idea of the unconscious 'knowingness' of practice in relation to gender is that it highlights the ways in which gender identity cannot simply be conceived of as the internalization of an external set of representations, that is as a conscious process of memorization. Rather, it foregrounds the ways in which gender identity is in important respects enacted at a pre-reflexive level (McNay 1999a: 101). In terms of the understandings of identity found in both Foucault's later work and in theories of reflexive modernization this conceptualization of identity has a number of important implications. In particular, and as McNay makes clear, habitus points to aspects of embodied experience which are not amenable to self-fashioning and self-monitoring (although they are never closed off). Thus, in McNay's view, Bourdieu's work highlights a problematic voluntarism in theories of reflexively constituted identity, since it points to 'entrenched dimensions of embodied experiences that might escape processes of self-reflexive monitoring' (McNay 1999a: 103).

To illustrate these more entrenched experiences McNay discusses certain aspects of the detraditionalization of gender. She argues that on the one hand processes of detraditionalization have opened up certain aspects of gender relations for renegotiation. Here McNay pinpoints the detraditionalization of the gender division of labour and marriage in particular. However, on the other hand, she points out that men and women have entrenched 'often unconscious investments in conventional images of masculinity and femininity which cannot easily be reshaped and throw into doubt ideas of the transformation of intimacy' (1999a: 103). McNay also discusses women's entry into the workforce as an aspect of the detraditionalization of gender, but she suggests such movements may further entrench other conventional patterns. For example, such moves have not freed women demonstrably from the burden of emotional responsibilities (McNay 1999a: 103). Instead they have made the process of individualization for women more complex since the ideal of performing an individualized biography – 'living one's own life' – is in sharp conflict with the conventional expectation of 'being there for others'.

For McNay this kind of unevenness in the transformation of gender relations illustrates how an emphasis on strategic and self-conscious self-monitoring overlooks more enduring aspects of identity. She also points to sexual desire and maternal feelings as examples of unconscious, pre-reflexive, entrenched aspects of identity which question the process of identity transformation highlighted by writers such as Giddens. Importantly, McNay also notes that the entrenched nature of gender identity is related to the ways in which other social distinctions – such as those of class – may be played out through the categories of gender. McNay suggests that such unevenness in the transformation of gender is again indicative of how Bourdieu's work is of relevance for theorizing gender. In particular this unevenness is understood to illustrate Bourdieu's claim that the habitus may continue to work long after 'the objective conditions of emergence have been dislodged' (McNay 1999a: 103), that is, to illustrate what Bourdieu terms the hysteresis or inertia of habitus (Bourdieu 1977: 83; Bourdieu and Waquant 1992: 130).

Like Lash, via Bourdieu, McNay therefore also finds the reflexive modernization thesis wanting. Lash draws on Bourdieu to critique the objectivist notion of reflexivity in the accounts of Beck and Giddens, to problematize the assumption that reflexivity goes hand in hand with indi-vidualization, and to arrive at a hermeneutic or aesthetic reflexivity, that is, a reflexivity of our 'unthought, though bodily inscribed, categories' and a 'we' of reflexive modernity. McNay also draws on Bourdieu to critique the idea found in the reflexive modernization thesis that identity is an issue of self-conscious transformation. In so doing, however, her analysis suggests that in relation to gender there may be important limits to the kind of reflexivity talked about by Lash. Specifically, in highlighting the ways in which there may be certain embodied and pre-reflexive aspects of identity which are less amenable to self-transformation, McNay's analysis suggests that Lash's analysis of reflexivity, although not referring to a strategic, self-conscious, self-monitoring reflexivity, nonetheless may downplay the ways in which hermeneutic or aesthetic reflexivity may be unevenly constituted within and across fields. More particularly, McNay's analysis suggests that

Lash's reflexivity – that is, a reflexivity of background practices, unthought categories and bodily dispositions (which breaks with the reflexivity of Beck and Giddens) – assumes that such hermeneutic reflexivity may be evenly realized across fields. Put another way, Lash's account assumes that the uncovering of unthought categories and categories of habit is a fairly even process (albeit intensified in the informational and communication field). Thus in drawing attention to the ways in which certain embedded unthought categories, bodily dispositions and shared background practices may not only be less amenable to the self-conscious form of reflexivity discussed by Beck and Giddens, McNay's analysis suggests that such aspects of identity are also less amenable to the hermeneutic reflexivity discussed by Lash, that is, are less amenable to hermeneutic interpretation. Following McNay's analysis we may then ask if Lash's reflexivity is so exclusionary for women and his 'we' of reflexive modernity is so masculinist because he assumes hermeneutic reflexivity – that is a reflexivity of unthought, though bodily inscribed catergories – may be evenly realized. Does he overlook the ways in which certain background practices, unthought categories and bodily dispositions may be particularly embedded?

detraditionalization, gender, mobility and social fields

But McNay is not only offering a critique of the reflexive modernization thesis, she is also offering a more substantive thesis regarding transformations of gender. I want now to draw out this more substantive thesis as well as her conceptualization of these transformations. While it is clear that McNay finds the idea of reflexively constituted identity problematic, nonetheless she accepts that there is an ongoing detraditionalization of gender, which while uneven, is nevertheless understood as a powerful social force. McNay posits that detraditionalizing forces in relation to gender are currently expressed in women's entry into the workforce, the opening up of negotiations regarding marriage and the gendered division of labour, and current conflicts between achieving an individualized and a more traditional biography for women ('being there for others'). Moreover, she proposes that this detraditionalization of gender may be fruitfully understood and analysed as involving the transposition of the *feminine* habitus into different fields of action (McNay 1999a: 113). Thus women's entry into the workforce may be understood in these terms. This transposition, McNay argues, is the outcome of increasing social differentiation of fields, whereby individuals may increasingly *move* across fields. In terms of gender, such differentiation and associated mobility means that there may be an intensified lack of fit between gendered habitus and field. McNay suggests that it is crucial to give attention to this 'lack of fit' for understanding the constitution of gender in late modern societies. In particular, this is imperative in the light of the increased entry of women in to traditionally non-feminine spheres of action and in the light of the putative opening up of alternative definitions of masculinity which some theorists have identified.

(McNay 1999a: 107)

For McNay the detraditionalization of gender is therefore understood as an issue of an intensified differentiation of social fields, an increasing mobility across fields, a lack of 'fit' between gendered habitus and field, and the emergence of hybrid experiences in terms of gender. The intensified differentiation of social fields in late modernity means, for example, that it is no longer possible to map masculine and feminine identities on to a straight division between public and private, as the relationship between the two realms has become more complex. This differentiation of social realms means that masculinity and femininity need, McNay argues, to be understood as imbricated in certain ways rather than as opposed and separate categories. McNay takes the example of the 'private' sphere to illustrate this claim. She notes the tendency in a range of social thought to conflate the private with both the domestic and the intimate and argues instead that it is important to break down the private into discrete arenas of action. Intimacy, for example, is now increasingly separated from the domestic and is central to conventionally defined impersonal fields of social action. Thus in many service industry occupations affective and intimate skills may be routinely enacted in relation to both customers and co-workers (see e.g. Hochschild 1983; Adkins and Lury 1992; Adkins 1995; Illouz 1997).

McNay's point here is that understanding the increasing differentiation of the social in terms of overlapping but distinct fields – rather than as opposed or separate areas of activity – opens up a way of conceptualizing the uneven process of detraditionalization in relation to gender. For example, it provides the conceptual space to read gender in the context of such differentiation not simply as an eternal opposition, but to give what she terms a differentiated account of gender identity that considers 'multiple disjuncture, overlap and conflict'. But more than this, McNay argues that this reading of detraditionalization as it relates to gender also provides a way of exploring claims about the increasingly reflexive nature of gender identity. Drawing on Bourdieu once again, McNay argues that such claims need to be assessed in relation to a Bourdieuian understanding of reflexivity. In particular they need to be assessed in the light of Bourdieu's argument that the emergence of reflexivity is itself linked to social differentiation, and in particular to the tensions and conflicts constitutive of a particular field. Thus rather than a generalized, universal capacity, 'reflexivity is an irregular manifestation dependent on a particular configuration of power relations' (McNay 1999a: 109). Indeed McNay suggests reflexivity can only emerge from distanciation provoked by the conflict and tension of social forces operating within and across specific fields. Reflexivity is therefore understood by McNay not to be a generalized capacity of subjects living in a detraditionalized era but to arise unevenly from subjects' embeddedness within differing sets of power relations. On this conceptualization, any recent shifts in conventional notions of masculinity and femininity are understood as a discontinuous process arising, as McNay argues, from the 'negotiation of discrepancies by individuals in their *movement within and across fields of social action*' (1999a: 111, emphasis added).

To illustrate this claim regarding the constitution of reflexivity, McNay considers the example of women entering the workforce after child-rearing. Such women, she argues, may experience difficulties since their expectations and predispositions (constituted largely through the experience of the domestic field) may sit rather uneasily with the 'objective requirements of the workplace' (1999a: 110). At the same time however, such dissonance may lead to greater awareness of the shortcomings of a patriarchally defined system of employment. McNay's point here is that in this instance reflexivity – a reflexive awareness towards gender – is based on what she terms a 'distanciation of the subject with constitutive structures'. Thus gender reflexivity – for example, a questioning of conventional notions of femininity – is understood to arise from the tensions in negotiating a lack of fit between habitus and field, in this case the tensions inherent in the negotiation of increasingly conflictual female roles. Indeed, McNay argues that if the notion of reflexivity is to have any relevance for feminism, it needs to be qualified with such a differentiated analysis of attendant social relations which in turn will lead to a more qualified analysis of reflexivity as a capacity of agents that is unevenly realized.

Other writers have agreed with this approach to understanding the constitution of reflexivity. In his discussion of Bourdieu's analysis of reflexivity Christopher Bryant (1995), for example, also draws attention to the constitution of reflexivity via mobility across fields and to its uneven realization. Like McNay, Bryant notes that for Bourdieu the habitus is not fixed in relation to specific fields but is potentially transferable from one field to another (see also Postone *et al.* 1993), and this 'may lead to clashes or prompt reflection' (Bryant 1995: 74). He argues 'patriarchy at home, for example, might clash with educational opportunity for girls and women at school and university' (1995: 74). Thus for Bryant, like McNay, reflexivity is understood to arise via the negotiation of discrepancies in the context of movement across fields. Moreover, Bryant similarly draws attention to the ways in which gender reflexivity is not a universal capacity of individuals but is unevenly realized in the context of tensions and conflicts between, across and within fields.

I want to draw attention to a number of issues regarding this form of conceptualization of gender transformation put forward by writers such as McNay and Bryant and consider its implications for some of the issues I have considered so far in this chapter. First, in such analyses reflexivity is understood to arise in the context of the differentiation of social fields, and moreover to be *constituted by mobility within and across fields*. Thus it is such mobility which is understood to be productive of the kind of discrepancies and conflict through which reflexive awareness may arise. This analysis of reflexivity therefore directly parallels Dean's in that in both accounts reflexivity is understood to be constituted by mobility in regard to the social, whether this be a mobility in and between different groups (Dean) or a mobility within and across fields (McNay and Bryant). But such analyses also highlight that mobility is a hidden issue in Lash's analysis of reflexivity. In particular, through her detailed exposition of the implications of Bourdieu's sociology for understanding specific forms of the detraditionalization of gender, McNay's analysis draws attention to some of the assumptions which Lash makes in his Bourdieuian influenced account. Specifically, in drawing attention to the ways in which Bourdieu links the emergence of reflexivity to social differentiation, and especially to the conflicts constitutive of fields, McNay reminds us that Lash's analysis is also one about differentiation, and in particular that his is an analysis of the emergence of the information and communication field, or as Lash sometimes also puts it, the cultural field.[8] This is an important point, for as I have repeated throughout this chapter, in terms of gender, what stands out from Lash's analysis is the exclusion of women from reflexivity. And this is so even though Lash argues that the cultural field is increasingly de-differentiating, that is, 'the delimited [cultural] field is itself now forming a mass market' (1990: 243), or as he terms it elsewhere, the social world is increasingly becoming like Bourdieu's theoretical world.

This account of de-differentiation notwithstanding, and bearing in mind McNay's reminder that for Bourdieu reflexivity arises in the context of the differentiation of fields, what we can now say about Lash's analysis in terms of the issue of gender, is not simply that women tend to be excluded from hermeneutic or aesthetic reflexivity, but from the post-traditional (de-differentiated) cultural field. Indeed, and keeping in mind McNay's reminder, we may well ask if women end up being reflexivity losers *due to a lack of mobility between social and cultural fields and within the cultural field* (that is the information and communication field). That is, are women reflexivity losers due to a lack of mobility between and within the cultural field? In short, considered in light of McNay's analysis, it seems that Lash's account of reflexivity has some hidden issues regarding mobility in relation to fields of action and the relationship between mobility and reflexivity.[9]

I hope to have illustrated so far in this chapter, that recent analyses of reflexivity link reflexivity either explicitly or implicitly to issues of mobility across and within fields – but this begs the question of how mobility is constituted. We might want to ask, for example, who gets to be mobile and how? This question seems particularly crucial to ask of Lash's analysis where reflexivity is linked to position in the mode of information and there are reflexivity 'winners' and 'losers' and Dean's analysis which suggests that reflexivity is a cultural resource.

As was highlighted above, McNay characterizes the differentiation of social fields in late modernity as 'the transposition of the feminine habitus into different fields of action' (1999a: 113). Her analysis therefore implies that forms of gender detraditionalization involve a kind of feminization of social fields, and that it is this feminization which is at issue in terms of mobility (that is, movements within and across fields), the lack of fit between habitus and field, and the constitution of reflexive awareness (a distanciation of the subject with constitutive structures). The differentiation of the intimate and the domestic and women's entry into the workforce are, for example, understood by McNay to involve the transposition of the feminine habitus into different fields of action.

In this analysis mobility across and within fields and the emergence of reflexivity are therefore above all understood as issues of the feminization of social fields. Indeed, as I will go on to illustrate in Chapter 3 the idea that the detraditionalization of the social is linked to feminization is widely taken up in contemporary analyses of socio-cultural change, particularly as such change relates to gender. Yet I shall also point to the ways in which to understand mobility and reflexivity as an issue of the feminization of social fields may limit understandings of the constitution of gender in late modernity. This is because ironically it does not allow the kind of understanding of gender which McNay argues is important in the context of the differentiation of social fields. Thus rather than as imbricated, an understanding of detraditionalization in terms of feminization reproduces the idea that masculinity and femininity are opposed and separate categories. A take-up of the idea of feminization thus ironically short-circuits the kind of work which McNay herself argues is central to an adequate understanding of gender in late modernity.

A further issue remains, however. If, as McNay claims, reflexivity (at least in terms of gender) is currently being realized (albeit unevenly) in the context of a feminization of social fields – indeed that contemporary reflexivity is a matter of the transposition of the feminine habitus into different fields of action – this implies that such a feminization is not at issue in regard to the information and communication field discussed by Lash, where, as we have seen women not only tend to be excluded from, and have a lack of mobility in and between this field, but where reflexivity tends to be masculinist. But as we have also seen Lash's information and communication field is cultural, while the fields with which McNay is concerned are social. Thus while McNay locates certain tendencies towards a social detraditionalization of gender, and (uneven) forms of gender reflexivity across and between (differentiated) social fields, Lash's analysis highlights an exclusion of women from the post-traditional de-differentiated cultural field. Indeed on the basis of the analyses of McNay and Lash, we may well surmise that while the social is (unevenly) detraditionalizing in relation to gender, the cultural field is now central to new forms of inequality, exclusion and difference. What this suggests is that it may be imperative not just to consider, as McNay argues, the lack of fit between gendered habitus and social fields, but also the relations between social and cultural fields for understanding the constitution of gender in late modern societies (Lury 1995; Adkins and Lury 1996).

aesthetics and reflexivity

But McNay tends to rule out of court a consideration of the relation between social and cultural fields through her insistence that reflexivity must be considered as a thoroughly *social* phenomenon and through her understanding of the social and the cultural as discrete and separate fields. This insistence is on view, for example, in her discussion of aestheticization and reflexivity, for in forwarding her analysis of reflexivity McNay not only questions the idea implied in analyses of reflexive modernity that reflexivity is an evenly distributed capacity of subjects in late modernity, but also the idea that reflexivity has an important aesthetic dimension. In particular, McNay takes issue with the analyses of writers such as Featherstone (1992), Maffesoli (1996) and the early writings on aestheticization (Lash 1988, 1990). In such analyses, McNay claims, identity transformations are conceived primarily as an aesthetic process where the possibility of reflexive awareness arises from processes associated with an aestheticization of everyday life. Here McNay is referring broadly to arguments where symbolic change (which McNay links to the issue of aestheticization) is understood as opening up possibilities for (social) identity transformation and in particular for reflexive awareness towards issues of identity. She has in mind, for example, arguments where an intensification of stylized or aestheticized images of gay, lesbian and 'queer' sexualities are understood to problematize the normative and incite reflexivity in regard to gender and sexuality through deliberate forms of experimentation with sexual and gender codes.

Throughout the 1990s a number of authors forwarded such arguments in relation to the proliferation of images (in the context of consumer capitalism) of a diverse range of sexual desires. So for example, regarding lesbian identity, the targeting of lesbians as a specific consumer group (Clark 1991; Smith 1997), the proliferation of signs of the lesbian body in everyday popular culture (Griggers 1997), and the proliferation of images seeming to address particularly lesbian pleasures (Gibbs 1994; Allen 1997; Lewis and Rolley 1997) throughout the 1990s were understood by some to produce the kinds of possibilities for reflexive identity transformation to which McNay refers. Creith (1996), for example, argued that the aestheticization of lesbian desire opened up the possibility of new forms of politics around sexuality, and in particular new ways of critiquing and destabilizing the hetero/homo binary. She looked, for example, at the re-emergence from the late 1980s onwards of a highly stylized butch/femme – or as she terms it neo butch/ femme – which she suggested challenged the gender binaries of heterosexuality since 'such performances demonstrate the ease with which gender identities can be constructed, no longer on the map of genital geography – showing that all gender is a performance, a masquerade' (Creith 1996: 138). For Creith the stylization of lesbian desire therefore concerned the emergence of a new aestheticized postmodern 'lesbian' and a new stylized politics of sexuality involving a blurring of the boundaries between heterosexuality and homosexuality (see also Lamos 1994).

What McNay finds particularly problematic about such arguments, as well as those of Lash, Featherstone and Maffesoli, is the assumption that such symbolic forms of destabilization invoke an opening up of social identities to produce a less fixed positioning of subjectivity. Thus she finds in such understandings a problematic conflation of processes of symbolic destabilization with processes of social and political transformation, or, and as McNay herself puts it, an elision of symbolic detraditionalization with social detraditionalization. Discussing shifts in images of gender, for example, she suggests that while there may have been a loosening of dominant images of femininity, nevertheless the transformatory impact of these images 'is far from certain' (McNay 1999a: 106).

For McNay such an elision of the symbolic with the social not only overestimates the significance of the expressive possibilities and reflexivity available in late capitalist society, but also involves problematic claims regarding identification which she argues are not able to sustain a notion of reflexivity. For instance she takes issue with Lash's (1988, 1990) understanding of how such reflexive identity transformations may take place in the relationship between subject and symbolic structure. In particular, she takes issue with the idea found in this account that identification operates not through meaning (discourse) but through direct impact (figure) (see also Featherstone 1992; Lash and Urry 1994).

What is problematic for McNay here is that this understanding of identification is primarily conceived of as visual, a form of identification which she argues 'operates through direct instantiation or the unmediated investment of the spectator's desire in the cultural object' (1999a: 110). This understanding she argues is unable to account for reflexivity as it assumes a total submission of the subject to cultural objects and hence presupposes that any space for a self-conscious shaping of identity is closed off. In short, while claiming to account for reflexivity in regard to identity, McNay suggests that such accounts which focus on aesthetic forms of reflexivity ironically cannot account for, or leave little space for an account of reflexivity. Against such accounts, McNay insists that reflexivity can only occur from distanciation provoked by the conflict and tension of *social* forces operating within and across specific fields. Thus in terms of gender, rather than through a processes of aestheticization, shifting forms of visual codes, and identifications with such codes, and as outlined earlier in this chapter, McNay wants to understand any shifts in conventional notions of masculinity and femininity and gender reflexivity as concerning the negotiation of the discrepancies arising from mobilities across and within fields constituted by a feminization of social fields.

This argument against an understanding of identity transformation in relation to processes of aestheticization and the insistence that identity transformations must be understood as primarily *social* clearly has certain parallels with the feminist sociological critiques of the techniques of 'deconstruction' and 'destabilization' for understanding identity transformations in late modernity discussed in Chapter 1. In particular, like many of the feminist sociological critiques of deconstruction and destabilization, McNay sees in analyses of aesthetic forms of reflexivity a problematic conflation of social and political transformation with symbolic transformation. In addition, and again with the sociological critics of deconstruction and destabilization, McNay finds analyses which stress the performative character of gender and sexuality wanting. In a discussion of the work of Judith Butler, for example, McNay suggests that such analyses focus too heavily on the symbolic and lack social and historical specificity (1999b: 178). Thus she suggests that in Butler's account of performatively constituted identities the relation between resignificatory practices and other social structures remains unexplored. In particular, McNay finds in Butler's account a tendency towards a valorization of the linguistic act of resignification as 'inherently subversive' at the expense of 'a more sustained consideration of the extent to which attendant social relations are dislodged or reinforced by such as act' (1999b: 181). Thus, and discussing the emergence of queer identities, although McNay suggests there is no question that the resignification of the term queer has been a powerful force for such forms of identification, much like Hennessy, she suggests also at issue here are the structures of consumerism associated with a 'detraditionalization of social relations in late capitalism' (1999b: 183). McNay argues however that a consideration of the latter – that is of the specificity of sociohistorical relations and their connections with symbolic identification – is ruled out of court in Butler's analysis because of the valorization of the act of resignification, the primacy accorded to symbolic identification, and the conflation of the latter with the social and historical.

But while McNay shares with many of the sociological critics discussed in Chapter 1 a concern that a focus on symbolic (or as she also sometimes sees it aesthetic) processes sidesteps the historical and social, nevertheless she does not simply assert the primacy of the social and historical as if that was enough to dislodge the significance of analyses such as those of Butler. For via Bourdieu, McNay articulates an account of the social made up of a differentiation of fields, mobility, a lack of fit between habitus and field and uneven reflexivity. Thus unlike many of the other accounts described in Chapter 1 which tend simply to assert the primacy of social, McNay provides an account through which different claims regarding identity transformations – including arguments regarding increasing reflexivity, detraditionalization and individualization – can be assessed. As I indicated earlier in this chapter, in the chapters that follow I will take up aspects of this account, particularly the ideas that detraditionalization vis-à-vis gender concerns a feminization of social fields and that reflexivity is constituted via mobility across fields. In particular I critically assess the usefulness of these ideas in regard to the problematic of understanding gender and sexuality post social structure.

While providing these analytical levers, nonetheless McNay's rejection of the significance of an aesthetic dimension to transformation of identity and reflexivity is curious. There is, for example, a well documented tradition in writings on modernity regarding the significance of figural regimes of signification for the experience of modernity, that is of the significance of the aestheticization of everyday life through such forms of signification (Featherstone 1992). This is particularly so in writings on the experiences of the big European cities of the nineteenth century (Simmel 1950; Benjamin 1973; Frisby 1985) which stressed that modernity involved a distinctive aesthetic mode of experiencing social reality, and in particular that this experience is characterized by the fleeting, transitory and contingent.

What is important regarding these analyses is that rather than as a separate or differentiated sphere, the aesthetic is understood as part of modern life (Frisby 1985; Featherstone 1991). More than this, however, in such writings the aesthetic is not simply understood to be part of modern life but a mode of knowing. Simmel's social theory of modernity, for example, concerns, as Frisby (1985: 53) has argued, an 'aesthetic stance vis-à-vis social reality' where the systematic, logical analysis of the fleeting and transitory experiences of modernity is rejected in favour of an aesthetic interpretation. Here social 'facts' are not differentiated by their 'truth value' but rather on the basis of analogies. In such a mode of knowing symbols replace ideas, a method which Frisby (1985, 1992) argues is akin to the notion of style in art, indeed makes Simmel a sociological impressionist in which the aesthetic is not just located as a part of modern experience but is also a way of knowing that experience. Thus Frisby comments that in Simmel's social theory the aesthetic dimension 'provides a degree of "self-understanding" with regard to its own role in delineating modernity' (1985: 53). In short, in Simmel's social theory this mode of knowing or 'method' concerns a *reflexive mode of knowing* in regard to the aesthetic itself.

As I will discuss in Chapter 4 this aesthetic reflexivity is certainly not confined to Simmel's social theory. Such reflexivity, for example, provided an alternative to positivism and realism for the literary avant-garde of the late nineteenth century (Felski 1995).[10] And in contemporary debates in the social sciences such reflexivity is also understood to offer an alternative to dominant ways of knowing. Reflexivity and the aesthetic are then not as sharply divided as McNay's analysis implies. Moreover, as I will also illustrate in Chapters 3 and 4, to downplay aesthetic reflexivity is to make invisible a key dimension of the unevenness of reflexivity with respect to gender which McNay herself seeks to make visible.

In addition, although McNay claims that analyses of the aestheticization of everyday life cannot sustain a notion of reflexivity, she also overlooks the ways in which such analyses foreground the emergence of a reflexive attitude in relation to the aesthetic, in particular in relation to consumption

(Lury 1996: 76). This is for instance at issue in Featherstone's (1992) historical analysis of aestheticization, and in particular of the significance of what he terms a controlled decontrol of emotions, senses and tastes in relation to the cultivation of an aesthetic stance in relation to everyday life. For Featherstone the latter has its roots in modernity and in particular concerns the cultivation or imitation of aspects of the lifestyles of the artistic and intellectual counter-cultures of the turn of the nineteenth century. Specifically, Featherstone suggests such a stance has its roots in the avant-garde movements engaged in the project of turning life into a work of art and with aesthetic consumption including 'the heroic concern with the achievement of originality and superiority in dress, demeanor, personal habits and even furnishings – what we now call lifestyle' (1992: 269). What Featherstone draws attention to in regard to this stance is that rather than simply being naive or uncontrolled, these practices involved what he terms a controlled decontrol of the emotions which involved the development of specific techniques of the self through which such an aesthetic sensibility could be cultivated. Such techniques, for example, 'can be developed to foster sensibilities which allow us to enjoy the swing between the extremes of aesthetic involvement and detachment' (Featherstone 1992: 285). That is, such techniques enable the enjoyment of both the pleasures of immersion and detached distanciation. Featherstone notes the take-up of such techniques by the emergent middle classes in the nineteenth century and how their cultivation served as a way of establishing the distinctiveness of this emergent class. In addition though, Featherstone argues that such practices are increasingly widespread, this more generalized take-up being connected to the development of mass consumption involving processes of de-differentiation (Lash 1990), that is, the reversal of the process of cultural differentiation involving the de-auraticization of art (Benjamin 1975). Indeed, it is this more widespread take-up of the techniques of the self in relation to cultivating an aesthetic stance in relation to the everyday and in particular in relation to consumption which for Featherstone constitutes the aestheticization of everyday life.

In foregrounding how an aesthetic stance requires the cultivation of techniques of the self which allow controlled decontrol, Featherstone's analysis questions McNay's claim that analyses of the aestheticization of everyday life leave no room for a notion of reflexivity. In particular, and as Lury has noted in a discussion of Featherstone's analysis of the controlled decontrol characteristic of such an aesthetic sensibility, the emotional distancing involved in such a stance introduces the possibility of reflection which 'facilitates the adoption of playful or ironic ways of consuming' (Lury 1996: 76). Such a stance, Lury argues, may therefore be understood to contribute to the emergence of a reflexive attitude towards identity. In short, and contra to McNay's claim, Featherstone's analysis of the aestheticization of everyday life does not only leave room for the kind of reflexivity which she is concerned to delineate, but also points to an *intensification* in this kind of reflexivity with the aestheticization of everyday life. In addition though, in highlighting the historical connection between the cultivation of an aesthetic sensibility and class formation, Featherstone's analysis suggests that the aesthetic and the social should not be understood as separate fields or as divided as McNay's analysis implies.[11] Indeed it suggests that by rejecting the significance of aesthetic reflexivity in the processes and practices of identity transformation, McNay's approach may put out of view some important irregular and uneven manifestations of reflexivity, that is, precisely those manifestations of reflexivity with which she states her analysis aims to make intelligible. Indeed, as I will go on to suggest in Chapters 3 and 4, in rejecting the significance of the aesthetic dimensions of reflexivity via her critiques of aestheticization, McNay may be limiting an assessment of uneven realizations of reflexivity. In particular, via analyses of cultural economy and a consideration of the reflexivity and the politics of knowledge I will suggest that a rejection of the aesthetic in attempts to assess transformations of identity limits attempts to do the kind of work which McNay argues is required for analysing such transformations, that is to consider reflexivity not as a universal, but as unevenly realized. In so doing I also hope to illustrate that reflexivity should not be considered as *either* social *or* cultural, but that it is important to consider the relations between the two if the politics of reflexivity are to be adequately assessed.

In closing this chapter, I want finally to return to Hennessy's analysis discussed in Chapter 1. For in highlighting the historical connection between the cultivation of an aesthetic stance and (middle)-class formation, Featherstone's analysis clearly has certain resonances with Hennessy's, especially her claim that such a stance or a stylized identity is only available to the urban middle classes of industrialized economies. Yet there is an important, if not major, difference in these analyses. Specifically, while Featherstone's suggests that social difference may be a consequence of the struggles around the ability to claim or take up such a stance, Hennessy's suggests that social difference and various forms of (class) inequality are not related to such struggles as such, but rather pre-exist such forms of contestation. Thus in her analyses the western metropolitan middle classes take on such an aesthetic stance in a seamless reproduction of class inequality. However, as I will suggest in the following chapters, such a position negates the ways in which first, the take-up of such a stance is a point of contestation, and second, how such a stance – involving as I have argued reflexivity – is not a matter of a seamless reproduction of social difference, but of the articulation of differences differently (Ahmed 1998).

three

feminization, mobility and cultural economy

introduction

Part of my discussion in the previous chapter drew attention to the ways in which recent analyses of reflexivity often rely on an explicit or implicit assumption that reflexivity is constituted via mobility across and within fields of action. I also drew attention to a strand of argument where in late modernity such mobility (and hence reflexivity) is understood to concern a feminization of social fields, that is, the transposition of the feminine habitus into different fields of action. Thus McNay proposes that it is feminization which accounts for mobility within and across fields, the lack of fit between habitus and fields and the constitution of a reflexive awareness towards gender. In short for McNay, it is the feminization of social fields which accounts for (certain kinds) of the (uneven social) detraditionalization of gender which she argues is characteristic of late modernity. I suggested also that social and cultural theorists interested in the detraditionalization of the social more broadly often discuss this process by invoking ideas of feminization, and it is this association between detraditionalization and feminization which I am concerned with in this chapter. In particular, I turn to recent arguments where changes in the economic sphere are understood in terms of feminization. That is, and to invoke a Bourdieuian frame, where such change is understood to entail the transposition of a feminine habitus into (certain) economic fields, especially post-industrial service sectors of the economy in metropolitan centres.

The economic sphere is of interest here on a number of counts. First of all, and as was made clear in my discussions in the previous chapter, the economic sphere has been located as a privileged site of reflexivity.

Second, the economic sphere has been located as an important site of reflexivity vis-à-vis gender. So as discussed in the previous chapter, McNay argues that the economic sphere is one in which there is an increasing transposition of the feminine habitus. She therefore locates the economic sphere as an important site for the constitution of gender reflexivity and for detraditionalization. Third, a number of recent analyses of the economy appear to support this feminization thesis. Finally, and significantly in the light of my discussions and arguments made towards the end of the previous chapter, this feminization is understood by some to be linked to processes of aestheticization. In particular, such feminization has been assumed to be linked to an increasing aestheticization or what is sometimes referred to as a 'culturalization' of economic life (see e.g. Lash and Urry 1994; Du Gay 1997; Bauman 1998) that is, a stylization of work, workplace identities, production processes and products.

Specifically, in terms of gender, the aestheticization of economic life is assumed to mean that performances of femininity – for all workers – are constitutive of workplace resources and that this aesthetic feminization undoes the categories, boundaries and binaries which make up gender, and in particular the gendered ordering of the economic. Thus a cultural or aesthetic feminization is assumed to be at play in relation to the economy, involving the transposition of the skills of femininity into the economic field, a transposition which involves both a detraditionalization and the emergence of a reflexive stance towards gender.

While this is an increasingly popular interpretation of post-industrial service work, nevertheless in this chapter, I question the view that the aestheticization of the economic is best understood as an issue of feminization. I question, for example, the logics of reversal and substitution at play in this argument as well as the claim that performances of femininity universally secure workplace rewards. Indeed instead of a feminized worker I suggest that the ideal worker of post-industrialized service work is one who can claim to possess a flexible or mobile relation to gender performance and hence to have taken up a reflexive stance towards gender. Yet I also highlight ways in which a mobile or flexible relation to gender performance may be denied to some workers through a naturalization of the performance of particular aesthetic styles which disallows reflexivity in relation to gender. In this sense I stress that while the new workplace ideals of flexibility and mobility may signal an end of a traditional masculine/feminine binary, gender in contemporary cultural economies is not simply being undone or straightforwardly detraditionalized, but rather is being arranged in new ways, an arrangement which I suggest involves positions of mobility and immanence in regard to cultural styles.

The arguments put forward in this chapter will therefore certainly support claims such as McNay's that reflexivity is unevenly realized and is not a universal. But they will nevertheless question the claim that transformations of gender identity in late modernity are best understood as concerning mobility within and across fields constituted by a process of feminization (whether that be conceived as social and/or cultural). As I suggested in the previous chapter, the notion of feminization ironically does not allow such transformations to be considered. Moreover, in discussing this issue with reference to the aesthetic, this chapter will also underline a further claim made in the previous chapter: that to reject the aesthetic as a source of reflexivity is to make invisible important uneven realizations of reflexivity, and in particular to make invisible how such reflexivity is central in understanding the constitution and articulation of differences post social structure. To begin to address these points I turn first to the idea of feminization and in particular to its recent history in analyses of economy and gender.

from political economic to cultural feminization

The idea of feminization is a familiar one in analyses of work, employment and economy. During the 1980s, for example, many analyses stressed the ways in which work may be understood as increasingly feminizing (see e.g. Massey 1984; Beechey 1988; Jenson *et al.* 1988). At this time the notion of feminization was used to refer to increasing labour force participation rates for women and declines in participation for men, but also at issue were a range of political–economic shifts that were understood to be connected to these changing participation rates.[1] So, for instance, (sometimes major) restructuring of state regimes, processes of de-industrialization, declines in traditional forms of men's employment (especially manufacturing work), the growth of the service sector, involving an increase in the kinds of jobs (such as servicing and caring jobs) traditionally performed by women and an expansion in the number of jobs involving terms and conditions often associated with women's work (including low pay, insecurity and deskilling), as well as changes in household and family forms were all at issue in discussions of the feminization of the labour force. Indeed given the issues linked to feminization, including new arrangements of gender, class, ethnicity and sexuality, and the emergence of new political and economic regimes (see e.g. Hagen and Jenson 1988; Haraway 1991; McDowell 1991) it was hardly surprising that it was claimed 'the feminization of the labour market is amongst the most far-reaching of the changes of the last two decades' (McDowell 1991: 417). Although the notion was clearly used to refer to a great deal more than an acknowledgement that women were increasingly active in the labour force, the wide-ranging set of changes brought together in discussions of feminization tended to overload the concept, with the complexities and specificities of the various processes at issue seeming to be obscured and written out by the use of the term.[2] This overloading, together with a general vagueness regarding the precise meaning of feminization, meant its use appeared somewhat limited. Indeed the focus on feminization as a possible way of thinking through and coming to grips with many of the shifts in work, employment and economy proved to be rather short lived.

Despite its limited purchase however, some of the discussions around 'feminization' contributed towards one of the major innovations in analyses of gender and employment. Specifically, some urged the need to go beyond the assumption that jobs were gender neutral and consider the ways in which jobs may be gendered (see e.g. Beechey 1988; Hagen and Jenson 1988), particularly because at that time declines in men's employment in manufacturing and expansions in women's employment in service sector jobs seemed to be making such a gendering explicit.[3] While the idea of the gendering of jobs does not seem to be an especially profound one today, especially as a range of writers have since turned attention to this issue, nevertheless the recognition that jobs are not simply empty places opened up a number of very significant developments in analyses of gender and work.[4] It led, for example, to redefinitions of workplace power, where power at work was no longer understood as a neutral economic domination or oppression, but to entail issues such as sexuality, desire and pleasure, as well as to a questioning of problematic distinctions which had previously pervaded the field, for instance, between the economic, the material and the cultural.[5] These moves in turn have fed into the more recent concerns to consider the performativity of economies (see e.g. Joseph 1998; Adkins and Lury 1999).

While the early discussions of feminization certainly contributed to some of the momentum which led to these kinds of moves, nevertheless analyses of the gendering of jobs also made clear that these early discussions often took for granted that particular kinds of jobs are quite fixed in terms of gender. Thus the growth in the number of service sector jobs was understood to be part of a 'feminization' of the labour force as it was simply assumed that service work would be performed by women. McDowell and Court (1994a), for example, argued that for the UK 'eight out of ten new jobs created in the 1980's have been for women'. Yet such jobs were understood to be 'women's' because 'these "new" occupations rely on the marketing of attributes conventionally associated with the "natural" attributes of femininity – sociability, caring and, indeed, servicing' (McDowell and Court 1994a: 229). At this time there certainly seemed to be an overlap between service sector jobs and women's employment, but analyses of the gendering of jobs questioned the taken-for-grantedness of such assumptions, in that they stressed that such gendering is by no means fixed, but rather is continuously made, remade and contested.

The importance of this point has been underlined by recent shifts and emerging trends in terms of employment. For instance there is increasing evidence of processes of desegregation of occupations in terms of gender, a loosening of the boundaries between 'men's work' and 'women's work'.[6] Thus rather than being segregated within a limited range of occupations women are now moving into a wider range of jobs, are increasingly working in the same jobs as men, and are moving into higher status occupations. At the same time, there is an increasing movement of men into occupations which have traditionally been understood as 'women's jobs'. Crompton (1997) for example has noted some significant moves of men into service occupations. In particular she has noted that 'between 1979 and 1990 more men have taken up catering, cleaning and other personal service occupations, as well as professional and related jobs in education, welfare and health' (Crompton, 1997: 139).[7] Such moves have been linked to some important shifts in workplace and organizational arrangements. In a recent study of organizational change in the UK, Halford *et al.* (1997), for example, have suggested that organizational and career hierarchies are moving away from an ascriptive gender order based on familial and gendered ideals and are increasingly figured in terms of principles of performance, a shift which has involved 'an undeniable decoupling of gender (as well as age) from organisational position' (1997: 262).[8] In short, in regard to gender and economy, a range of evidence points to the undoing of the kinds of social structures (such as the segregation and definition of jobs in terms of gender) which had previously been understood as key to the very constitution of gender (see e.g. Walby 1986, 1990).

Such processes of desegregation and redefinitions of jobs clearly question the easy association made in early discussions of feminization between service occupations and women. Indeed one would think that such moves render the idea of feminization as it was conceived in the 1980s debates entirely redundant, revealing as it does both an unworkable essentialism in terms of the gender of jobs and an inability to come to grips with recent changes in employment. Yet ironically, in the context of these recent changes, the notion of feminization is again being invoked to think about some of the recent shifts in terms of gender at work. But feminization is now being used to refer to a very different phenomenon to that at issue in the earlier discussions. Specifically, 'feminization' is no longer being mobilized in a political economy or socio-structural framework to think through labour market participation rates, terms and conditions of jobs, and the relationship between state, economy, labour market positions and class and gender formations. Rather, it is now being used to refer to a new sovereignty of appearance, image and style at work, where the performance of stylized presentations of self has emerged as a key resource in certain sectors of the economy, particularly in new service occupations. This is thought to constitute a feminization of work in that appearance, image and style are understood to be closely aligned to the aesthetics of the feminine, and moreover, to concern an aesthetics characteristic of workplace acts and jobs traditionally performed by women. 'Feminization' is therefore now being used to think through an aestheticization or 'culturalization' of labour linked to the more general processes of the de-differentiation of culture and economy and the aestheticization of everyday life pointed to by writers such as Lash (see also Du Gay 1993, 1997) and Featherstone and Hennessy respectively. Thus, with the shift from a focus on political economy to that of cultural economy, there has been an accompanying shift from a concern with political economic feminization to a concern with what might be thought of as a cultural feminization of work.

However, those who are now interested in the matter of feminization do not assume – as was the case in the early discussions of feminization – that femininity pertains only to women. Hence it is not assumed that the aesthetics of femininity relate only to women workers. Rather, the issue to be explored is the ways in which for range of jobs, both women and men are increasingly performing the aesthetics of femininity, and in these ways those who are concerned with such processes aim to shed light on the desegregation of jobs, the movement of men into 'women's jobs' and women into workplace positions which have traditionally been associated with men, as well as on the ways in which work and workplace identities are currently constituted. That is, the idea of cultural feminization is being invoked to shed light on detraditionalizations of gender in the economy post social structure.

the feminization of culture and the cultural feminization of work

The idea that work is culturally feminizing may be understood to be connected to the much broader view that there has been a recent feminization of contemporary culture (Baudrillard 1983; Felski 1997), a feminization which is often perceived to be linked to the ways in which contemporary culture is predominantly figured and defined as a consumer culture.[9] In particular, the characteristics of consumer culture – including the sovereignty of the sign, appearance, image and style; surface, simulation and masquerade; the authority of the consumer; and a de-differentiation of the social, involving, for example, a domestication of the public sphere – have been understood to involve such a feminization. This is so not only because of an 'ongoing interpellation of women as consumers' (Felski 1997: 136), but also because the dominant aesthetics and practices of consumer culture – for instance, style, surface, image, simulation and masquerade – are understood by some to be closely associated with the feminine, indeed to concern the very fabric of the feminine.[10] Commenting on the de-differentiation of the public and the private sphere in television culture, especially through daytime television, critic and journalist Mark Simpson (1996: 54) makes the view that contemporary culture is a feminized culture explicit:

> In making public the private world of home and 'feelings' – the inside outside – [daytime television] extends the bounds of the 'feminine' into the world . . . until 'the feminine' becomes the world and there is no inside/outside any more.

Indeed for some, the feminine has 'become the world' to such a degree that masculinity is also to be understood in these terms.[11] Such a feminization of masculinity is understood to take expression in the increasing representation of masculinity as a sign – as a signifier of desire, pleasure and difference – in contemporary culture, that is, in the representation of masculinity in terms traditionally associated with the representation of femininity (see e.g. Segal 1990; Nixon 1996; Carter 1998). A feminization of masculinity is also understood to be evidenced in the ways the performance of masculinity is now perceived to involve techniques and practices which have been characteristically associated with femininity, such as parody and masquerade (see Stern 1997 for a discussion of these moves), as well as in the ways men are increasingly considered to be performing the aesthetics of the feminine through stylized presentations of self (see e.g. Gullette 1994). Indeed,

> femininity would . . . appear to have lost its terrors, to have settled in like magic dust, over the terrain of culture generally, and in the process to have transformed masculinity itself: from he-man to her-man. Everyone may . . . 'become woman'.
>
> (Modleski 1991: 101)

Thus Gullette (1994) points to the ways in which (some) men are increasingly performing the corporeal aesthetics of femininity. She discusses, for example, the emergence of male cosmetics and perfumes, the normalization of the 'male makeover', and the performance of more 'expressive' corporeal styles by men. In addition, Gullette suggests that men are spending more than women on 'beauty aids' and are the fastest growing market for plastic surgeries (1994: 228). For Gullette such practices are understood to mean 'that some men now share the condition that women are forced to live . . . the genders are not opposed but in some freaky new way are overlapping' (1994: 224). Thus she suggests men may now be experiencing the traditional cultural traps of femininity, for instance, are becoming the subjects of an objectifying gaze (1994: 232). Indeed, it has been suggested that the relations of looking may themselves be understood to be increasingly feminizing, that is, moving away from being structured in terms of a normative male gaze (see e.g. Nixon 1996; Craik 1997; MacInnes 1998).

Such moves may clearly be read as troubling many understandings of gender in that they call into question both the usefulness and relevance of many of the key tropes and concepts used to understand the constitution of gender, including subject–object relations, the masculine/feminine binary and the idea that contemporary culture may be understood to be predominantly structured and may be analysed in terms of a male gaze. Cultural feminization has therefore been understood to call for sometimes major revisionings of social and cultural theory as not only does it suggest that the masculine/feminine binary may well be being undone, but also that power and its operations may have to be rethought. For example, it has been suggested,

> the typical . . . equation of the symbolic order with a regime of phallic authority and repression seems inadequate for dealing

with much of contemporary culture; here the dominant motifs
are no longer those of self-discipline, control and deferred gratifica-
tion, but rather of hedonism, abundance and instant pleasure.
Capitalism is increasingly portrayed as the good mother rather
than the repressive father, the munificent breast rather than the
phallus.

(Felski 1997: 136)

Given that consumer culture is in many ways understood to be a
totalizing culture, to the extent that workplace identities have been read as
consumer identities (see e.g. Du Gay 1996), and consumer culture is so often
thought to be a feminized culture, it is perhaps unsurprising that one of the
themes in recent analyses of work is that of cultural feminization. Nor is it
surprising that some of the concerns in relation to work parallel some of the
arguments made more generally in relation to contemporary culture. So it
has been suggested that a 'feminization' of masculinity is taking place at
work whereby men workers, rather than women, are new objects of desire,
pleasure and difference at work. On the movement of women into high
status occupations traditionally occupied by men, Grace (1991: 118), for
example, comments,

As women have entered certain sectors of the workforce, a certain
anxiety seems to have emerged and a displacement of women as
representation of desire and pleasure has begun to take place.
Increasingly, the sex-objects are men, partly in terms of their
bodily attributes but partly also because of what might be called
their mind attributes; the bright young executive or bond dealer,
who outsmarts the competition.

Even though as was made clear in Chapter 2 writers such as
McNay may object to the emphasis on culture and the aesthetic in such
interpretations, nonetheless there seems to be a general broad agreement
that the movement of (certain) women into the labour market (and in particular into high status jobs) is related to processes of feminization (whether
conceived of as social and/or cultural). And such processes in turn are understood to be linked to the detraditionalization of gender in the domains of
work and economy.

the cultural feminization of work: a hybridization of gender?

While claims such as Grace's are clearly suggestive of a major reordering of
work in terms of gender, what is less clear is how the 'culturalization' or
aestheticization of work relates to such changes. However, in a recent analysis
of the 'money, sex and power novel', a new form of mass-market fiction

which has at its core the theme of the cultural feminization of work, Felski (1997) presents some interesting hypotheses and provokes some important questions in this regard. The narrative structure of the genre is characterized by Felski as: 'a glamorous, ambitious heroine fights her way to the top of a corporate empire while engaging in conspicuous consumption of men and designer labels' (1997: 130). Thus in the 'money, sex and power' novel the feminine is located at the centre of consumer culture, and the traditional masculine script of corporate achievement and success is rewritten through the figure of a woman. For Felski this narrative structure is located as import-ant for analysis because of 'its surprising congruence with many current theoretical concerns' (1997: 142), a congruence evidenced in its focus on the relations between refashionings of gender and the cultural logics of late (consumer) capitalism. Indeed, Felski suggests the 'money, sex and power' novel might be seen as an 'exemplary instance of late capitalist semiotics' since it has for its focus a commodity culture where the desire to consume 'bears no relationship to the use value of what is bought; rather, it is triggered by the aesthetic and erotic aura of the commodity' (1997: 133). As with many analyses of contemporary consumer culture, however, the genre references and reconfigures the longstanding association between femininity and con-sumption. For instance, while the affinity of women with the commodity is central to the narrative, this affinity is not devalued but is rather reconfigured as a key source of the heroine's power. Specifically, the consumption skills of the heroine are the essential preconditions for her economic power and are central for her professional success in the cutting-edge economic sectors of late capitalism: the lifestyle, marketing and image industries, or what are sometimes referred to as the 'culture' industries. In the 'money, sex and power' novel the traditional affinity between women and the commodity is therefore,

> no longer devalued but triumphantly affirmed as a source of their economic power; this affinity equips them with new-found authority and professional expertise as media magnates and captains of industry in a culture increasingly feminised in its preoccupation with image, surface and style.
>
> (Felski 1997: 133)

More than reconfiguring women's affinity with the commodity as a new source of economic and professional power in the 'money, sex and power' genre, the semiotics of late capitalism are also linked to a

> novel reconfiguration of gender identities and relations. Rather than either reiterating the age-old story of feminine romance or reinvigorating conventionally masculine plots . . . it offers a dis-tinctively new script of femininity which is characterised by its hybrid and transvestite qualities.
>
> (Felski 1997: 129)

Felski suggests such hybrid qualities in relation to femininity are apparent in the way the heroines of novels are contradictorily gendered. So, for instance, one heroine 'combines a "masculine, piratical swagger" with the feminine body of a "great courtesan of the Belle Epoque"', and another 'usually identified with "feminine, long-legged grace" could also "almost have passed for a young man"' (Felski 1997: 141). What is important for Felski regarding this contradictory process of gendering is the way in which 'gender is a form of *self-conscious* and strategic artifice rather than a natural, internal attribute' (1997: 141, emphasis added), which she argues is particularly evident in descriptions of sexual encounters where 'women are alternatively dominating and submissive, objects but also desiring and active subjects of the gaze' (1997: 141–2). Thus Felski's analysis suggests that cultural feminization is linked to increasing fluidity or mobility in regard to gender performances, especially for women. Moreover, it suggests that such mobility is linked to the emergence and take-up of a reflexive attitude towards gender and to significant forms of detraditionalization, including a refiguring of women's affinity with the commodity as a source of power, and a denaturalization of gender.

While Felski claims that her analysis of the relations between late capitalist semiotics and refashionings of gender at work in this genre cannot be read in mimetic terms as a simple and accurate description of the lives of women, nevertheless she suggests 'the narrative trajectory of the . . . heroine . . . bears witness to a profound ideological shift in conceptions of women's position vis-a-vis the public and social world, a shift which in turn possesses real material effects' (1997: 140). Felski singles out the multiple modes of self (and multiple temporalities, for instance of the modern and the postmodern) actualized in the 'money, sex and power' novel as especially important in this regard. In particular, she suggests the idea of multiple subject positions 'speaks in particular to the diverse and rapidly shifting social roles of women' (1997: 141), especially as the exploration of 'the fluid and multivalent meanings of gender does not lose sight of the changing social and economic conditions which make such fluidity possible' (1997: 142). In this sense Felski argues that the genre provides 'suggestive insights' into the conditions of capitalist consumer culture, as such an acknowledgement of multiple subject positions is understood to be central to the analysis of contemporary women's culture (1997: 142).[12]

Given Felski's claims regarding the 'suggestive insights' of the 'money, sex and power' genre in terms of the relations between the semiotics of late capitalism and refashionings of gender, we might therefore ask what insights the genre, and Felski's analysis of the genre, may offer for understanding the aestheticization of work and current shifts in terms of the gendering of work. For instance we might ask if the cultural feminization of work, including the significance of consumption, style, and image for late capitalist production, is connected to the constitution of new forms of authority for women at work, to new forms of professional expertise, skill, and other workplace resources for example, and hence to the recent movement of (some) women into high status occupations. In particular, we might ask if it is the mobility and reflexivity in regard to gender which cultural feminization seems to afford women that is at the heart of these shifts. So we might take up Felski's claim that an acknowledgement of mobility vis-à-vis subject positions is crucial for understanding contemporary culture, and consider the possibility of multiple positionings at work and what this might mean for understanding the constitution of work and workplace gender identities. Indeed we might ask if the 'culturalization' of work is linked to a hybridization of workplace gender identities, and if such a hybridization is linked, for example, to the 'feminization' of masculinity at work (such as the new definition of men as sex-objects at work noted by writers such as Grace), as well as to redefinitions of jobs and processes of desegregation in relation to gender. In short, we might ask whether processes of the culturalization of work are linked to the kinds of refashionings of gender which Felski suggests may well characterize contemporary culture, and if such refashionings lie at the heart of some of the recent shifts in the gendering of the labour market described at the start of this chapter.

It is clear however from discussions in previous chapters, that many writers on transformations of gender in late modernity would question the emphasis found in Felski's analysis on the cultural. Thus while, as already mentioned, McNay may well agree that there is an ongoing feminization of the economic field, and that this process is a source of (uneven) gender reflexivity and is linked to certain (uneven) forms of detraditionalization, nonetheless she would reject the emphasis in Felski's analysis on the aesthetic. In particular, writers such as McNay may well reject the emphasis in Felski's analysis on the aesthetic dimension of gender reflexivity. Indeed, we can surmise from her discussions of Lash and Featherstone that McNay might view such an analysis as overemphasizing the possibilities for such gender reflexivity, that is, as overemphasizing the extent to which gender has become a reflexive, strategic artifice for women in late capitalism. McNay may well also see in Felski's analysis a conflation of symbolic forms of detraditionalization with social detraditionalization, and therefore a far too utopian and exaggerated account of gender transformation in late modernity. For as was stressed in Chapter 2, McNay sees reflexivity as a thoroughly social phenomenon, and as such would probably query the validity of the questions posed above stemming from Felski's analysis. But while Felski and others have linked processes of feminization to major transformations in gender in late capitalist societies, and in particular, understand the reflexivity that such processes incite to be linked to such transformations, nonetheless others would disagree that aesthetic reflexivity has such transformative powers in relation to gender. As was discussed in Chapter 2, Lash argues that many women are what he terms 'reflexivity losers'. Thus, Lash's analysis suggests that women are excluded from aesthetic reflexivity and implies that aesthetic reflexivity is masculinist. Indeed in the previous chapter I suggested that

Lash's analysis implies that (many) women somehow lack mobility between and within the (increasingly de-differentiating) cultural field, and it is this lack of mobility which is at issue in regard to losing out on reflexivity.

hybrids or reversals?

For the moment I will put these rather conflicting views on the relations between the aesthetic, reflexivity and transformations of gender to one side (I will return to them later in the chapter) and instead consider Martin's (1994) analysis of the emergence of the ideal of the flexible body. In particular, I focus here on Martin's discussion of workplaces and corporations, where she shows the flexible body to be rapidly emerging as a new ideal for employees, and to increasingly secure workplace rewards. While Martin is not concerned with thinking through how this new ideal of the flexible body for employees may relate to shifts in the gendering of work outlined at the beginning of this chapter, nevertheless what interests me here is that aspects of her discussion suggest that some of the refashionings of gender – for instance, the emergence of multiple subject positions in relation to gender – which Felski suggests may be characteristic of contemporary culture, may well be at issue in contemporary workplaces. For example, she describes training exercises,

> in which teams of men and women workers and managers of all ages and physiques ... climbed forty-foot towers and leaped off into space on a zip line, climbed forty-foot high walls and rappelled down again, climbed a twenty-five-foot high telephone pole, which wobbled, stood up on a twelve-inch platform on the top, which swiveled, turned around 180 degrees, and again leaped off into space.
>
> (Martin 1994: 212)

Martin notes how such exercises are designed to break down traditional workplace hierarchies, for instance, those between management and labour, men and women. Thus she comments such exercises were intended

> to *scramble* the characteristics usually associated with males and females. Men can feel fear on the high ropes course and thereby learn to express their vulnerability; women can feel brave and thereby learn to see their ability to lead. Men and women can also learn to appreciate these unaccustomed capacities in each other.
>
> (1994: 213, emphasis added)

From the point of view of my concerns in this chapter, what is so interesting about such 'scrambling' exercises (although Martin herself does not comment on them in these terms) is that they suggest flexibility at work now involves not just flexibility in relation to, for example, production processes, products and employment practices, but also flexibility in terms of gender. That is, such practices establish – and the ideal of the flexible body involves – a principle of flexibility or mobility in relation to gender. Hence in such training practices gender is not assumed to be a signifier of essential sex, nor to be a characteristic that workers simply 'possess' by virtue of 'natural', 'social' or some other form of determination. Rather, gender is denaturalized and established as mobile, fluid and indeterminate. Indeed far from being an issue of essences or determination, such 'scrambling' practices establish gender as a matter of performance. Hence masculinity, femininity and new gender hybrids may be performed, mobilized and contested by workers in a variety of ways in order to innovate and succeed in flexible corporations. Thus 'men' may perform (and indeed be rewarded for performing) traditional acts of femininity – such as showing fear and confessing it – and 'women' may perform (and also be rewarded for) traditional acts of masculinity – for instance physical exertion and bravery – when gender is established as flexible.

Indeed, many of the management specialists quoted by Martin make reference to the necessity of 'scrambling' sexual difference for corporate success and growth. Thus one specialist recommends that growth may now involve a process of *'sexual fusion and recombination'* dependent on recognizing and integrating 'those parts of ourselves – *male/female identities*, left/right brains, divergent/convergent thinking – that we have all neglected while striving for a strong sense of "self"'(Martin 1994: 208, emphases added). If, as my reading of Martin's evidence suggests, the flexible body involves a denaturalization and the establishment of a principle of flexibility and mobility in relation to gender at work, then it seems that Felski may well be correct in her hypothesis that multiple subject positions and hybrid gender performances characterize contemporary corporations and workplaces. Indeed, more than this, Martin's analysis is supportive of the general hypothesis being critically explored in this book: that gender post social structure is an issue of mobility and flexibility.

But in a further commentary on the ideal of the flexible body at work, Martin suggests that what is often at issue in processes of 'scrambling' is what she terms 'gender reversal'. Martin notes such a logic of reversal in an advertisement for a large banking corporation based in the US in which 'a woman sailor makes it clear to men rowers, "Be innovative or be gone"' (Martin 1994: 281), especially since,

> An amazingly precise reversal of this image was used in a poster 'Handicapped!' for women's suffrage in nineteenth century England . . . In this poster, the positions of men and women are the reverse of the . . . bank version: a woman rows laboriously in an unsuccessful effort to keep up with a man sailing far ahead in a sailboat.

Moreover, and importantly, Martin notes that such forms of gender reversal are increasingly being called for in today's business environment. Here then flexibility and mobility in regard to gender seems to be less a matter of hybridity and more a matter of a reversal of traditional workplace hierarchies, that is, a reversal of the values of an 'original'. In which case flexibility and mobility in relation to gender at work would seem to concern not so much the emergence of new positions which erase the idea of an 'original' and of 'origins', but rather a reversal of workplace positions traditionally associated with men and women, whereby women come to occupy positions traditionally associated with men, and men those associated with women.[13] Flexibility may therefore not involve the making of hybrid positions outside of a binary framework, but a reversal or substitution of positions defined by a traditional binary logic.[14]

Indeed, while warning of new forms of inequality connected to the new ideal of flexible bodies at work (especially the exclusion of groups defined as in possession of non-flexible rigid, unresponsive bodies), Martin herself registers some delight at certain elements of current organizational change, including 'the elimination of some old hierarchies between management and labor, the effort to include women and minorities, the wish to treat workers as whole people' (1994: 248). She therefore implicitly connects the emergence of the ideal of the flexible body at work – which I have suggested involves a principle of flexibility in relation to gender performance – to the kinds of shifts noted earlier in relation to employment, for instance to processes of gender desegregation and new definitions of jobs which seem to break with gender categorization, that is to detraditionalizations of gender in relation to the economy. We might then ask if what is at issue, for example, in men's movement into service occupations, and the movement of women into high status positions, is not so much a mobility concerning a logic of hybridity but rather one of 'reversal'.

the cultural feminization of work as 'money, sex and power' for women

To consider this question I now return to the issue of the cultural feminization of work, especially the claim that such a feminization is evidenced in an emphasis on style and image at work, that is, in an emphasis on the performance of aesthetics understood to be closely associated with the feminine. Thus I ask if a logic of hybridity or reversal is at issue in terms of this process, but in so doing I want to bear in mind Haraway's point that 'reversals . . . never just . . . reverse the values of the original. Rather, reversals . . . open up the story in unexpected ways' (1997a: 35). To do so I consider a study of professional financial service sector workers in the City of London by McDowell (1997; see also McDowell and Court 1994b) where a version of what I have termed the 'cultural feminization' thesis is made explicit.[15] Specifically, it is suggested that 'in the 1990s workplace performances are . . . increasingly influenced by feminine characteristics' (McDowell 1997: 298), an influence which is understood to take expression in the increasing emphasis on appearance, image and a style at work, indeed in the ways that stylized workplace performances increasingly secure rewards. Such stylized performances are understood by McDowell to be particularly at issue in new service sector occupations where 'the personal performance of workers, their ways of being and doing, are part of the service that is sold' (1997: 139). This organization of service labour is read as involving a ' "feminization" of all workers in the sense that bodies and personal appearance have become an integral element of workplace success' (McDowell 1997: 139). For McDowell the stylization of work is therefore interpreted to mean that both men and women workers are increasingly performing femininity at work. Indeed she argues that it is now 'in men's interests to co-opt femininity, or a version of it' (1997: 208). Thus McDowell looks at the ways many of the young men in her study (in contradistinction to their older workplace 'fathers') were conscious of the significance of bodily discipline in their work, especially in the areas of dress, style and weight. For example, they often worked out regularly and spent considerable time, effort and money on the production of a stylishly adorned, sleek, sexy body. So strong is this emphasis on body work for men workers that following Grace, it is suggested that such moves mean that men may now be positioned as sex objects at work, with desire and pleasure being displaced from women to men workers (McDowell and Court 1994b: 742).

What McDowell is concerned with here therefore are the kind of processes discussed by Featherstone as part of the aestheticization of everyday life outlined in the previous chapter. That is, she is interested in the ways in which the take-up of an aesthetic stance increasingly characterizes (certain kinds of) post-industrial service work, a stance which she aligns closely with the feminine. Thus here the 'cultural', or more particularly, the 'aesthetic' is understood to involve a process of feminization. Such processes of cultural or aesthetic feminization are understood by McDowell to have a number of important consequences for understanding the current constitution of service work, workplace gender identities and shifts in the gendering of the labour market. For example, she suggests that processes of feminization challenge many of the longstanding principles and ideals of bureaucracies, especially those which have worked to make men's advantage and women's disadvantage at work. For instance, it is suggested that the ideal of a disembodied, rational worker – which a number of writers have shown to be key in the creation of gendered workplace hierarchies in that it has been an ideal from which women have typically been excluded (see e.g. Pateman 1988; Acker 1990) – is being challenged by processes of cultural feminization. This challenge is understood to be taking place through the establishment of the necessity of a masculine as well as a feminine corporeality in service work. In particular it is argued that masculine corporeality disrupts the disembodied/ embodied binary and its association with male/female. In short, service based, 'culturalized' economies and the associated establishment of masculine corporeality at work are read as opening up a space for the disruption of techniques of the making of men's advantage and women's disadvantage at work, that is, for the undoing of conventional gendered workplace hierarchies.

But more than unsettling some key workplace ideals connected to traditional workplace hierarchies, the cultural feminization of work is also understood to constitute new forms of workplace power and authority for women. In particular, cultural feminization 'necessitates a reappraisal of workplace attitudes and behaviour by many men and may reposition women in a more powerful place' (McDowell 1997: 139). Indeed, 'the characteristics associated with femininity, conventionally assumed to be part of the reason for the disadvantaged position of women, may become a positive advantage' (McDowell 1997: 207). Thus as in the 'money, sex and power' novel where the heroine finds her consumption skills to be reconfigured as a new source of economic power, here the culturalization of the economic is understood to mean that the skills of femininity – in relation to appearance, style and image – are now new sources of workplace authority for women. Moreover, and also as for the heroines of the 'money, sex and power' novel this involves a take-up of a reflexive stance towards gender. Thus McDowell notes that older professional women self-consciously perform parodies or masquerades of femininity at work to gain workplace advantage. Discussing femininity at work one woman respondent in her study, for example, commented,

> You should use it to your best advantage. You can get a chance to speak maybe when others don't; you can dress for a certain meeting in a way that will instantly change the atmosphere slightly or I mean you can start to learn that there are things you can do to manipulate things. You can influence things by being more or less female.
>
> (McDowell 1997: 198)

Another remarked, 'as long as you are very competent you can use being a woman to your advantage. It might be easier, to gain a client and his confidence' (McDowell 1997: 198).

As already mentioned in this chapter, this view of the cultural or the aesthetic as a source of power for women clearly stands in opposition to that of Lash's where the detraditionalized, de-differentiated cultural 'field' is located as exclusionary of women. Indeed, despite her differences with Lash, and even though she too understands (social) feminization as being linked to specific (albeit uneven) forms of the detraditionalization of gender, McNay may well see McDowell's interpretation as lacking an analysis of power in regard to processes of feminization. Despite this however, a range of writers appear to concur with this view that femininity is now a labour market resource. In a Bourdieuian influenced analysis Lovell, for example, has argued that femininity as a form of cultural capital is beginning to have broad currency in what she says are unexpected ways. In particular she discusses a general increase in demand for feminine skills in the labour market (Lovell 2000: 25), while Pringle (1988), discussing her study of medical doctors in Australia and the UK, and also in a Bourdieuian frame, suggests similarly that within the medical profession there is an increasing demand and recognition of such feminine skills, that is, that there is a shifting gendered habitus in medicine. Indeed Pringle writes 'doctors have been compelled to take on a more feminine style, more holistic, and more concerned about communication' (1998: 8). She locates this shift as being part of what she sees as a more general repositioning of gender and work, involving shifting relations between the public and the private and the conditions of modernity. Thus much like McDowell, Pringle sees the feminization of work as relating to a detraditionalization of gender.

A similar line of argument is also put forward by Illouz, who in an analysis of recent transformations of the capitalist workplace suggests that with the emergence of the service economy (which demands an orientation towards persons rather than commodities) workers 'had to incorporate . . . in their personality . . . so called feminine attributes such as paying attention to emotions, controlling anger and listening sympathetically to others' (1997: 39). Indeed, and again drawing on Bourdieu, Illouz suggests that in service economies such feminine attributes are defined as forms of capital to be traded, a trade which was made possible via the articulation of a new language of selfhood.[16] Thus she too suggests that work in service economies is feminized, involving the breakdown of the distinction between public and private spheres, which she argues 'tends to blur distinctions of gender and gender roles' (Illouz 1997: 51), a blurring which she understands to have led to an increasingly prominent model of selfhood characterized by androgyny.

The feminization of the economic is therefore not only widely understood by many to constitute new forms of power for women through a revaluing of the skills of femininity at work, but also to signal, as Felski puts it in relation to the 'money, sex and power' genre, a 'reconfiguration of gender identities and relations'. In her study McDowell notes, for example, that for women in professional service jobs gender is often understood as a fluid, reflexive, strategic performance rather than as a fixed essence or attribute. Thus, professional women workers' descriptions of their performances of femininity in terms of 'being more or less female' and as strategically adaptable – 'it depends who I am going to be seeing. Sometimes I'll choose the "executive bimbo look"; at others . . . [a plain but very smart tailored blue dress] looks tremendously, you know, professional' (McDowell 1997: 198) – are understood as 'a clear recognition of the significance of a fluid gender performance in the workplace' (McDowell 1997: 198). As for the heroines of the 'money, sex and power' novels, femininity for such professional women service sector workers is therefore a matter of reflexivity: it is a self-conscious artifice characterized by multiplicity and fluidity. The aestheticization of the economic therefore appears to involve the take of a reflexive stance towards gender for women.

On this reading of the cultural feminization of work, it would seem that Felski's analysis of the semiotics of late capitalism in terms of gender may indeed have much in common with understandings of current shifts at work, such as the movement of women into higher status occupations and the desegregation of jobs. It also suggests that feminization – the transposition of the feminine habitus 'into' the economy (whether understood as social and/or aesthetic) – is a significant source of reflexivity in relation to gender which is connected to powerful forces of detraditionalization. However McDowell's analysis of the refashioning of gender in professional service sector work departs from the themes of the 'money, sex and power' genre in one crucial respect. Specifically, in McDowell's study a self-conscious, reflexive and fluid relation to gender does not only concern women, but is also understood to be at issue for men workers. This relation to gender is suggested to be apparent in the ways men workers, like their women colleagues, understand their service work to be a performance. In particular they are 'aware of the interactive nature of service work – the inseparability of their bodily performance from the product being sold' (McDowell 1997: 186). As such, men workers as well as women workers are understood to have a reflexive relation to gender. Specifically, rather than an internal, fixed attribute men workers understand gender as a self-conscious stratagem in interactive service work, a sign to be made, deployed and used as an item of exchange. Moreover, this refashioning of 'masculinity' at work is understood to represent a major shift in terms of gender at work:

> Rather than the centred and singular concept of a masculine identity that is used as a comparison to a more fluid feminine sense of self, it seems that young men in service occupations have a view of themselves and their gendered subjectivity as complex and multiple.
>
> (McDowell 1997: 190)

Indeed, for McDowell, this shift in 'masculinity' at work is understood as yet further evidence of a cultural feminization of work because a self-conscious, reflexive relation to gender is understood to be characteristic of femininity; younger men workers are beginning 'to do gender in ways that parallel the social construction of femininity' (1997: 182). In these ways McDowell understands the cultural feminization of work to be suggestive of perhaps a major refiguring of gender and gender identities at work, especially since it is not only understood to involve processes the denaturalization of gender, but also, following Butler (1990), to open up possibilities for '"complex and generative subject positions" for men and for women' (McDowell 1997: 207). Hence she suggests the current organization of service work may contain a 'liberatory promise' (1997: 207) in terms of gender at work.

On this account then, the 'feminization' of the economic is understood to be constitutive of a reflexive attitude in relation to gender for both women and men. Thus the changes McDowell describes suggests that certain sectors of post-industrial economies may be characterized as encouraging a self-conscious and strategic stance in relation to gender. That is, these shifts may be described as involving the cultivation of techniques which allow the enjoyment of 'the swing between the extremes of aesthetic involvement and detachment' (Featherstone 1992: 285) in regard to gender performances. They seem therefore to concern an intensification of the kind of aesthetic reflexivity discussed by Featherstone and Lury, involving the cultivation of techniques of controlled decontrol vis-à-vis the aesthetic styles of gender. As was discussed in the previous chapter however, writers such as Featherstone do not assume that the intensification of such aesthetic reflexivity simply undoes differences in the manner that McDowell argues in relation to gender. Indeed they suggest that such aesthetic reflexivity is linked not to a simple dispersal of differences but to their reworking. In the next section I take up this latter point in a consideration of the 'complex and generative subject positions' which McDowell suggests are at issue for workers in post-industrial service economies. In particular, I consider these positions more closely in relation to the question of hybridity and/or reversals raised earlier in this chapter. I do so because on my reading of McDowell's findings it seems that current refashionings of gender at work may involve more complex logics than those of either hybridity or reversal.

transtextual masculinity, immanent femininity?

So far in this chapter I have illustrated the ways in which the professional service workers in McDowell's study may be seen to be contradictorily gendered, to perform gender hybrids (for example, mix masculinity with femininity) and reversals (for instance, men may perform as sex objects). Nonetheless, McDowell's findings also suggest that only some workers are able to achieve such mobility in relation to subject positions. In particular, on my reading of this study, it seems reversed and hybrid positions are only available to workers who have a particular relation to workplace performance. Thus while McDowell notes mobility and fluidity for men professional service workers in relation to gender, what is so striking regarding her findings (although McDowell herself does not comment on it in these terms) is that they suggest women professional workers may have more limited mobility in relation to these positions. Specifically, while men professional workers can 'take on' the aesthetics of femininity, perform 'reversals' and gender hybrids, women professional workers not only find it difficult to 'take on' masculinity, but performances of masculine aesthetics often have negative workplace consequences. While McDowell stresses that certain masculinized performances by women may potentially be disruptive of gender – for instance, performances of emphatic gestures and facial grimaces by women on trading-room floors are understood to 'challenge conventional images of feminine passivity' (1997: 195) – many of the professional women stressed difficulties in relation to performing masculinity at work. Some, for example, were found to adopt a 'feminised version of the male uniform' (McDowell 1997: 146) and others to perform as 'honorary men', but such performances are shown to be 'doomed to failure' (1997: 197), counterproductive and to often backfire. Indeed for many of the women 'masquerading as a man was impossible' (McDowell and Court 1994b: 745). One of the respondents commented, for example, 'that it is difficult, even demeaning to try to be one of the boys' (McDowell 1997: 154); another said, 'You can't go out and get ratted with one of the boys in the pub; it just won't work' (1997: 154). Indeed, these professional women stressed that such performances often had negative workplace consequences with, for instance, colleagues and clients finding such performances inappropriate and out of place at work.

These problems for professional women service workers with performances of masculinity at work may be understood to be linked to what Halberstam has described as 'a widespread anxiety about the potential effects of femaleness and masculinity' (1998: 273). Indeed she argues that, 'Gender it seems is reversible only in one direction . . . masculinity one must conclude has been reserved for people with male bodies and has been actively denied to people with female bodies' (1998: 269). This thesis seems to have immediate purchase in relation to McDowell's study, not only because of the difficulties for women in performing masculinity at work, but also because no similar difficulties are described for men workers in relation to performances of femininity (or at least, those aspects of femininity focused on in this study, namely self-conscious emphases on style, image and appearance). Indeed performances of feminine aesthetics for men workers are achievable, recognized and moreover, may be converted into workplace resources to the extent that in contemporary service occupations it is 'in men's interests to co-opt femininity, or a version of it' (McDowell 1997: 208). In this sense one may therefore question the claim made by McDowell that in terms of gender, service labour is a matter of fluidity, mobility and 'complex and generative subject positions', for it seems from her findings that some workers have far greater mobility than others, evidenced, for example, in the way many men workers may 'take on' (and be rewarded for) performances of femininity, yet women do not seem to be able to unproblematically 'take on' (and be rewarded for) performances of masculinity. The women professional workers in McDowell's study do have some mobility in relation to gender, but this seems to operate *within* the genre of femininity. Hence while women professional workers talk of strategically adaptable performances of gender, these performances are understood in terms of being 'more or less female' and not 'more or less male'.

Interestingly, this uneven distribution of mobility in relation to gender at work is visible in other contemporary work narratives. For example, it may be seen in Tasker's (1998) discussion of work narratives in 1980s and 1990s 'new' Hollywood film, especially in her discussion of the significance of the theme of cross-dressing for these narratives. Here Tasker looks at films such as *Tootsie* (1982) and *Mrs Doubtfire* (1993), whose central male characters are cross-dressers and whose impersonations and performances of femininity take place for and at work. Indeed, both films 'emphasise the *need* to cross-dress for work' (Tasker 1998: 33, emphasis in original). What Tasker thus draws attention to is how these popular work narratives figure performances of femininity as forms of labour and exchangeable as economic and professional resources for men. But while Tasker's discussion of cross-dressing for men focuses on performances of male femininity, her discussion of cross-dressing for women focuses not so much on the performance of female masculinity, but on different forms of femininity by women. For instance, in films such as *Working Girl* (1988) cross-dressing for women is not a matter of an imitation or performance of masculinity, but of class cross-dressing. In particular, in *Working Girl* the narrative of cross-dressing for women concerns the performance of a (white) middle-class femininity by a (white) working-class woman in order to achieve career advancement and success. While, as Tasker points out, this transformation involves elements of a masculinization of femininity, for example, 'from the big hair and jewellery that signifies her working class status, to a guise of short hair and business suit' (1998: 42), nevertheless, at issue in this transformation is a desire for mobility within femininity rather than 'the adoption of male (dis)guise' (1998: 41).

In raising the theme of cross-dressing in relation to popular work narratives here I am certainly not suggesting that men's performances of femininity in professional service work as discussed by McDowell concern forms of cross-dressing.[17] Rather, my point is to highlight the way in which popular work narratives not only define a mobile and flexible relation to gender performances as a workplace resource, but also associate such mobility more often with men than with women. This association of men with mobility and fluidity in regard to gender at work clearly displaces more established narratives of male success and power at work where performances of, for example, paternalism, adventure, heroism, self-reliance and self-improvement have typically been linked to the achievement of workplace authority and power for men. Indeed this association not only appears to disrupt such links between men, the performance of traditional masculine scripts and workplace power, but also the very idea of gendered work narratives. However, my suggestion is that mobility and fluidity in relation to gender performances at work concerns not so much the end of work narratives, but a new narrative of workplace success. Moreover, Tasker's discussion of popular work narratives, together with my reading of McDowell's study, suggests that such a narrative and the mobility associated with this narrative may well be more available to men than to women.

The emergence of mobile subject positions and the association of such positions with cultural resources has also been discussed by Diawara (1998) in relation to masculinity. Commenting on the recent re-emergence of 1970s Blaxploitation films Diawara notes that within this new-old genre, black masculinity has become transtextual, that is, has become a mobile cultural style which may move from character to character. In *Pulp Fiction* (1994), for example, he suggests this mobility takes expression in the ways white characters play blackness. Thus white characters, such as those played by John Travolta and Bruce Willis, take on the aesthetics of blackness – including black 'esthetique du cool' and black male style language – as deployed in earlier Blaxploitation films by black characters themselves. Indeed 'Tarantino's [the director's] discovery was that white characters can play Blaxploitation roles, and that black maleness, as embodied in esthetique du cool, can be transported through white bodies' (Diawara 1998: 52).

Yet Diawara stresses that transtextuality – achieving a mobile or flexible relation to cultural styles – and therefore occupying (and claiming) a transtextual subject position, is not distributed evenly among characters. In *Pulp Fiction*, for instance, white male characters achieve transtextuality while black male characters tend to be excluded from performing mobility in relation to subject positions. Indeed, black male characters tend only to play blackness. Commenting on this uneven distribution of transtextuality Diawara notes 'Travolta has literal mobility, in terms of coolness and language and dress code; no door can be closed to him' (1998: 57). Black characters, such as the character played by Samuel Jackson, by contrast, have their own coolness: 'Jackson has the coolness of his own – immanent – blackness. To me, Jackson, who's a great actor, appears not to be acting; he just appears to be "a black guy"' (Diawara 1998: 57). What is important here for Diawara is that the blackness of Jackson's character – his coolness – unlike in the case of Travolta, is fixed and 'trapped' in the character. To use Diawara's terms, the blackness of Jackson's character is made 'immanent'. When a cultural style becomes 'trapped' or naturalized in this way, transtextuality is denied. Thus in terms of subject positions Jackson's character may only occupy the position of black maleness. But so strong is 'the trapping of a cultural role in a character' (Diawara 1998: 51), that not only is a mobile, flexible relation to cultural styles denied to black characters, but also to 'performing' or to acting itself. Hence the actor (Jackson) 'appears not to be acting'.

Similarly for the film *Boyz N The Hood* (1991) Diawara comments 'the single mother of Doughboy and Ricky is acting, but she looks so much like a typical welfare mother that she could not even be considered for an award for supporting actress' (1998: 57). Yet while the positioning of black characters–actors in terms of immanence means they may not be recognized as 'actors', for white characters when black masculinity becomes transtextual it is 'not only a source of fun and role-playing, but also *a source of revalorization of the white characters' cultural capital*' (Diawara 1998: 52, emphasis added). At issue in terms of this revalorization, and as Diawara also notes, is the way in which such mobility accords white characters' *reflexivity* in respect to masculinity. Thus such mobility suggests that masculinity is understood not as a fixed internal state, but rather as a self-conscious artifice. In short, such mobility is constitutive of reflexivity. Moreover, this reflexivity is disallowed when a cultural style is made immanent, since the fixing of a cultural style 'in' a character – an immanent relation to cultural style – makes a self-conscious relation to masculinity unintelligible.

This analysis of transtextuality and immanence, especially in relation to masculinity, appears to have some currency in relation to the shifts currently being documented in terms of gender at work, including those outlined by McDowell. For example, while white male characters in more recent Blaxploitation films are mobile in relation to various masculine aesthetics, and such performances constitute reflexivity and forms of cultural capital, the male professional service workers in McDowell's study 'take on' various aesthetics of gender, are attributed with reflexivity in relation to gender, and such performances may be converted into workplace resources. Thus while white male characters have mobility in relation to a range of subject positions, so too it seems do these male professional workers. Indeed, McDowell's male professional service workers may be said to occupy a transtextual position in relation to gender at work. But more than this it also seems that some workers occupy positions of immanence in regard to gender. For example, while McDowell's findings show that women's performances of masculinity are often denied, they also show how performances of femininity by women are often made immanent in workplace practices. Thus women's performances of femininity are widely defined as not concerning skills or competencies, but rather, as one respondent commented, 'natural advantages' which should not receive workplace recognition and rewards, for instance, be rewarded by promotion (McDowell, 1997: 154). Thus (many of) the professional women workers in McDowell's study are not recognized as taking up a reflexive stance in relation to gender since they are positioned as having an immanent relation to femininity. In this sense Diawara's 'transtextuality/immanence' scheme may give us some purchase not only on the flexibility of male professional service workers in relation to gender in McDowell's study, but also on the research finding that as women move into professional and managerial jobs, this involves 'an abandonment' (Halford *et al.* 1997) or 'loss of femininity' (Coates 1997) for women.[18] Specifically, such 'losses' or 'abandonments' may be understood not, as is so often claimed, that performances of femininity are somehow out of place for women in high status jobs, but rather that such performances are naturalized and unrecognized.[19] Thus rather than a set of workplace skills, strategies or performances, femininity is made immanent for such professional women workers. As writers on consumer culture have argued and writers on the culturalization of work imply, femininity may now be a key aesthetic resource, and this may especially be the case for new service occupations. But if performances of femininity *by women* at work are not recognized as performances, they will not be recognized as styles which are made up, deployed, and exchangeable as workplace resources. That is, they will not be recognized as concerning the take-up of a reflexive stance towards gender.

What this suggests is that the idea of feminization (whether conceived of as cultural and/or social) – and in particular the idea of the transposition of the feminine habitus 'into' the economy, which leads to mobility and reflexivity with regard to gender and to a process of detraditionalization – may be a less than adequate conceptualization of the reconfiguring of gender and gender identities in the context of late modernity. This is especially so as the feminization thesis blocks out of view the ways in which a mobile and reflexive relation to gender is not universally available to all workers and is a cultural resource, that is may be converted into forms of economic capital. Indeed it blocks out of view the ways in which a mobile and reflexive relation to gender is a privileged identity position in late modernity (see also Cronin 1999, 2000a, 2000b; Skeggs 2002). Rather than registering this latter point, the feminization thesis reads such mobility as transgressive, 'liberatory' and as involving the detraditionalization of gender. In short, the feminization thesis fails to register that such mobility and reflexivity is not transgressive, but involves a new arrangement of gender, one which I have argued concerns positions of flexibility and immanence in relation to cultural styles.

   If as writers such as Felski, Martin and Diawara suggest, mobility and flexibility increasingly constitute both reflexivity and cultural resources, and yet as I have indicated in the case of femininity, and as Diawara has shown in relation to masculinity, such flexibility (and hence reflexivity) is by no means universal, then it seems that a politics may well need to be developed around immanent and flexible subject positions. But such a politics needs to keep in mind, as I hope to have shown in relation to cultural economy, that these positions cannot easily be divided from issues of 'distribution' or 'production' since, as the case of post-industrial service labour implies, such positions may be made in (late capitalist) distribution–production networks, circuits and exchanges themselves.[20] The development of such a politics may be particularly pressing if the undoing of binaries associated with the new workplace ideals of flexibility, mobility, hybridity, substitution, reversal and reflexivity continue to be read as 'liberatory' and there is a failure to address the ways in which such mobility may entail new forms of power. While in this chapter I have focused on the politics of mobility in terms of gender performance, Diawara's analysis of mobile and immanent masculinities and Tasker's discussion of cross-dressing clearly indicate that transtextual positions at work involve a complex politics of performance in terms of race, class, ethnicity, sexuality and gender. In terms of gender, although it is clearly the case that mobility and fluidity signal the end of a simple masculine/feminine binary and there are significant moves towards the denaturalization and desocialization of gender at work, what I have tried to stress is that the undoing of an 'original', in this case of traditional gendered hierarchies and categories at work, has certainly opened up the story in some unexpected ways. Men's performances of the aesthetics of femininity at work, for example, may not necessarily indicate that men are now experiencing the traditional cultural traps of femininity, nor that men are now positioned as sex objects at work with women as subjects.

Rather my argument suggests that analyses which rely on these kind of logics of reversal where the values of an 'original' are simply reversed or substituted for each other – as is so evident in analyses of the feminization of work where the trope of masculinity is simply replaced with that of femininity – should themselves be put into question.[21] While it seems that service work in late capitalist economies involves the making of a mobile femininity, it cannot simply be assumed that this necessarily leads to 'money, sex and power' for women, but rather seems to concern the emergence of a new ideal worker figured in terms of mobility and flexibility in relation to gender performance at work.

cultural economy, reflexivity and detraditionalization

All of this puts in question the claims of writers such as McNay who suggests that the cultural or the aesthetic has little, if any, effectivity in the constitution of gender and sexuality, and in particular is of little significance in terms of the constitution of gender reflexivity. For in the case of cultural economy it seems that the aesthetic is not only an important source of gender reflexivity, but also that the aesthetic dimension involves uneven manifestations of reflexivity. Specifically, while the broad shifts in the economy I have described in this chapter may be characterized as encouraging the take-up of a self-conscious and strategic stance in relation to gender, the take-up of this aesthetic gender reflexivity is by no means a universal. For instance, and as my discussion in this chapter has illustrated, only some workers are recognized as having cultivated such a stance. In particular, it is only those whose relation to gender is mobile and is not made immanent who can claim reflexivity, while for those whose relation to gender is made immanent, a reflexive or self-conscious stance is rendered unintelligible. Thus while on the one hand this chapter has pointed to the ways in which in cultural economies gender has been established as mobile, fluid and indeterminate, on the other it has pointed to the ways in which this has provided a very ground for the articulation of difference. Specifically, instead of via social or natural determinants, differences of gender are articulated in terms of positions of mobility and immanence in regard to cultural styles.

What this suggests is that it is crucial to consider the aesthetic not only as source of reflexivity but also how such reflexivity is unevenly distributed, and how this relates to current articulations of difference. Indeed it suggests that the aesthetic may be a key dimension of everyday life for the making of such differences. In addition though, given that the take-up of a reflexive stance (for instance gender reflexivity) may be converted into resources (including cultural and economic capital), to ignore the aesthetic dimension of reflexivity would not only make such differences invisible, but also forms of inequality related to these kinds of exchange. To ignore the aesthetic dimension of reflexivity is therefore ironically to put out of view those very issues – including the constitution of resources, their uneven distribution, and forms of inequality – which many of the sociological critics of 'the cultural' and/or 'the aesthetic' claim to be able to illuminate. Thus, and as I suggested in Chapter 2, and as I hope to have illustrated in this chapter, to understand the constitution of gender in late modern societies it seems that it is crucial to consider neither the social nor the cultural but rather to consider the (shifting) relations between the two.

The argument I have put forward in this chapter therefore certainly endorses the view put forward by writers such as Lash and others that reflexivity has an important aesthetic dimension. It is therefore also supportive of the view that it is crucial to consider winners and losers with respect to aesthetic reflexivity. But here I have suggested that many women may lose out on reflexivity not simply (as Lash's analysis implies) because of processes of 'ascription' which operate independently of the politics of reflexivity. Rather it suggests that processes of 'ascription' – of being made immanent – are part of this very politics. Losing out on reflexivity is therefore not an issue of pre-existing ascribed characteristics but being dispossessed of mobility and hence reflexivity via processes of naturalization in regard to cultural styles (Adkins and Lury 1999). Thus while 'in-the-world' reflexivity may be a source of a 'we' for some, as suggested by Lash and Dean, it is also crucial that such reflexivity is recognized as being the grounds for the making of difference and as linked to emergent forms of inequality. But while my analysis in this chapter suggests that in Lash's analysis not enough attention is paid to the issue of how aesthetic reflexivity is constitutive of processes of 'ascription', nonetheless in suggesting that reflexivity in de-differentiated cultural fields is very masculinist, his view comes far closer to the kind of politics at issues in relation to reflexivity and gender than many of the other analyses of reflexivity considered in this book. This is because Lash does not understand reflexivity to be straightforwardly connected to detraditionalization but rather insists on breaking with the equation between the two. This equation of reflexivity with detraditionalization may well be assumed to be the case if the focus is merely on the social and especially the socio-structural, for instance, on the undoing of the socio-structural determinants of gender (such as occupational segregation) outlined at the beginning of this chapter. Yet to focus solely on the undoing of such social structures and then to assume that gender has simply been undone and transgressed as a result is to forego an analysis of the 'freeing of agency from structure' or of mobility post social structure, and in particular to forego an analysis of the articulation of differences, power and inequalities post structure.

Indeed, even those analyses which do not stress that mobility is transgressive but are reproductive of existing differences, divisions and inequalities bypass such an analysis. Thus as we have seen a number of writers have argued that gender mobility (and reflexivity) is reproductive of differences of class. It was noted in Chapter 1, for example, that Hennessy has suggested that,

> the once-rigid links between sex, gender, and sexual desire that the invisible heterosexual matrix so firmly secured in bourgeois culture have become more *flexible* as the gendered divisions of labor among the middle class in industrialized countries have shifted. While these more accommodating gender codes are not pervasive, they have begun to take hold among the urban middle class particularly.
>
> (1995: 169, emphasis added)

Hennessy's argument then is that a mobile relation to gender performance is increasingly characteristic of the new middle classes. Indeed the 'androgynous' worker discussed earlier in this chapter located by Illouz (1997) as the optimal worker of service economies – that is workers with a flexible relation to gender 'attributes' and especially to femininity – is also a middle-class subject. Thus Illouz suggests that this model of selfhood is at issue for the new middle-class occupations of service economies, indeed is characteristic of the habitus of the new middle classes of post-industrial societies. A direct consideration of refashionings of class in terms of flexibility (and hence reflexivity) in relation to gender has clearly been beyond the scope of my considerations in this chapter (although see Skeggs 2002). Nonetheless, my analysis in this chapter and in Chapter 2 suggests that assuming that a take-up of an aesthetic stance in regard to gender is an expression of already existing social divisions and differences, is to fail to consider how the take-up of such a stance is a point of contestation and indeed how aesthetic reflexivity may be a source of these very differences. That is, it suggests that rather than reflecting already existing differences of class, flexible and immanent relations to gender codes may be a source of their very inscription.[22]

In Chapters 1 and 2 I asked if the reflexive modernization thesis may offer feminist sociology, and the sociology of gender and sexuality more broadly, the kind of empirical, analytic and political purchase that it has offered sociology in general, and in the introduction I asked a similar question of the sociology of mobilities. Clearly the analysis of cultural economy in this chapter suggests that issues of both mobility and reflexivity are quite central to the current constitution and politics of gender. In this sense it seems that many of the concepts mobilized by these branches of sociology may be of some significance for the analysis of gender and sexuality. But as I have repeated throughout this chapter this will only be so if a sharp distinction and separation is not made between 'social' and 'cultural' issues, and related to this, if it is recognized that neither mobility nor reflexivity concern straightforward forms of detraditionalization but are implicated in a politics of difference. For an analysis of gender it seems vital therefore that reflexivity and (social and cultural) detraditionalization are unhinged and the relations between them are explored rather than assumed (Adkins 1999, 2000b).

With this in mind in the chapters that follow two further aspects of reflexivity are explored: reflexivity in respect to modes of knowing and reflexivity towards sexuality. As I shall make clear in both of these areas reflexivity has been located as significantly detraditionalizing. Thus, and as I mentioned in the Introduction, reflexivity in relation to knowledge has been understood to offer an alternative to dominant ways of knowing, while reflexivity towards sexuality has been located as challenging the heterosexual/ homosexual binary. However in line with the analysis of reflexivity and cultural economy offered in this chapter I suggest that such reflexivity should not be read as transgressive but rather as involving the very inscription of difference and the making of hierarchies.

four

reflexivity and the politics of knowledge

introduction

In the previous chapter, I questioned the idea that recent transformations of gender (and of identity more generally) are best understood in terms of a feminization of social fields, constitutive of both gender reflexivity and detraditionalization. In so doing I suggested that aesthetic reflexivity is a central source for the making of differences and relates to emerging forms of social inequality. I did so with particular reference to cultural economy, especially general processes of denaturalization and desocialization in regard to gender in this context, and especially the emergence of a reflexive stance towards gender. In so doing I also questioned the idea that such reflexivity should be understood as transgressive or 'liberatory'. In Chapter 2 in my discussions on reflexivity in relation to recent feminist and social theory more generally, I mentioned that such aesthetic reflexivity has been understood to be transgressive in another kind of way, namely as a mode of knowing. Specifically, reflexivity enacted at an epistemological level has been understood to undo the conventions of dominant ways of knowing and provide a ground for the creation of alternative knowledges.

My concern in this chapter is with this latter form of reflexivity and in particular with how reflexivity has been understood to break down subject–object relations in ways of knowing and to lead to a kind of reflexivity akin to that talked about by Lash, that is a hermeneutic or aesthetic reflexivity involving subject–subject forms of knowledge. What I shall point towards in this chapter however is the ways in which such reflexivity enacts not so much subject–subject relations but a configuration of the relation between subjectivity and knowledge or knower and known which only allows certain subjects to speak. Specifically, I shall argue that reflexivity in relation to knowledge practices concerns a speaking position constituted in terms of a vision of a mobile relation to identity on the side of the knower in relation to the known, a position from which there are a number of exclusions. I address these issues with reference to recent debates over reflexivity in relation to social research and through a discussion of some of my qualitative empirical research regarding sexuality and labour markets, and especially sexuality and service labour (see e.g. Adkins 1995, 2000a). What I draw attention to in relation to the latter is a recent review of some of my research in this area, especially some of the points of critique raised in this review. I do so not because I want to take this opportunity to mount some kind of defence of my research. Rather, I do so because these points of critique highlight for me some of the issues at stake in current disputes over reflexivity. In particular they highlight the limits of the form of reflexivity which is currently being encouraged in social research. To begin to lay out these limits I turn first to some recent discussions of reflexivity in relation to social research.

reflexivity and social research

From the early 1990s and even before, reflexivity has been recommended as a critical practice for social research (see e.g. Steier 1991, Woolgar 1991a; Alvesson and Skoldberg 2000), especially as it is often understood to serve as an antidote to the problems of realism. For example, reflexivity has been recommended as a response to and indeed is often represented as an answer to the crises of representation and legitimation in social research widely associated with postmodernism and poststructuralism (Denzin and Lincoln 1994: 10–11; Alvesson and Skoldberg 2000). These crises made problematic a number of central assumptions of social science research. Thus the idea that researchers can somehow directly capture lived experience has been troubled by the argument that experience is created in the social texts written by researchers. In addition, the criteria for evaluating and interpreting social research have been problematized. Thus terms such as reliability, generalizability and validity have come into scrutiny in regard to what totalizing and universalizing assumptions they make regarding the social, knowledge and ways of knowing. Denzin and Lincoln suggest that the result of these crises is that 'any representation must now legitimate itself in terms of some set of criteria that allows the author (and the reader) to make connections between the text and the world written about' (1994: 11). One way in which social researchers have attempted to perform such legitimization is through a turn to reflexive practice (Game 1991; Alvesson and Skoldberg 2000), including new forms of textual expression and analysis.

This is clearly visible in the social studies of science where one consequence of applying the argument that 'natural' scientific knowledge is a social construct to the knowledge generated by the social sciences has been a turn to reflexivity. Thus in their introduction to 'the reflexive project' of the social studies of science Woolgar and Ashmore (1991) have posited reflexivity as a kind of corrective to the problems of both realism and relativism. They discuss the ways in which, as they see it, the conventions of realism constrain explorations of knowledge practices and inhibit the development of reflexive practice in the social sciences. Such practice is itself illustrated by the self-conscious, reflexive style of the introduction to the collection. Here, Woolgar and Ashmore (1991: 4) explicitly give presence to more than one textual voice in dialogic form to remind the reader

> that interpretation goes on all the time, that the idea of one reading – a singular correspondence between text and meaning – is illusory. In particular, the dialogue is one way of introducing some instability into the presumed relationship between text and reader.

Thus such forms of textual expression are located as potentially overcoming the problems of realism in social research through a self-consciousness regarding the role of the author in producing accounts of the social world. Such self-reflexivity is understood to destabilize the relations between text and reader, author and text, researcher and social life. In short, such practices are understood to destabilize all that realism held in place. Consider, for, example, the following (abridged) section of dialogue in which such a self-consciousness is enacted both to take account of its own production and to illustrate the ways in which realist conventions inhibit the development of reflexive practice (I shall return to this dialogue in a later section of this chapter).

... REITERATING THE TIRED OLD PLATITUDE THAT ALL TEXTS ARE
        MULTIVOCAL ... ?
Certainly not.
... TRYING TO FIND A NEW WAY OF SUPPLYING REFERENCES THAT HAVE
        USED OR DISCUSSED THE SECOND VOICE DEVICE ... ?
Look, it's your intervention. I don't see why you're asking me ... And while
        you're thinking about that you might explain why you appear in
        UPPER CASE this time?
WHAT DO YOU MEAN?
... the use of UPPER CASE makes it seem like you're shouting!
... YOUR MONOPOLY OF THE CONVENTIONAL IDIOGRAPH MAKES ME
        SEEM LIKE THE ODDBALL. BESIDES I THOUGHT WE'D BOTH
        AGREED THAT THERE WAS NO REAL DIFFERENCE BETWEEN
        US: THAT WHEN ALL WAS SAID AND DONE WE ARE NOT TWO
        VOICES BUT TWO SETS OF INTERCHANGEABLE SCRIPTED RE-
        MARKS; THAT OUR ORIGINS SHOULD NOT BE HELD AGAINST
        US AS SOURCES OF SANCTIONABLE CONSISTENCY, AS LABELS
        TO WHICH OUR REMARKS ARE HELD ACCOUNTABLE, AS ...

... Why don't you just say that actors' voices can emanate from quite different
        and interchangeable identities, and that this can be done without
        any evident contradiction on the part of actors themselves?
YOU THINK THAT'S LESS OBSCURE?
Not very.
BUT THE BASIC POINT IS THAT WE COULD SWITCH ROLES WITHOUT
        ANYONE NOTICING?
Yes.
AND THAT WE COULD DROP THIS UPPER CASE/lower case DISTINCTION
        IN ORDER TO DELIBERATELY CONFUSE OUR SUPPOSEDLY SEP-
        ARATE IDENTITIES?
Right.
(Woolgar and Ashmore 1991: 3)

Such textual self-consciousness is understood however not only to overcome
the problems of realism, but also relativism. Woolgar and Ashmore discuss
how in the relativist (or constructivist) social study of science, while the topic
of investigation – science – is relativized, a realist methodology is maintained.
The consequence of this adherence to a realist methodology is the construction of a new metascientific reality – that 'scientific knowledge is built in
such and such a way and has such and such a character' (Woolgar and
Ashmore 1991: 4). Within such relativist approaches, however, the nature of
the reflexive similarity between findings and methods is itself not an issue;
'reflexivity is either treated as an inherent but uninteresting characteristic of
such work ... or, by contrast, is actively opposed' (Woolgar and Ashmore
1991: 8). Thus Woolgar and Ashmore point to a lack of reflexivity regarding
the role of method in social world construction in such approaches. In short,
such approaches do not problematize the role of the author in producing
social worlds, and as an escape from such problems the abandoning of the
commitment to realist methods is recommended along with a take-up of the
reflexive project, a project described as concerning 'some of the most exciting intellectual work currently being undertaken anywhere' (Woolgar and
Ashmore 1991: 9).

two reflexivities

May (1998) has, however, recently noted a number of limitations of such
reflexivity for social research. He distinguishes two dimensions of reflexivity:
endogenous and referential. By endogenous reflexivity he refers to the ways
in which the actions of members of a given community are seen to contribute
to the constitution of social reality itself. This dimension of reflexivity includes
not only 'the methods of people within lifeworlds who are the subjects of
social investigation but also those within social scientific communities in
terms of how they construct the topics of their inquiries and conduct their

investigations' (May 1998: 8). By referential reflexivity May refers to 'the consequences that arise from a meeting between the reflexivity exhibited by actors as part of a lifeworld and that exhibited by the researcher as part of a social scientific community' (1998: 8). Through a review of reflexivity in the social sciences in relation to social research – from Weber, through the ethnomethodologists, to the methodological changes brought about by poststructuralist and postmodern arguments – May shows how in all of these different traditions there is a tendency to bracket referential reflexivity. He argues this has the effect of producing an inward-looking practice that results in a failure to adequately understand the role and place of the social sciences in the study of social life (1998: 18). The methodological implications of 'postmodernism'[1] for social research – including the critique of the idea that the relation between research production and the representation of the social world may take place according to universal concepts of reliability and validity – are, for example, understood to have resulted in such a bracketing of referential reflexivity and a focus on endogenous reflexivity alone. For instance, May notes a tendency 'to take the words that are written about social life as *the* central topics for the social construction of reality' (1998: 17, emphasis in original) with the consequence that the authority of the author often becomes an important focus. Indeed, certain critiques of the authority of the author have led 'to research accounts that reproduce ego-identity!' (May 1998: 18). Thus he sees the problematization of social science methodology, especially the techniques of representation of the social world, to have led in some quarters to a (rather ironic) privileging of a new form of authority – that of the author. Instead of turning inwards in this way and relieving social science of engagement with the social world, May suggests the social sciences need also to embrace referential reflexivity. Quoting Fay, he agrees that the worth of social science should be judged in terms of 'what it tells us about those under study, not just what it reveals about the social scientist' (Fay quoted in May 1998: 20).

May's distinction between endogenous and referential reflexivity and his claims regarding the limits of reflexivity for social research may be paralleled to Latour's (1991) arguments regarding the problems of reflexivity for the social studies of science. Latour distinguishes between what he terms meta- and infra-reflexivity. By meta-reflexivity he refers to 'the attempt to avoid a text being believed by its readers', while infra-reflexivity concerns the 'attempt to avoid a text *not* being believed by its readers' (Latour 1991: 166, emphasis in original). Latour's meta-reflexivity is similar to May's endogenous reflexivity. It is based on the idea that

> the most deleterious effect of a text is to be naively believed by the reader as in some way relating to a referent out there. Reflexivity is supposed to counteract this effect by rendering the text unfit for normal consumption.
>
> (Latour 1991: 168)

Latour argues this position makes a number of assumptions, including that people easily believe what they read, and that believing always involves relating an account to some referent 'out there'. Yet the most bizarre assumption involved in meta-reflexivity, Latour suggests, inheres in arguments regarding self-reference. Here Latour refers to Woolgar's (1991b) discussion of reflexivity, where there is an assumption that an ethnographic text which discusses the ways in which ethnography is produced, is more reflexive than an ethnographic text which talks, say, about the Balinese. But Woolgar goes further, to suggest that such a reflexive account could be replaced by another account (or layer of reflexivity), since the reflexivity involved in discussing the ways in which ethnography is produced could be a naive way of telling a true story about ethnographic production. But still more, this third layer may not be reflexive, and thus Woolgar imagines 'many other rungs on this Jacob's ladder' (Latour 1991: 168). The problem Latour has here is that an nth degree account is no more and no less reflexive than any of the others in the chain,

> A text about . . . [a] way of writing about the Balinese is no more and no less reflexive than . . . [a] text about the Balinese and this is no less and no more reflexive than what the Balinese themselves say.
>
> (Latour 1991: 168)

The whole vertigo regarding self-reference, Latour argues, stems from a very naive belief that the same actor appears in the first and last text, while at the same time believing that when a text does not have an author as one of its characters it is less reflexive than when it does, 'as if these were not, in semiotic terms, two similar ways of building the enunciation' (1991: 169).

In place of piling layer upon layer of self-consciousness to no end and holding on to the possibility of reaching a meta-language – searching for a meta-meta-language that would judge all others – Latour asks, why not just have one layer, the story, and obtain the necessary amount of reflexivity from somewhere else? This strategy entails what Latour refers to as infra-reflexivity and is close to May's notion of referential reflexivity. Instead of focusing on the knower, infra-reflexivity focuses on both the knower and the known, 'displaying the knower and the known and the work needed to interrupt or create connections between A and B [elements to provide explanations and elements to be explained]' (Latour 1991: 172). This he says is a non-scientific way of studying the natural and social sciences. Instead of turning to the word, Latour urges, let us go back to the world. He considers, for example, completely 'unreflexive', 'journalistic' accounts of the world in which it is things – such as computers – that appear as reflexive, active, full of life, and ready to take part in dramatic stories, and thus are not objects in the way that empiricists would have them. Latour proclaims, 'there is more reflexivity in one account that makes the world alive than in one hundred self-reflexive loops that return the boring thinking mind to the stage' (1991: 173). Thus while Latour agrees that the problems located by the reflexivists are correct, and that the reflexive trend is inescapable – 'otherwise our field would . . . be self-contradictory' (1991: 176) – like May, he also agrees that meta or endogenous reflexivity is too limited as an alternative, especially since in the end it endorses a scientistic agenda by believing that there is no other way out of empiricism than language and self-reference. For Latour, a better strategy is to search for non-scientific and weaker explanations, and to look for reflexivity not 'in' the author but in the world.[2]

reflexivity 'in the world' (again)

But are these problems only at issue in regard to textual self-consciousness or to endogenous or meta-reflexivity? In what follows I suggest that many of the same points – especially the location of reflexivity 'in' the self – may be made in relation to the research practices social researchers have taken up in relation to 'the world', that is, in the kind of research which both May and Latour suggest is the domain of referential or infra-reflexivity, the kind of reflexivity which is about the knower and the known. To do so, and with May and Latour's distinctions between endogenous and referential or meta- and infra-reflexivity in mind, I want to now turn to a review (Williams 1997) of some of my research regarding sexuality and labour markets. Here the reviewer compares aspects of my research account with a research project on masculinity in British corporate culture (Roper 1994). The latter involved life histories conducted with 25 men and five women executive managers, while my own research involved two case studies of service (tourist) organizations in the UK (a hotel and a theme park) and a study of the organization of the occupation of public house management.[3] Like some other commentators on organizations Roper foregrounds the operation of homosocial relations between men in organizations, while in my own account I stress that in service organizations a heterosexual imperative may be central to understanding the organization of service labour. Here then we have two accounts that are squarely in the world, yet, as we shall see, the reviewer attributes referential reflexivity to Roper's account (and to Roper himself) and discounts it from my own. The grounds on which the reviewer makes this move I believe may tell us much about the limits of reflexivity as a critical practice for social research.

The reviewer describes my own and Roper's study, charts out her points of contention, and then makes what for me are some interesting moves in terms of the current debates regarding reflexivity. She says that reading these two books together made her 'ponder some epistemological issues involved in gender research on organizations when it is conducted either by a man or a woman' (Williams 1997: 519). In particular, she was 'struck by the different depictions of male sexuality in the two studies' (1997:

519). She describes a portrayal of men as hostile to women in my study, and in Roper's study a 'much more humane and sympathetic view of his subjects' (1997: 519). Williams is anxious to get to grips with these differences, and on this she has two proposals. The first of these concerns empathy, which she understands to be an effect of the social characteristics of the researchers. She suggests,

> Part of the difference may stem from empathy: as a young woman, Adkins no doubt had difficulty seeing the world from the vantage point of the sexist managers and ride operators she interviewed. In contrast, Roper admits to experiencing countertransference in his interviews: he describes tensions he felt 'between affection and criticism, sympathy for the organization man's masculinity, and an often uncomfortable identification with it' (p. 40).
>
> (1997: 519)

The second proposal, which Williams suspects is more important than the first – indeed, she says 'something more than differences in empathy may be going on here' (1997: 519) – involves the relations between researchers and research subjects. To illustrate this issue, Williams turns to Roper's study. In particular, she discusses how Roper's study points to the importance of the business world as an arena for intimacy among men. Summarizing this aspect of Roper's research Williams (1997: 519) writes,

> Men are drawn into the competition, aggression, and risk of business because it is one of the only avenues available to them to establish close, personal, emotional bonds with other men. Women represent a threat to this homosocial world. In fact, Roper found that men were much more inhibited with their emotional expressiveness with women than with other men. Career women provoked fears in the men about the security of the gender order and their own masculinity.

Crucially for Williams, it is this aspect of Roper's study which is held to explain the differences in the 'depictions of male sexuality in the two studies'. On Roper's research regarding homosociability in organizations she says, 'If this finding is correct – *and I believe that it is* – this could help to explain the different depictions of men in the two works' (Williams 1997: 519, emphasis added). In effect, Williams argues that my research was an outcome of the kind of homosocial logic identified by Roper. In Williams's view, I was positioned by such a logic in that my experiences in the two tourist organizations were mediated by organizational homosociability, and as a consequence, my research was a direct effect of this logic. She suggests,

> Adkins's male respondents may have seen her as an intruder and an interloper – a challenge to their masculinity and to their authority over women – and treated her accordingly. Roper's male

respondents, in contrast, clearly saw him as 'one of them' or at least a younger version of themselves: many projected their own values and ambitions onto him, offering him unsolicited advice about his career and giving him business contacts.

(Williams 1997: 519–20)

Roper's account of homosociability in organizations is therefore held by Williams to be correct ('if this finding is correct – and I believe that it is') and is mobilized to position my research as the effect of this logic. Moreover, according to Williams, unlike Roper, I could neither escape nor be aware of this logic as a result of certain social characteristics: 'as a young woman, Adkins no doubt had difficulty seeing the world from the vantage point of the sexist managers and ride operators she interviewed'. In effect, Williams is claiming that certain immanent characteristics (in this case age and sex) on the part of the knower meant that a 'meeting of the reflexivity exhibited by actors as part of a lifeworld and that exhibited by the researcher as part of social scientific community' (May 1998: 8) was not possible in my research. Thus for Williams age and sex ensured that this research could not involve referential or infra-reflexivity, including the various forms of identification between knower and known described by Roper in his research project. Indeed, Williams goes on to write that it is unfortunate that I have not provided any information about how I was treated or how I felt doing the study (1997: 520), that is, that I did not provide a more self-conscious account of fieldwork of the sort given by Roper. In making these claims however, Williams assumes or reads in an antagonism between myself and the various men I interviewed in the course of this research project. Yet in assuming such an antagonism, she ignores the accounts provided by the men and women interviewed of their experiences of work in tourist organizations and their explanations of aspects of service work organization including selection criteria, rules and regulations and the specifics of service work, especially the significance of issues of self-presentation in relation to customers. Williams therefore not only discounts referential reflexivity from this research on the grounds of age and sex on the part of the knower, but also on the grounds an assumed antagonism and hostility in relation to the knower on the side of known.

What interests me about Williams's review is the kind of politics around reflexivity being enacted here, about who is and who is not recognized as capable of being both self and referentially reflexive in regard to social research *in the world*, that is reflexive in terms of the knower and the known. Let me pose a number of questions to get at this politics. Why is Roper's account read as concerning self and referential reflexivity but reflexivity discounted in my own on the grounds of age and sex on the side of the knower and antagonism on the side of the known? Why is my research discounted on the grounds of a logic which my own positioning did not allow me to 'see', while Roper's positioning is understood to be constitutive of both self-reflexivity and the kind of reflexivity between knower and known (referential or infra-reflexivity) which writers such as May and Latour suggest the social sciences need to embrace? Why does the reviewer foreground the relationships between the researchers and the men interviewed in Roper's and my own study and ignore the relationships between the researchers and the women interviewed in the respective studies? Why doesn't the reviewer see similar problems in Roper's research with respect to his relationship with the women executive managers he interviewed to those she accredits to mine in relation to interviewing men? In short why does my sex (and age) matter while Roper's does not?

My answer to these questions is that it has something to do with the concept of reflexivity, and in particular that reflexivity entails a particular figuring of the relationship between the knower and the known, not only in relation to textual and other forms of endogenous reflexivity, but also in social research 'in the world'. Specifically, and in the section which follows I will suggest that reflexive social research puts in place a relationship between the knower and the known which positions the researcher as able to 'speak' (and be viewed as 'correct') via a particular figuring of identity. However, I suggest that this speaking position does not concern a claim of a transcendental positioning as in realism, but rather that in reflexive social science practice such a speaking position is constituted in terms of a vision of a *mobile relation to identity* on the side of the knower in relation to the known. In short, I shall argue that calls for reflexivity in social research comprise this kind of vision of mobility in regard to identity. One implication of this argument is that the kinds of problems located by May and Latour in relation to reflexivity are not simply confined to meta or endogenous reflexivity but also to the reflexivity associated with being-in-the-world. Another implication, however, as I shall make clear, is that there are a number of exclusions from reflexivity.

To make this argument I turn to Felski's (1995) analysis of the emergence of self-conscious textualism in the writings of the literary avant-garde. That is, I turn to an analysis of the cultivation of a reflexive stance in the artistic and intellectual counter-cultures at the turn of the nineteenth century. As I mentioned in Chapter 2 in my discussion of Featherstone's analysis of the aestheticization of everyday life, it is such cultures in which the more contemporary (and more widespread) forms of aesthetic reflexivity are understood to have their roots. In turning to Felski's account I therefore suggest that the reflexivity at issue in regard to knowledge and modes of knowing (whether endogenous or referential) is the very same form of reflexivity at issue in respect to the aestheticization of everyday life, that is the kind of reflexivity which has been the topic of discussion in previous chapters. I turn to Felski's analysis not only to illustrate this point, but also because it highlights the kinds of politics operating around reflexivity which I want to suggest are at issue in relation to contemporary calls for reflexivity in relation to social research. If my turn here to textual reflexivity seems odd in the light of the way May and Latour tend to associate textual reflexivity with endogenous or meta-reflexivity and their distinctions between endogenous/ meta-reflexivity and referential/infra-reflexivity, I hope it will become clear that part of my argument is to question whether or not these distinctions can be so easily drawn.

self-reflexivity and the politics of subversion

In *The Gender of Modernity* Felski (1995) discusses how during the late nineteenth century the literary avant-garde pursued a self-conscious textualism as a strategy of subverting sexual and textual norms. Such a strategy was deployed in the context of the emergence and rise of consumerism for the middle classes, particularly for middle-class women. This 'feminization' and aestheticization of the public sphere, Felski suggests, was threatening to bourgeois men whose social identity had been formed 'through an ethos of self-restraint and a repudiation of womanly feelings' (1995: 90). Yet for men who were disaffected from the dominant norms of middle-class masculinity, Felski argues the emergence of an aestheticized and feminized modernity offered hope of an alternative to the forces of positivism, progress ideology, and the sovereignty of the reality principle. It was this alternative that offered the literary avant-garde a ground to challenge traditional models of masculinity via an imaginary identification with the feminine (Felski 1995: 91). This took the form of a self-conscious textualism which

> defined itself in opposition to the prevailing conventions of realist representation, turning to a decadent aesthetic of surface, style and parody that was explicitly coded as both 'feminine' and 'modern'.
>
> (Felski 1995: 91)

While as Felski points out these practices were limited to a small, if influential group, nevertheless in questioning dominant ideals of masculinity this group aimed at 'the heart of bourgeois modes of self-understanding' (1995: 92), in particular, these practices denaturalized masculinity. Thus masculinity could no longer be assumed to be fixed, unitary and stable. But, Felski argues, it is a mistake to understand the feminization of texts as simply undoing gender, since the appropriation of an aesthetic of parody and performance 'reinscribes more insistently those gender hierarchies which are ostensibly being called into question' (1995: 92). This, she argues, is the case as the transgressive power of feminine in such texts is predicated on a 'radical disavowal of and dissociation from the "natural" body of woman' (1995: 92).

Felski considers a number of avant-garde texts to give flesh to this proposal. Here, she draws attention to the ways in which femininity was crucial to the self-reflexivity of such texts. She considers, for example, how the trope of femininity is mobilized to epitomize artifice rather than authenticity and acts 'as a cipher for the very self-reflexivity of poetic language itself' (1995: 94). The key precondition of this move was the aestheticization of woman in relation to consumerism, and in particular how the everyday practice of femininity gradually came to concern practices of adornment and self-presentation. This aestheticization of woman decoupled femininity from the natural body, and as a set of signs femininity lent itself to appropriation. Through this very artificiality 'femininity was to become the privileged marker of the instability and mobility of modern gender identity' (Felski 1995: 95).

For example, in avant-garde texts the 'modernness' and supposed gender transgressiveness of the male protagonists is portrayed in terms of femininity. Thus the protagonists possess traits usually associated with women such as a love of fashion, sensitivity and vanity and they spend much time in private space codified as feminine rather than in the public sphere of work and politics, often locked into practices of self-reflection and self-contemplation regarding their aesthetic practices. In addition, language itself in such texts is an object of display, with description taking priority over narrative, form over substance, style over history, characteristics which the protagonists also share. This abandonment of realist conventions in such texts leads, Felski argues, to a self-conscious preoccupation with the surface of language, a self-consciousness which is evident in the use of techniques of cliché, stereotype and paradox which undermine any referential dimensions. Thus in these texts the transgressiveness of the protagonists (their mobility in terms of gender) and the challenges to realism and to conventional codes of masculinity all converged on the appropriation of the trope of femininity, whose very stylization, denaturalization and artificiality provided the grounds for such moves.

But while Felski draws attention to the ways in which the trope of femininity is central to such moves, she also highlights a number of key exclusions from this textual strategy. For example, while women's bodies in such texts are often portrayed as aestheticized – for instance, through portrayals of women as actresses, performers, images and works of art – nevertheless women are denied mobility in regard to gender and an ironic self-consciousness in relation to this aestheticization. Indeed, women are portrayed as embodying 'artifice naively . . . without being able to raise it to the level of philosophical reflection' (Felski 1995: 110). The subversion of gender norms is therefore not available to women 'whose nature renders them incapable of this kind of free-floating semiotic mobility and aesthetic sophistication' (Felski 1995: 106). For example, Felski points to Huysmans's text *Against the Grain* (1884), where after fantasizing about the possibility of erotic perversity with a masculine female athlete, the male protagonist is dismayed to find that she is 'unable to transgress the limits of her own gender' (1995: 111) and possesses 'all the childish weaknesses of a woman' (Huysmans, in Felski 1995: 111). In avant-garde texts women are thus excluded from a self-conscious transcendence of corporeality and identity.

In this context Felski draws attention to how the very strategy of subversion deployed in such texts is constitutive of new boundaries and gender hierarchies, as well as to the similarities between self-conscious literary texts and modern rationalism. In particular, the latter share a vision of,

> overcoming the constraints of psychological determination and dissolving the power of sexual difference. Reducing the body to a free floating play of signs and codes, aestheticism, like science, positions itself as being against (female) nature.
>
> (Felski 1995: 112)

With writers such as Featherstone, Felski therefore draws attention to how this strategy of subversion served to establish the class distinctiveness of the avant-garde. More than this, however, she shows how this strategy reinscribed gender hierarchies even though it appeared to challenge the conventions of gender. Her analysis of the gender politics of such reflexivity therefore suggests that in his analysis of these intellectual and artistic counter-cultures, and more generally of the aestheticization of everyday life, Featherstone tends to downplay the significance of aesthetic reflexivity in this regard. Specifically, and as my analysis in the previous chapter also pointed towards, Felski's analysis suggests that Featherstone downplays how the cultivation of an aesthetic stance involves such forms of inscription in relation to gender. And this is so even as he recognizes the significance of the cultivation of an aesthetic stance in the making of class distinctions. Felski's analysis also underlines a number of further points made in previous chapters. These include her insistence (albeit somewhat in tension with her analysis of the 'money, sex and power' novel) that a mobile and denaturalized femininity and 'feminization' of the public sphere is not straightforwardly detraditionalizing of gender; that the take-up of an aesthetic stance should not be read as undoing gender (even though it appears to unsettle or subvert gender norms); that reflexivity entails a mobile relation to gender styles; and that women are often excluded from such mobility and hence such reflexivity. Felski's analysis therefore appears to support the very broad argument made in the previous chapter, that to ignore the aesthetic dimension of reflexivity is not only to make invisible uneven distributions of reflexivity but also the significance of the aesthetic in regard to the making of differences.

Indeed, Felski extends her analysis further, and notes the similarities between the early modernist endeavour to overcome gender via the feminine, and more recent interests in the destabilizing power of feminine textuality, especially in the 'deployment of the motif of "Becoming woman" as a trope for the crisis of Western philosophical thought' (1995: 113). Felski argues that in such contemporary strategies the fantasy of becoming woman is often defined in opposition to the naivety of feminists' struggles for social change which are read as either essentialist or as concerning phallic identification. On such strategies she writes,

> Without wishing to exaggerate the similarities between very dif-
> ferent intellectual and political contexts, one might note that this
> strategy appears to enact an uncanny repetition of the dandy's
> affirmation of his own 'feminine' semiotic at the expense of women.
> (Felski 1995: 113)

A similar logic is also located by Ahmed (1998) in her analysis of
the postmodern genre of meta-fiction – a genre of writing which is often
understood to involve an extreme form of self-reflexivity and as overcoming
the conventions of realism. Ahmed notes that while often fascinated with
sexual difference and sexuality, nevertheless this genre is often read as overcoming such differences.[4] But she argues while postmodern fictions are frequently read as such, they 'may re-constitute those differences differently,
through the very experimentations with literary form' (Ahmed 1998: 150).
Via a detailed analysis of meta-fictional stories, Ahmed suggests that such a
reconstitution may take place through the way in which the self-reflexivity
of such narratives concerns a masculine mode of enunciation. For example,
she draws attention to how the self-reflexivity of such narratives often entails
a liberal and masculinist freedom to create woman, as well as phantasies of
'over-coming gendered and generic limits as an aspect of a masculine mode
of enunciation' (Ahmed 1998: 158).

reflexivity and the politics of mobility

With similar caveats as Felski's in mind with regard to issues of historical,
intellectual and political specificity, what I want to draw attention to is the
affinity between the kinds politics of reflexivity at issue in relation to the
self-consciousness of the literary avant-garde and post-modern fictions located
by Felski and Ahmed respectively, and the politics of reflexivity at issue in
social research 'in the world'. And specifically I want to do so in regard to
gender. Consider for example, the disembodied textual mobility enacted by
Woolgar and Ashmore in their self-conscious dialogue above ('BUT THE
BASIC POINT IS THAT WE COULD SWITCH ROLES WITHOUT ANYONE
NOTICING? Yes. AND THAT WE COULD DROP THE UPPER CASE/lower case
DISTINCTION IN ORDER TO DELIBERATELY CONFUSE OUR SUPPOSEDLY
SEPARATE IDENTITIES? Right'). Thus, as Felski argues in relation to the literary
avant-garde the apparent transgressiveness of such self-reflexivity – indeed
the speaking position of such self-reflexive texts – is constituted through a
vision of a self-conscious transcendence of corporeality and identity. But
consider also the non-textual, non-endogenous, referential, *'in-the-world'*
mobility accredited to Roper by Williams in terms of the relationship between
knower and known. Specifically, Williams accredits Roper's social research
with referential or infra-reflexivity (and his account is understood to be
'correct') on the grounds of an account of a recursive identification between

knower and known, that is, on the grounds of Roper's identification with the male organizational executive managers he interviewed, and an account of the latter's identification with Roper, evidenced in offers of career advice and business contacts. Thus what constitutes Roper's account as reflexive for Williams is a vision of mobility in regard to identity on the side of the knower in relation to the known, that is a mobility both in terms of identity and identification (in this case a mobility in terms of different forms of masculinity) as well as a self-consciousness regarding this mobility. For example, according to Williams, such mobility ensured that Roper's research involved the kind of challenge to subject/object relations in relation to the knower and the known which a more reflexive social research reaches towards. By contrast, in regard to my research Williams disallows such a reflexive dimension by attributing a *lack* of mobility in regard to identity and identification to the knower in relation to the known. In short, Williams suggests that the problems of my particular research project related to the inability to overcome identity – age and sex – and that this fixity in turn led to a lack of reflexivity (referential and endogenous) and to problematic research. Hence her claim that I 'had difficulty seeing the world from the vantage point' of those I interviewed and her assumption of hostility between those interviewed and myself.[5] It seems therefore that the capacity for reflexive social research, and in particular the precondition of referential reflexivity (for example, claims of a recursive identification between knower and known) is an issue of overcoming fixity on the part of the knower through a vision of a mobile relation to identity in relation to the known.

While for the literary avant-garde and for the contemporary textual self-reflexivists reflexivity is constituted through a vision of a self-conscious transcendence of corporeality and identity, it seems that reflexivity 'in-the-world' – that is, aesthetic or hermeneutic reflexivity – is constituted through a similar vision of mobility in regard to identity. As we have seen, Felski has shown how the reflexivity of the literary avant-garde was constituted through a mobility in relation to gender, yet this mobility was predicated on a 'radical disavowal and dissociation from the "natural" body of the woman' (Felski 1995: 11). Hence in avant-garde texts women are denied such mobility 'whose nature renders them incapable of this kind of free-floating semiotic mobility' (Felski 1995: 12). So too it seems that a similar politics of exclusion is at issue in reflexive social research. Thus according to Williams age and sex may render women incapable of mobility 'in the world' and hence of referential and self-reflexivity in the social research process. Indeed, much like the 'in-the-world' reflexivity in cultural economies discussed in the previous chapter, it seems that in terms of the research process women may be denied such reflexivity on the grounds of an immanent relation to gender identity.

In this context, and along the lines of Felski's and Ahmed's questioning of the subversiveness of literary avant-garde and of postmodern meta-fictions respectively, the progressiveness so often ascribed to reflexive social research (not only endogenous, but also referential) must surely be questioned. Indeed, reflexivity as a critical practice may be far from neutral and in particular may have a hidden politics of gender. Specifically, if reflexivity between knower and known is constituted via a vision of a mobile relation to identity on the part of the knower in relation to the known, and women are excluded from such mobility on the grounds of their 'nature', then much like the self-reflexivity of the literary avant-garde, such strategies 'in the world' may also concern the inscription of new gender hierarchies. Here the issue is one of who can speak 'for whom, why, how and when' (Probyn 1993: 2) in the age of reflexive social science. For as I hope to have illustrated through the example of two research projects, reflexivity in terms of the knower and the known may inscribe a hierarchy of speaking positions in relation to gender. The inscription of this hierarchy is however hidden by claims that reflexivity is a 'good' and 'progressive' thing in regard to the gender politics of social research. Indeed what is ironic regarding this inscription is that reflexivity is often understood in part to be a response and antidote to feminist critiques of universalism in social research (see e.g. Gergen and Gergen 1991). Thus a more reflexive politics of location in regard to both the knower and the known in social research developed in part due to feminist critiques of universalism in social research. Yet while reflexivity ostensibly calls into question such universalism, and in particular appears to call into question assumptions of a masculine speaking position and the normalization of masculine experiences, at the same time reflexivity may be constitutive of new hierarchies in social research, particularly if reflexivity is attributed to certain selves and not to others (see also Cronin 1999, 2000a, 2000b; Skeggs 2002).

On this point, it is interesting to note that although, as was made clear in Chapter 3, McDowell has interpreted the apparent questioning of universalism associated with the take-up of an aesthetic towards gender (that is, in-the-world reflexivity) as potentially 'liberatory', somewhat ironically Barnes *et al.* (2000) have denied McDowell this very form of reflexivity in relation to the research process. Specifically, in a discussion of her research project on professional financial sector workers, Barnes *et al.* suggest that McDowell may not have treated the men and women she interviewed in her research project equally, and in particular suggest that she was 'often more sympathetic to women than she was to men' (Barnes *et al.* 2000: 276). For example, they argue that McDowell makes 'snide asides' when discussing the comments of high-up male directors in a way that she does not for the women she interviewed. Thus Barnes *et al.* question McDowell's research on the grounds of a lack of mobility in regard to identity on the side of the knower in relation to the known – that is, on the grounds of an implied inability to overcome identity in the context of the research evidenced in a lack of identification with (some of) the men she interviewed. Barnes *et al.* therefore imply that this lack of mobility vis-à-vis identity and identification did not allow for the development of referential or infra-reflexivity in this project, and question the research on these grounds. Thus the very politics (the politics of in-the-world, hermeneutic, or aesthetic reflexivity) that McDowell sees as potentially 'liberatory' are here enacted to call into question her research, indeed to enact a hierarchy of social science speaking positions arranged in terms of mobility and fixity.

situating reflexivity 'in the world'

In a critique of the reflexive ethnographic turn in anthropology, and in particular a turn to self-reflexivity (where 'the reflexive gaze stops at the author'; 1993: 80) Probyn has also discussed the politics involved in reflexive social science. In particular, she has drawn attention to the ways in which self-consciousness on the part of reflexive ethnographers often relies on making respondents as well as 'the field' stationary. What I am suggesting is that for referential reflexivity a similar logic is also at issue regarding speaking positions on the side of the knower. Thus while some social scientists are deemed mobile (and their research hence reflexive and sound), others are deemed fixed (their research unreflexive and hence questionable). Discussing self-reflexivity further, Probyn has argued that the problem is not that there should not be reflexivity regarding one's research practices, but rather that it 'is the conception of the self at work within this reflexivity that is at fault' (1993: 80), a conception which she characterizes as concerning an ontological egotism. Against this conception of the self, Probyn insists that it is vital to always ask 'what had to be held in place in order for this self to appear at all' (1993: 80). Thus, she posits an understanding of the self as a speaking position based on a questioning 'of how it is that I am speaking' (1993: 80; see also Skeggs 1995). It is precisely this kind of questioning which I am suggesting may be disallowed in reflexive social science through a *normalization* of a speaking position based on a vision of a mobile relation to identity, a normalization which makes invisible exclusions from this vision. Thus while Probyn, along with writers such as May and Latour, have questioned the version of the ego-centred self at issue in endogenous and self-reflexivity, I would suggest that this questioning also needs to be extended to referential or infra-reflexivity, particularly if, as I have suggested, the politics of reflexivity only allows some people to speak.

Felski denaturalized the speaking position of the avant-garde and called into question the apparent transgressiveness of their textual strategies by showing how a self-conscious speaking position relied on an appropriation of femininity, an appropriation made possible by the emergence of consumerism for the middle classes. Following this strategy, alongside Probyn's suggestions regarding the importance of historically situating speaking selves and questioning conceptions of selfhood at work in social research, we might ask how it is that the referentially orientated social researchers are speaking? What has to be held in place in order for a vision of the self with a mobile relation to identity to appear? Following my analysis of gender reflexivity in the previous chapter I would suggest that such visions of mobility need to be situated in terms of general processes of denaturalization and desocialization, but where such processes are understood to be an important ground for the making of contemporary axes of difference. That is, such visions need to be situated in terms of broad processes which are undoing forms of socio-structural classification (such as the aestheticization of everyday life), but where this does not imply straightforward forms of declassification, but also new forms of classification. As with the previous chapter, this chapter suggests that positions of mobility and immanence in regard to aesthetic reflexivity – in this case, the take-up of a reflexive stance towards the relations between the knower and the known – are central to the latter, and in particular that differences of gender as well as class are currently being articulated in these terms. Situating such a vision in this way suggests that the version of the self at issue on the side of the knower in relation to reflexivity 'in the world' – that is, a vision of the self with a mobile relation to identity – may be the ideal and privileged self of late modernity. Reflexivity may then be far from the critical practice it is often understood to be for social research. Indeed, while reflexive social research practice ostensibly aims to redress the norm-alization of particular privileged speaking positions both in relation to the knower and the known it seems, as Haraway has argued, that 'reflexivity, like reflection, only displaces the same elsewhere' (Haraway 1997b: 16).

five

reflexivity, risk and the (neo-liberal) politics of sexuality

Introduction

In the previous chapter through a consideration of reflexivity and the politics of knowledge particularly in regard to recent debates in social research I suggested that rather than offering a mode of knowing which breaks down self–other relations and produces subject–subject forms of knowledge, reflexivity involves a vision of a mobile relation to identity on the side of the knower in relation to the known. Moreover, I suggested that such reflexivity inscribes a hierarchy of speaking positions in relation to gender whereby women may be denied such 'in-the-world' mobility. Indeed, I argued that the mobile speaking position at issue in reflexive social research is a version of the ideal self of late modernity made possible by processes of denaturalization and desocialization in relation to gender. Thus much like the reflexivity at issue in cultural economies discussed in Chapter 3, while such processes enable mobility in regard to identities and identifications, and moreover, the cultivation of techniques which allow such flexibility, they should not be understood as 'liberatory' but rather should be read critically, and in particular should be understood as involving new articulations of difference and power.

    In this chapter I explore the politics of 'in-the-world' reflexivity further, but here I am concerned with sexuality. In particular, in this chapter I am interested in the politics of reflexivity in regard to sexuality and HIV testing. I have chosen the latter as important for analysis since the discursive and administrative procedures associated with HIV testing have been located as inciting reflexivity. That is to say HIV testing has been located as an important technology that incites the kind of reflexivity which the reflexive modernization thesis posits as both characteristic of and intensifying in the late modern world. In addition though, the techniques and procedures associated with HIV testing have also been understood to involve the mapping of a new politics of sexuality. Specifically, the techniques involved in HIV testing have been understood to challenge the heterosexual–homosexual binary via a responsibilization of heterosexuality in relation to HIV/AIDS. Thus the techniques associated with testing have been located as involving a process of detraditionalization in respect to sexuality. However, in this chapter I suggest that rather than straightforwardly challenging the heterosexual–homosexual binary, the techniques and procedures associated with HIV testing make self-reflexivity only fully available to the category of heterosexuality. Thus I suggest that reflexivity is bound up not in an undoing of sexual hierarchies but in their very inscription. Before turning to discuss HIV testing however, I turn first to the idea of risk, and specifically to the idea of risk society.

reflexivity and risk

Throughout this book so far I have broadly focused on increasing tendencies towards reflexivity in late modernity and with the politics of such reflexivity. One aspect of the reflexive modernization thesis that I have so far neglected however concerns the relations between reflexivity and risk. Specifically in the reflexive modernization thesis tendencies towards intensified capacities for reflexivity are sometimes understood to be connected to the increasing cultural significance of risk as an organizing principle of contemporary life. Most notably, Beck (1992, 1994) has argued that reflexivity is bound up with a shift from industrial to risk society. Risk society for Beck is post-traditional where, for instance, social position and conflicts are defined not by a logic of the distribution of goods, but by the distribution of risks, hazards and insecurities, such as ecological hazards, which themselves have been produced by the successes of industrialism (1992: 20). Thus for Beck risk society is one where the threats produced by industrial society predominate, indeed where risks are the axial principle of social organization, but where risks themselves are incalculable, unaccountable, uncompensatable and unlimited (Beck 1994; and see Lash and Urry 1994: 32–7). Risk society is therefore characterized by an increasing identification, awareness and concern of and with risks, whose utopia is not equality but safety.

For Beck risk society involves increasing reflexivity on two counts. First, risk society is understood as reflexive since it involves a *self-confrontation* of industrial society with industrial society itself, where modernization processes 'produce threats which call into question and eventually destroy the foundations of industrial society' (Beck 1994: 6). Indeed, for Beck, risk society is understood to be constituted by industrial society turning back in on itself and reflecting on itself, where modernization is confronted and undermined by its own limits and consequences. Second, in risk society reflexivity arises in attempting to deal with contemporary risks, where risks 'make us aware of a new reflexive self-determination' (Beck 1994: 8). In particular, in risk society 'the recognition of the unpredictability of threats . . . necessitates self-reflection on the foundations of social cohesion and the examination of prevailing conventions and foundations of "rationality" ' (Beck 1994: 8). Put another way risk society is reflexive in that society is understood as a problem for itself, and there is a reflexive monitoring of risk involving attempts at assessing, defining and regulating risks. Such reflexivity is however intensified by the ways in risk issues, 'no one is an expert, and everyone is an expert' (Beck 1994: 9) where, for example,

> insurance experts . . . contradict safety engineers. While the latter diagnose zero risk, the former decide: uninsurable. Experts are undercut or deposed by opposing experts. Politicians encounter the resistance of citizens' groups, and industrial management encounters morally and politically motivated organized consumer boycotts. Administrations are criticized by self-help groups. Ultimately, even polluter sectors (for instance, the chemical industry in the case of sea pollution) must count on resistance from affected sectors (in this case the fishing industry and the sectors living from seashore tourism). The latter can be called into question by the former, monitored and perhaps even corrected.
>
> (Beck 1994: 11)

This proliferation of knowledges regarding risk and of 'risks' themselves means risk society is also one characterized by uncertainty, doubt and ambivalence. As the certainties and traditions of industrial society dissolve and people are being expected to live with a broad variety of different global and personal risks they are therefore 'now expected to master . . . "risky opportunities", without being able, owing to the complexity of modern society, to make the necessary decisions on a well-founded . . . basis' (Beck 1994: 8). This leads to a 'reflexive conduct of life' (Beck 1992: 98), a planning of one's own biography and social relations where the opening up and dis-integration of industrial society and the untying of individuals from its rules, norms and expectations such as class and status compel people not only to create and invent their own certainties, forms of authority and regulation but also to create and invent their own self-identities and themselves as individuals. In risk society the standard biography therefore becomes a chosen, do-it-yourself, reflexive biography mediated by categories of risk. For Beck, self-reflexivity is therefore understood to be an *effect* of the culture of risk. Thus the reflexive project of self-monitoring, self-regulation and self-building becomes a necessity because of the break up of old certainties and narratives of self (such as those of nation, class, status, gender, sexuality) in the move to risk culture.

risk and techniques of government

While Beck's thesis on risk has been widely influential, nonetheless it has been subject to critique from governmentalists, that is, by those who have taken up aspects of Foucault's work on the practices and techniques of governing. Mitchell Dean (1998, 1999) has for example argued that Beck's account works with a far too realist understanding of risk and in particular does not register enough that what is significant about risk is that it is a way of ordering reality, that is of rendering it into a calculable form (see also Ewald 1991; Lupton 1999). Risk he says 'is a way of representing events so they might be made governable in particular ways, with particular techniques, and for particular goals' (Dean 1998: 25). Thus what is problematic for Dean in Beck's account of risk society is that it operates with an ontological and totalizing understanding of risk. As a consequence it fails to register that it is not that the social or 'society' that is increasingly characterized or mediated by risk, but that risk is central to the constitution, ordering and indeed intelligibility of the 'social' itself. Hence Dean comments 'society perhaps is as much an artefact of risk as the other way around' (1998: 40). In particular, he suggests that the contemporary proliferation of risk rationalities (in which he includes epidemiological risk, clinical or case management risk, and risk management) order reality or the social in such a way which is consistent with neo-liberal modes of rule. Specifically, such rationalities individualize risk, that is, make individuals responsible for their own risks.

This attachment of risk technologies to contemporary neo-liberal programmes of governance has been noted by a range of commentators (see e.g. Lupton 1995; Peterson and Lupton 1996; Nettleton 1997; Peterson 1997). Higgs (1998), for example, has shown the ways social and health policy is increasingly organized in terms of a logic of risk identification and risk assessment. Here risk is defined as the result of lifestyle choices made by individuals, a logic which results, for example, in health promotion strategies aimed at changing behaviours. Higgs points, for instance, to the ways in Britain a 'Salience of Lifestyle' index has come to be used as a diagnostic measure in the targeting of health promotion towards those most vulnerable to strokes. Using this measure individuals are categorized as 'lifestylist' or 'fatalist', where 'fatalists' are defined as less amenable to health promotion and therefore more at risk of strokes. Higgs notes that what is important in the adoption of such measures is that, rather than a matter of government responsibility, the pursuit of public health comes to be defined as a matter of individual action, where primary responsibility is located with the individual who is expected to adopt certain lifestyle choices. An ideal of a choosing, self-monitoring, self-regulating, self-forming – a subject who makes use of their own agency to govern their self – is therefore being figured through and by social and health policy newly arranged in terms of risk.

While it is possible to point to numerous examples of how the contemporary proliferation of risk rationalities conjoin with neo-liberal modes of governance (and in particular how such rationalities involve both a refiguring of the social in terms of categories of risk and the individualization of risks) nonetheless, and as was discussed in Chapter 2, those who have been concerned to evaluate the reflexive modernization thesis in regard to sexuality and gender have rejected the significance and usefulness of Foucault's work for this task. Thus, as was mentioned in Chapter 2, McNay sees Foucault's work to set a limit to the reflexive modernization thesis since she suggests it is precisely the influence of Foucault's later analyses of the aesthetics of existence and of practices of the self which makes the reflexive modernization thesis problematic for understanding the constitution of sexuality and gender in late modernity. Specifically, she suggests it is this influence which prompts theorists of reflexive modernity to understand identity as amenable to reflexive self-transformation, an understanding which ignores the embodied and embedded aspects of identity, that is, reproduces the very problem found in Foucault's (later) analysis of identity (see also Lash 1990).

However, while this may be the case, to reject the significance of more Foucauldian understandings of reflexivity and risk may be to close off a number of important issues. First is the issue of historical specificity, for as Dean's analysis suggests, from a governmentalist point of view, the reflexive modernization thesis tends to universalize and totalize risk and reflexivity and in particular fails to locate the latter as central to the practices and techniques of neo-liberal modes of governance. In this context the rejection of Foucauldian tools to analyse gender and sexuality in late modernity by writers such as McNay and by some of the sociological feminists discussed in Chapter 1 strikes as somewhat ironic, particularly because it is these writers who specifically state that they are in search of historical specificity and imply that analyses which have such Foucauldian influences are unable to deliver on this issue. For example, despite a stated concern with historical specificity, in McNay's analysis of reflexivity and detraditionalization in relation to gender and sexuality there is little acknowledgement of the alignment of reflexivity and especially a reflexive relation to identity with neo-liberalism. Indeed on the basis of analyses such as Mitchell Dean's (1998) it is possible to suggest that the privileged subject of late modernity at issue in the previous two chapters – that is a reflexive subject with a vision of a mobile relation to identity and identification – may be the privileged subject of neo-liberal modes of governance, a position from which (as I have illustrated) there are a number of exclusions.

But analyses such as Dean's not only alert us to the ways in which the self-reflexive subject and reflexively constituted identities are aligned with neo-liberal modes of rule, but the questioning of the ontological status of risk (and hence reflexivity) in such governmentalist accounts also adds weight to a point made so far in this book. Specifically, it adds weight to the point made in previous chapters that reflexivity should not be conceived as a straightforward *outcome* of the social, for instance be understood as an outcome of a cultural feminization of fields, or of already existing social divisions and differences, and nor should it be conceived of as straightfor-wardly undoing the social. For as I have suggested in preceding chapters, reflexivity is constitutive of new forms of classification, difference and division, indeed is constitutive of fields and the distinctions between them. Thus what is therefore at issue in terms of reflexivity is a reworking of the 'social' and this is especially so since reflexivity provides a ground for post-structural forms of classification. To repeat Dean's quote on risk, 'society perhaps is as much an artefact of risk as the other way around' (1998: 40).

surveillance, risk and reflexivity

Taking up these points, in what follows I critically evaluate Beck's under-standing of reflexivity as an effect or outcome of risk society. In particular, and as mentioned at the start, I do so via a consideration of the politics of sexuality in regard to HIV testing. This will serve to show that reflexivity in relation to sexuality does not concern a simple breakdown of the homosexual–heterosexual binary but the inscription of a sexual hierarchy. In addition, and taking up Dean's points regarding risk, the discussion which follows suggests that HIV testing in specific 'western' contexts must be understood as a tech-nique aligned to neo-liberal modes of rule and in particular is a technique of the neo-liberal mode of governance of sexuality. Finally, in what follows I suggest that reflexivity towards sexuality is not simply an outcome or effect of ontologically prior risks or 'risk society' as suggested by Beck. Rather it will be suggested that categories of risk which order and are constitutive of the social are actively constituted by the practices, techniques and technologies of risk themselves.

To do so I turn first to David Armstrong's (1995) thesis regarding the rise of surveillance medicine, involving the figuring of a self-reflexive, responsibilized subject in relation to risk. I do so for, as I shall go on to illus-trate, HIV antibody testing is best understood as a technology of surveillance medicine, that is a technology which serves to make risk management the responsibility of individuals. Emerging from the early twentieth century on-wards alongside the then hegemonic hospital medicine, but now dominant, Armstrong argues that one of the characteristics of surveillance medicine is its concern not with the ill patient (as was the case in hospital medicine) but with the surveillance of 'normal', healthy populations. A central feature of surveillance medicine is therefore the targeting and monitoring of everyone, a monitoring which takes place through techniques of testing, surveys and health promotion. Armstrong suggests the main expansion in such techniques occurred after World War II 'when an emphasis on comprehensive health care, and primary and community care, underpinned the deployment of explicit surveillance surveys such as screening and health promotion' (1995:

398). But a defining feature of the techniques of surveillance medicine is the way they deploy a logic of giving responsibility for surveillance to patients themselves. In health promotion, for example,

> concerns with diet, exercise, stress, sex, etc. become the vehicles for encouraging the community to survey itself. The ultimate triumph of Surveillance Medicine would be its internalization by all the population.
>
> (Armstrong 1995: 399–400)

The techniques of surveillance medicine therefore involve the constitution of self-monitoring, self-regulating, reflexive subjects in relation to health.

While 'the extension of the medical eye over all the population is the outward manifestation of . . . Surveillance Medicine' (1995: 400) Armstrong argues the shift to this framework also involved a fundamental reordering of the spatialization of illness. In hospital medicine a symptom was linked to the findings of a clinical examination (the signs) to indicate the presence of a hidden pathological lesion. In surveillance medicine however, the relations between symptom, sign and illness are reconfigured. Specifically, instead of through a linkage based on surface and depth 'all become components in a more general arrangement of predictive factors' (Armstrong 1995: 400). For instance, while in hospital medicine symptoms were understood to be produced by hidden lesions and were used to infer both the existence and nature of disease, in surveillance medicine symptom, sign and disease are reconfigured as contingent *risk factors*, which point to, but do not necessarily produce, future illness. Moreover, while in hospital medicine symptoms, signs and diseases were located in the body, in surveillance medicine risk factors concern any state or event from which a probability can be calculated. Thus

> Surveillance Medicine turns increasingly to an extracorporal space – often represented by the notion of lifestyle – to identify the precursors of future illness. Lack of exercise and a high fat diet therefore can be joined with angina, high blood cholesterol and diabetes as risk factors for heart disease.
>
> (Armstrong 1995: 401)

In surveillance medicine therefore 'the whole of the individual's life is subject to scrutiny for risky behaviours that might give rise to future health problems' (Higgs 1998: 189). Indeed so strong is this scrutinization that surveillance medicine is understood by Armstrong to map a different form of identity: a new risk identity for the 'normal' and 'healthy'. In short, surveillance medicine reworks 'health' in terms of categories of risk and makes the management of such risks the responsibility of individuals. Thus, and following Dean, surveillance medicine may be understood as a risk rationality that reworks and orders the social in a way which is characteristic of neo-liberal modes of governance.

surveillance medicine and HIV antibody testing

Armstrong's thesis regarding the rise of surveillance medicine as involving a new figuring of health in terms of risk and the creation of self-reflexive, self-managing subjects appears to have immediate purchase in relation to recent findings regarding HIV/AIDS. Recent analyses of HIV antibody testing, for example, suggest this diagnostic test may be understood as a technique of surveillance medicine involving as it does procedures of risk assessment, risk identification, (often) asymptomatic testing, and practices of subjection and subjectification. Lupton, for instance, has argued that discourses of health risk and diagnostic testing, such as HIV antibody testing, 'are highly inter-related' (1995: 104) since the logics of testing involve the identification of those defined to be 'at risk', that is, of those positioned as having a potential to develop a certain condition or disease; an incitement of those defined to be at risk to test, involving self-identification in relation to risk categories; and, if testing points to the potential of a future condition or disease, that such knowledge will lead to appropriate forms of self-management and self-regulation in relation to health, including the self-disciplining of behaviour to ensure potential conditions or diseases are not passed on to others.

In a more extended analysis of the micropolitics of power involved in HIV antibody testing Waldby (1996) expands on these themes. Along with other commentators (see e.g. Patton 1990a for a discussion in relation to United States and Danziger 1998 for a comparative analysis of Britain, Hungary and Sweden) she notes the ways in which HIV antibody testing represents a key technology in HIV policy for many 'first'-world nations. For example, Waldby argues that the general AIDS education strategy for Australia has 'involved asking every citizen to assess their own risk and decide accordingly whether to be tested' (1996: 114). However, it is not only self-assessment and self-identification in relation to risk categories which Walby shows to be at work in the techniques associated with HIV testing, for she also shows how HIV testing may be understood as a technology of sex, as a 'constellation of administrative and discursive techniques whereby subjects are classified and socially ordered through a securing of a confession as to the "truth" of their sexuality' (1996: 113). Thus Waldby describes the bio-administrative techniques involved in testing, including the taking of a blood sample, counselling, biochemical analysis of the sample, the reporting of results, and, if the test is positive, a confessional test for what she terms a transmission identity where

> each seropositive subject is asked to provide a history of their sexuality, to review sexual practices for the probable 'mode of transmission' so that they can be positioned in the classificatory schemas of AIDS epidemiology as a transmission type, for instance homosexual, (male) bisexual or heterosexual transmission, and so on.
>
> (1996: 113)

The techniques and procedures of HIV testing which oblige subjects to 'know themselves as sexual identities and to make themselves available for sexual identification' (Waldby 1996: 120) therefore not only work to position the virus in the particular body, to mark the positively tested with a sign of seropositivity, but also to authoritatively mark the positively tested with a sign of a sexual 'transmission category' 'type' or identity. Indeed in this way, Waldby argues that HIV testing is best understood as a technology through which the virus is *personified*, as diagnosing a type of person who is seropositive, a type of person who is often defined in terms of categories of sexual identity (see also Heaphy 1996 for a discussion of practices of 'personification' in relation to the medical and counselling experiences of people with HIV/AIDS).

Waldby also shows how such forms of marking render subjects visible to, and insert them into technologies of socio-medical surveillance. For example, a positive result both figures the tested person into a state of visibility in relation to public health surveillance, and inserts them into regimes of medical management which may include in- and out-patient hospital services, regular monitoring, referrals to counsellors and invitations to volunteer for clinical trials and epidemiological cohort studies. Such forms of administration and regulation concern not just subjection but subjectification since they attempt 'to induce the internalisation of the self as dangerous, as infected, and hence to precipitate a new ethics of sexual practice and institutional deportment for the seropositive person' (Waldby 1996: 124). Thus the medical management of seropositivity involves both an incitement towards a permanent state of self-examination and self-regulation and an obligation to adopt disciplined sexual practices oriented towards the protection of others. In these ways Waldby (1996: 114) suggests HIV testing must also be understood as a technology of the self, since testing

> not only compels subjects in certain ways but . . . also induces the internalisation of new norms of identity and self-management, above all the management of one's health and one's sexual practices, in the interest of minimising illness and HIV transmission.

But the administrative and discursive techniques of HIV testing make self-monitoring, self-regulation and 'responsibilization' not just desirable but *obligatory* for the seropositive, and in these ways Waldby argues that HIV testing has severe implications for particular subjects.

In this account of HIV testing the self-monitoring, self-assessing subject central to Armstrong's analysis of surveillance medicine is highly visible. So too is the scrutiny of 'the whole of the individual's life' for 'risky' behaviours evidenced, for instance, in the 'confessional' elements of testing. Also evident is the invention of new categories of risk identity which Armstrong suggests is a further feature of surveillance medicine. But, as Waldby shows through her analysis of HIV testing as a technology of sex, the risk, exposure or transmission identities constituted through testing are defined predominantly in terms of sexuality. And she goes on to show, as indeed have others both in relation to testing and in relation to epidemiological, public health and health education discourses on HIV/AIDS more generally (see e.g. McCrombie 1986; Patton 1990a; Schiller *et al*. 1994), that risk is defined not only in terms of sexual identity, but also that sexual identities are ordered hierarchically in terms of risk, with gay and bisexual men defined as high risk and heterosexuals as low risk. Thus in terms of health education strategies which ask every citizen to assess their own risk and to decide whether or not to be tested, this hierarchicization of sexual identities in relation to risk means

> the demand for risk assessment is far more rigorous for certain groups than it is for others depending on what position their self-identified categories occupy in the hierarchy of infectiousness determined by epidemiology . . . This category position will further determine the extent to which they are actively medicalised, sought out or 'targeted' by programmes designed to encourage testing.
>
> (Waldby 1996: 114)

This has amounted, Waldby suggests, to a strong sense of obligation to be tested for gay identified men (as well as for pregnant women, see also Treichler 1988; Patton 1990b). Indeed, she suggests that the classificatory logic of the discursive and administrative techniques of testing is so powerful that it 'resembles the general social drive to identify the "homosexual"' (Walby 1996: 121). This identificatory view of testing – as a drive to identify the 'homosexual' – is also supported by Treichler who has argued 'the ongoing fixation with HIV testing is in part designed to put a stop to gay men's successful passing as straight; refusal to take the HIV-antibody test is therefore similar to pleading the Fifth' (1988: 200). Thus what such analyses point towards is not only that processes of identification, classification and hierarchicization in regard to sexuality are characteristic of (neo-liberal) modes of regulation of HIV/AIDS, but critically that these forms of classification are articulated in terms of categories of risk.

the universalization of HIV/AIDS risk: the 'responsibilization' of heterosexuality

However, it is important to recognize as a number of writers have stressed, that the discursive and administrative techniques associated with testing should not be read as entirely determinate of identity. In his study of the ways the identities of people with HIV/AIDS living in Britain are formed and shaped Heaphy (1996: 153), for example, stresses that

> while people with AIDS/HIV are, in some senses, subject to dominant medico-moral and medico-scientific discourses on AIDS and HIV, they do draw on counter-discourses in making personal sense of the virus and syndrome, and do not accept dominant meanings uncritically.

He shows, for example, the ways medical and other dominant knowledges on HIV/AIDS are 'mediated in various ways through the gay press, alternative medical manuals and self-help groups' (1996: 149–50). Heaphy argues that the meaning of HIV/AIDS must therefore be understood as negotiated and that people living with HIV/AIDS play an active role in the creation of their own identities.

Bartos (1996) similarly argues that while AIDS policy in Australia may be understood in terms of a framework of governmentality – where populations are rendered calculable in terms of risk and where success is measured in terms of the adoption of governmental objectives by the targets of government themselves (Bartos 1996: 125) – there are important sources of disruption of the governmentalization of HIV/AIDS, sources which he terms 'the queer underside of government' (1996: 126; see also Patton 1993). Bartos looks, for example, at the ways people living with and against HIV work to defy governmentalization, to the ways, for instance, gay-identified men who have 'expert knowledge about safe-sex practices' (1996: 129) may practice unprotected sex as a way of resisting governmentalization, especially the tyranny of identification associated with AIDS policy. Indeed it has also been noted that the identificatory logics of testing have been challenged through resistance to HIV testing by gay identified men (see e.g. Hunter 1997).

While it is important to register that the classificatory and identificatory logics associated with HIV testing and other techniques of governance in relation to HIV/AIDS do not go unchallenged and are sometimes disrupted, it is also important to stress that analyses such as Waldby's, which suggest that testing and other techniques constitute a drive to identify the homosexual, tend to overlook other evidence which suggests that HIV antibody testing is increasingly being sought by heterosexuals, or, in epidemiological terms, is increasingly being sought by 'the general population' or 'general community'. For example, in a telephone survey of Sydney residents aged 16–50 conducted in 1988, 71 per cent of 651 respondents said 'yes' to the question 'Have you ever considered having an AIDS [sic] test?'.[1] And in a repeat study in 1989 80 per cent of 701 respondents answered in the affirmative to the same question (Bray and Chapman 1991: 110). In a large scale study designed to overcome what the researchers term a neglect of 'large scale surveys of HIV testing in the Australian population' Van de Ven et al. (1997: 26) looked at testing rates and factors associated with testing amongst first year heterosexual tertiary students in Sydney involving annual surveys over the period 1992 to 1995. They found that of 2,759 surveyed 'almost one in five of the students reported that they had ever had an HIV antibody test' (1997: 27). Moreover, the proportion tested was found to be significantly greater in later years of data collection. Thus in 1992, 14.5 per cent of 926 students surveyed reported having had an HIV antibody test and in 1995, 20.3 per cent of 506 students surveyed reported testing (Van de Ven et al. 1997: 27). While a number of the students cited various mandatory reasons for testing, for instance in cases of blood donations and for occupational, immigration or insurance requirements, the researchers found a broad group of what they termed 'voluntary' reasons for testing, including, for example, testing out of curiosity. Moreover, the researchers found 'that voluntary testing increased disproportionately over time' (Van de Ven *et al.* 1997: 29). Such intensifications of testing over time are reflected in generally high rates of antibody testing in Australia, and in the significant rises in the number of tests each year since its availability. Since 1987 over 9 million HIV tests have been conducted (Lupton *et al.* 1995a) with 700,000 tests performed in 1997 (Lamont 1998). In the state of Victoria alone in 1987 50,000 tests were performed and by 1993 the total had more than doubled with 120,000 tests conducted (Thompson *et al.* 1996: 166).[2]

Some commentators have suggested that the intensification of HIV antibody testing is linked to the ways testing is increasingly understood as a routine health check. Willis for example has argued that HIV 'testing is moving from the unusual to the usual to be part of the routine of "normal science" like other screening tests such as blood pressure' (1992: 180). This view of testing is supported by the findings of Lupton *et al.* (1995a: 177) who, in a study of 50 adults concerning their decisions to have one or more HIV tests, found

> many of the respondents appeared not to discriminate between the HIV test and other tests; they are all medical tests, serving the function of providing 'knowledge' of one's condition, and useful to undergo if offered as part of one's general maintenance of the body.

However, the intensification of testing in Australia has also been widely interpreted to be linked to processes of (what is sometimes referred to as) the 'degaying' of AIDS. Specifically, it has been argued that high rates of HIV testing are linked to health promotion campaigns and news media representations in the late 1980s which extended and universalized risk in relation to HIV/AIDS, a universalization which is often understood by AIDS researchers to have been constituted by the construction of heterosexuals as 'at risk' in relation to HIV/AIDS (see e.g. Morlet *et al.* 1988; Lupton *et al.* 1995b; Thompson *et al.* 1996; Tulloch and Lupton 1997) which caused 'panic, fear and anxiety' (Lupton 1993: 324) and led to demands for heterosexual HIV antibody testing (Morlet *et al.* 1988; Lupton *et al.* 1995a, 1995b; Thompson *et al.* 1996). Indeed it has been suggested that 'mass media campaigns or intense news media coverage of the risk of heterosexual transmission of HIV are frequently followed by upsurges in the numbers of heterosexuals seeking HIV tests' (Lupton *et al.* 1995a: 174; see also Morlet *et al.* 1988; Chippendale *et al.* 1998).

The construction of heterosexuals as 'at risk' in relation to HIV/AIDS is, however, considered not only to explain the growing demands for testing, but also to explain low levels of seropositive tests. Both the high numbers of tests and the low proportion of positive tests in the state of Victoria (where the proportion of positive tests has remained at less than

1 per cent since 1988) has, for example, been interpreted by medical researchers to 'reflect continued high demand for HIV testing by individuals
not at high risk of HIV infection' (Thompson *et al.* 1996: 168, see also
Lupton *et al.* 1995a; 1995b).[3] Thus Thompson *et al.* report for the period
1991–93 'many of those being tested for HIV do not fall into . . . identified
personal "risk" categor[ies]' (1996: 167), categories which the researchers
report as 'homosexual', 'injecting drug user' and 'prostitute'. For these latter
they say 'less than 10 % of tests [have been] undertaken on people identified
as having personal risks for HIV' (Thompson *et al.* 1996: 169). Moreover,
they report the majority of 'low risk' individuals who test identify as heterosexual, indeed that the majority of testing performed was on those identified
as heterosexual (Thompson *et al.* 1996: 169).

     While Thompson *et al.* were unable to consider the rates of
voluntary heterosexual testing in Victoria because the number of 'HIV tests
. . . ordered at the request of the patient . . . remains unanswered by . . .
[surveillance] data' (1996: 170), nevertheless, medical research in other contexts suggests that increases in heterosexual testing, especially those connected
to a 'universalization' of risk in relation to HIV/AIDS, concerns voluntary
testing. Chippendale *et al.* (1998) report such an intensification of voluntary
testing in a study of patterns of, and reasons for HIV testing in a central
London genito-urinary medicine (GUM) clinic for a six-month period in
1994–95. During this time 768 people attended for testing, 67 per cent of
whom self-identified as heterosexual, 4 per cent as bisexual and 29 per cent
as homosexual (Chippendale *et al.* 1998: 220). Moreover, on comparing this
data with rates and patterns of testing in 1986–87, the researchers found
that 'in relation to differences associated with year (1986–87 versus 1994–5)
significantly more heterosexual attendees in 1994–95 reported requesting
testing' (Chippendale *et al.* 1998: 220). And as with researchers in the Australian context, Chippendale *et al.* link this increase in requests for heterosexual testing to health promotion media campaigns which constructed the
'general population' (1998: 220) as at risk in relation to HIV/AIDS.

     Two points regarding this research on heterosexual testing stand
out as being of significance. First, the figuring of heterosexuality as 'low risk'
and homosexuality as a 'risk category' in and by medical research such as
that discussed by Thompson *et al.* clearly calls into question the argument
that there has been a simple universalization of risk in relation to HIV/AIDS,
revealing as it does a hierarchy of risk in relation to sexual identities. Second,
if, as Waldby and Treichler argue, the logics of the administrative and discursive techniques of testing constitute a drive to identify the 'homosexual',
what are we to make of heterosexuals seeking testing? As we have seen, part
of Waldby's argument regarding the identificatory logic of testing rests on
the claim that while health education strategies ask every citizen to assess their
own risk in relation to HIV/AIDS, the hierarchicization of sexual identities in
relation to risk means 'the demand for risk assessment is far more rigorous
for certain groups than it is for others' especially for gay men, for whom as

a result there is a strong sense of obligation to be tested. Are then heterosexuals now in some way also 'obliged' to test?

Some analyses suggest this may indeed be the case. Lupton (1993; see also Lupton *et al.* 1995a, 1995b), for example, suggests that the construction of heterosexuals as at risk in relation to HIV/AIDS has involved the creation of a new micropolitics of self-regulation in relation to HIV/AIDS for heterosexuals. She suggests that discourses of HIV/AIDS risk in relation to heterosexuality extended a micropolitics of self-surveillance to every individual, or 'responsibilized' every subject in terms of HIV/AIDS risk. Thus, and through emphasizing 'individual behaviour change . . . all individuals [became] responsible for stopping the spread of AIDS in the Australian community' (Lupton 1993: 317). Moreover, Lupton argues such moves were 'legitimized by the *pre-existing* discourse of risk which dominates public health discourses' (emphasis added), which she argues serve as 'an effective panoptic agent of surveillance and control that is difficult to challenge' (Lupton 1993: 324–5). For Lupton increasing demands for heterosexual testing are therefore understood to be connected to a new politics of subjection and subjectification in relation to heterosexuality, involving 'responsibilization' and the creation of self-managing, self-regulating heterosexual subjects in relation to HIV/AIDS. Similarly, Turner's analysis of governmentality and risk suggests that he also agrees that HIV/AIDS discourses have led to such a 'generalized' micropolitics of self-surveillance. For example, he comments,

> the notion of *generalised* risk in the environment may lead to greater surveillance and control through the promotion of preventative medicine. The AIDS 'epidemic' creates a political climate within which intervention and control are seen to be both necessary and benign. Individuals need, especially in the area of sexual etiquette, to becoming self-regulating and self-forming.
>
> (Turner 1997: xix, emphasis added; see also Peterson and Lupton 1996: 69–70)

Such analyses therefore seem to question Waldby's view that the administrative techniques and procedures of HIV testing simply concern the identification of the homosexual, since many of the techniques which Waldby associates with 'the drive towards the identification of the homosexual', including subjection, subjectification and self-management and self-reflexivity, appear from these analyses also to apply in relation to heterosexuality. Indeed, it has been suggested that the extension of HIV/AIDS risk discourse to the 'whole population' involves not so much a drive to identify the homosexual but to signal an important shift in relation to sexuality. Lupton has for example argued that the extension of risk discourse in relation to HIV/AIDS to heterosexuals involves a shift in representations of 'AIDS from a disease of the deviant and (primarily) homosexual Other to a disease of the heterosexual Self' (1993: 324), that is, to concern a kind of 'heterosexualization' of HIV/AIDS. Thus Lupton's analysis implies that rather that constituting a hierarchy of sexualities defined and articulated in terms of categories of risk, neo-liberal techniques of governance in relation to HIV/AIDS may be disruptive of the heterosexual–homosexual binary via an extension of a micropolitics of self-surveillance and self-regulation to the whole population. Yet while Lupton understands the universalization of risk in relation to HIV/AIDS to signal a new kind of regulation in terms of subjection and subjectification for heterosexuals, which incites testing as one such self-regulative act, nevertheless, she is curiously silent on the kind of heterosexual self being consti-tuted in practices and acts of self-surveillance and self-management in relation to HIV/AIDS risk. Indeed we might ask what kind of heterosexual self is being constituted in such moves?

testing and making self-reflexivity

While this may be an important theoretical and political question, for medical researchers the intensification of heterosexual testing is often inter-preted as unnecessary, excessive over-testing for a group defined as 'low risk' (see e.g. Thompson *et al.* 1996). This view has also informed social research concerned with heterosexual testing. For example, in discussing the findings of their large-scale survey of heterosexual students in Sydney, Van de Ven *et al.* ask 'Do these findings support the assertion that current levels of testing in "low-risk" populations are excessive?' In response they report 'The heterosexual tertiary students in our sample would not generally be regarded as being at high risk of HIV infection. On the whole they would belong to the so-called low risk group' (1997: 10). Nevertheless, Van de Ven *et al.* suggest on the basis of their findings that 'a great deal of their testing was done for good reasons . . . HIV testing among heterosexual tertiary students is based largely on reasonable medical, occupational, personal or interpersonal con-siderations' (1997: 10).

Similarly, questions concerning 'low risk' testing also informed Lupton *et al.*'s study (1995a, 1995b) of 50 adults who had had one or more tests. In particular the ways in which testing patterns have been interpreted to mean that the majority of people being tested for HIV are 'low risk', lead Lupton *et al.* to ask why heterosexuals seek testing. To approach this issue and for a sample of mostly heterosexual respondents who had recently had a test, Lupton *et al.* looked at the socio-cultural meanings of testing, and also at how people used the test result. From the point of view of my concerns here, especially those regarding the kind of heterosexual self figured through testing, the findings of this study are of particular interest.[4] In particular, my reading of the published data suggests testing makes self-reflexivity only fully available to the category of heterosexuality, defining other sexual categories as non-self-reflexive, that is, as incapable of adequately taking on technologies of the self and therefore in need of more obligatory *external* monitoring and checking. Indeed if this reading of testing has any purchase it suggests that heterosexual self-reflexivity in relation to HIV/AIDS should not simply be understood as an issue of the heterosexualization of HIV/AIDS and hence to challenge the hetero–homo binary, but rather as constituting new self–other relations in relation to sexuality: specifically, (hetero) reflexive-selves and non-hetero non-reflexive others.

To begin to address these points let me turn first to the issue of responsibilization. For a number of those interviewed by Lupton *et al.* HIV testing represented 'a sign of responsibility because it represented maturity and a concern for one's health' (1995a: 177). For instance, 'both sexes commonly used words such as "positive", "responsible", "sensible" and "right" to describe having the test'. Testing was therefore described as a 'responsible thing to do' (Lupton *et al.* 1995a: 176). One young woman, for example, described the way in which having the test 'was a statement about the "responsible" nature of her character' (Lupton *et al.* 1995a: 176). But for these respondents testing also provided a way of establishing not only self-responsibility but also self-regulation. Thus in discussing their experiences of testing, narratives of self-regulation and self-care were performed. One respondent, for example, said: 'I go for pap smears, I know [cervical cancer is preventable], so I go for those sorts of things. . . . It's something I can do something about, same with HIV, it's something I can do something about' (Lupton *et al.* 1995a: 177); and another: 'I've monitored everything as far as my body is concerned . . . I do look after myself, check and everything' (Lupton *et al.* 1995b: 103). Hence testing is understood as '"doing something" to keep the body in good order' (Lupton *et al.* 1995a: 179). For these respondents the technology of HIV testing therefore made available particular narratives of the self, those of self-responsibility and self-regulation. Put another way, testing figured their 'selves' in these terms. In this way it seems that doing the test – testing – may be understood as a technology of the self constitutive of responsibilized, self-reflexive heterosexual subjects.

Du Gay has shown how the 'responsibilization' of subjects involves a figuring of subjects as the agents of themselves, as reflexive subjects who are continuously engaged in a project to shape their lives as autonomous, choosing individuals driven by the desire to optimize the worth of their existence through the constant building and rebuilding of their own resources (1996: 181). In this context it is interesting to note as Lupton *et al.* do, that for their respondents the HIV test provides 'important social currency' (Lupton *et al.* 1995a: 176) or a 'bargaining tool' (Lupton *et al.* 1995b: 107) especially in the domain of intimacy and relationships (see also Van de Ven *et al.* 1997). In particular 'the ability to report oneself as being HIV negative involves a perceived dimension of character that is seen as congruent with enhanced sexual attractiveness' (Lupton *et al.* 1995a: 176). In this sense it seems that HIV testing for these respondents may constitute a technology for 'enterprising up' the self, for constituting not only a 'responsibilized' and reflexive self, but also resources of the self which may be mobilized and exchanged.

In addition, Lupton *et al.*'s respondents reported that, for them, testing made them feel 'better', 'confident', 'safe', 'less anxious', 'sure', giving them a 'sense of reassurance'. One respondent commented on the practice of testing as 'Just, for peace of mind – it's like any sort of test, you may be fairly certain that you haven't got it but you need a test anyway, just to make sure' (Lupton *et al.* 1995a: 177), and another, 'in the back of my mind, I know I always practise safe-sex, but I'm a bit of a hypochondriac, so I tend to go for those things, you know, if I go to the doctor's you know, "Give me a test"' (Lupton *et al.* 1995b: 94). These responses indicate that testing for these respondents may be a repetitive performance, and that the practice of testing constitutes not only an enterprising self, but one figured in terms of notions of 'safety'. Indeed, in the context of the universalization of risk in relation to HIV, Lupton *et al.* suggest that the ways in which the test allows 'safety' to be established may 'provide some explanation for the increasing numbers of HIV tests among anxious yet apparently "low risk" individuals' (Lupton *et al.* 1995b: 106).

However, in establishing their own safety through HIV testing, a number of Lupton *et al.*'s respondents simultaneously relied upon and invoked notions of the Other. In particular, respondents invoked 'other' categories of person to construct their own safety: 'impure', 'contaminating', 'out of control' others who were understood as a threat to their own safety and who were deemed to be in need of external regulation and control. Indeed, for these respondents 'the HIV antibody test serves as a means of guarding . . . boundaries against those . . . deemed risky', especially since

> those who felt at risk from HIV infection articulated feelings of extreme vulnerability and a strong need to re-establish subjectivity in the face of their exposure to 'contaminating' Others.
>
> (Lupton *et al.* 1995b: 106)

Moreover, these 'contaminating Others' were understood to be to particular categories of person in regard to sexuality, for example the 'gay man', the 'bisexual man' and the 'female prostitute'.

Here then are practices of the personification of risk as categories of sexual identity which Waldby and others have identified as at issue in relation to the administrative and discursive techniques of testing. But here it is not just that particular categories of sexually defined person are constructed as 'risky', but also that through the practice of testing, heterosexuality is imagined as 'safe' and 'low risk'. Indeed, Waldby's analysis of the techniques and procedures of testing shows that similar processes take place inside the bio-medical techniques of testing. Specifically, she shows how such techniques personify or perform heterosexuality as 'low risk', since the techniques of testing work on an explicit assumption of the cleanliness of the heterosexual. For example, she shows how the interpretation and classification of test results work 'to make the heterosexual category the most residual, the least likely to be nominated as a "source" of infection' (Waldby

1996: 126). Rather, 'sources' of infection are represented as outside of the category. Hence it is assumed that heterosexuality is 'regulated', 'checked' and 'safe', and that it may only be infected by the 'outside', by contaminating 'Others'. In this way heterosexuality is figured as at risk rather than risky, threatened rather than threatening.

On this kind of evidence it seems that HIV testing figures heterosexuality as internally checked and self-regulated and therefore as a 'safe', 'low risk' sexual identity. Thus, as has been seen, for Lupton *et al.*'s respondents, the practice of testing made available such narratives of the self. Indeed, on this evidence it seems that the universalization of risk in relation to HIV/AIDS involves not a straightforward shift of 'AIDS from a disease of the homosexual Other to a disease of the heterosexual Self', but new self–other configurations. Specifically, it suggests that, through the practice and techniques of testing, heterosexuality is defined as a self-reflexive identity, that is, as self-managing and self-regulating, while other sexual identities, for instance homosexuality and bisexuality, are defined as non-self-reflexive and, as a consequence, in need of more 'coercive' 'external' monitoring rather than voluntary, self-regulative measures. Put another way testing creates a hierarchy of sexual identities defined in terms of reflexivity.

This hierarchicization of sexual identities in terms of reflexivity is also visible in other studies of the procedures of testing. For example, in a study of post-test counselling McCrombie (1986: 456) has noted that in cases of negative results, gay men, injecting drug users and others classified as 'high risk' are often told

> that some people who test negative are actually infected and given advice on behaviours to limit the transmission of AIDS, i.e. limit the number of sex partners, limit body fluid exchange . . . avoid intravenous drug use, and don't donate blood, plasma, organs or sperm. Some recommend a follow-up test after 6 months.

Seronegatives defined as 'low risk' however, 'are told simply that their test results show they are not infected' (McCrombie 1986: 456). While gay seronegative men and others are therefore told to discipline themselves, especially in regard to sexual practices, and make themselves available for further medical surveillance, for seronegative heterosexuals no such measures are recommended. This hierarchy in terms of reflexivity is also visible in Bray and Chapman's two telephone surveys. Here, although the overwhelming majority of respondents said they had considered having a voluntary HIV test, over half in both surveys said 'testing should be *compulsory* for certain groups' (Bray and Chapman 1991: 110, emphasis added), the most common groups cited being homosexuals and prostitutes. Thus here it seems, as Patton (1990a) has argued in relation to HIV/AIDS education, that the administrative and discursive logics of testing constitutes the 'mainstream' as having a 'right to know, that is a right to protect *themselves*' (Patton 1990a: 14, emphasis added) and gay men and others with 'an *obligation* to know and act appropriately'

(Patton 1990a: 14, emphasis added). Moreover, more recent evidence on patterns of heterosexual HIV testing suggests that this 'mainstream' may concern not just a 'general' heterosexual 'community', but more specifically heterosexual men. In particular, there is some evidence that heterosexual men are more likely to seek voluntary HIV testing than heterosexual women (see e.g. Meyrick *et al.* 1997), suggesting that testing may figure male hetero-sexual sexual identities as the most charged in relation to self-reflexivity.[5]

risk culture and reflexivity

In these ways HIV testing can be understood as a technology which serves not only to identify the 'homosexual' but one which is also constitutive of a heterosexuality figured in terms of self-reflexivity: that is, a technology through which heterosexuality is constituted as a self-regulating, internally checked identity. It therefore comes as no surprise that Lupton *et al.* found that, for those in their sample, HIV testing offered a way of establishing a heterosexual subjectivity and identity based on self-responsibility and self-monitoring, for testing itself constitutes only heterosexuality as a sexual identity which can be understood in these terms. Thought of in this way it is clear that the now often asked question 'why are "low risk" groups – especially heterosexuals – increasingly opting for HIV testing?' misses the crucial point that testing precisely constitutes heterosexuality as self-regulating in relation to HIV/ AIDS, as 'low risk', and 'safe'. Indeed, put like this, the dominant assumption which informs many of the analyses of 'risk' and risk culture discussed throughout this chapter – that a generalized risk culture creates insecurity, uncertainty and doubt which then incites practices of self-reflexivity and a reflexive ordering of the self – comes into question. Specifically, it seems, from the example of HIV testing, that self-reflexivity is not a simple *effect* of risk culture – for instance, of *pre-existing* discourses of risk or of a risk society – but that the techniques and practices of risk (self) management, that is the techniques of self-reflexivity (such as those made available by the technology of testing) are constitutive of a social ordered in terms of categories and hierarchies of risk themselves, that is, to make up risk culture. In this sense it seems, as Higgs (1998) has argued in relation to technologies of risk for social and health policy more generally, that HIV antibody testing is a technology which serves not only to 'responsibilize' but also to define and identify so called 'risky' groups, who are deemed incapable of adequately undertaking technologies of the self, that is of being self-reflexive.

But while my analysis suggests that HIV testing is constitutive of such a hierarchy of sexualities defined in terms of categories of risk and reflexivity, nonetheless a range of social and cultural theory suggests that a responsibilized, 'deepened', self-reflexive subject is now the ideal subject of a range of domains, for instance of employment and citizenship (Du Gay 1996; Higgs 1998). For example, the voluntary governance of the self, involving demonstrations of capacities of self-control through the taking on of various technologies of the self, increasingly constitutes what it currently means to be a citizen (Higgs 1998). Thus, and as I indicated at the beginning of this chapter, such social and cultural theory suggests that the reflexive subject is the ideal and privileged subject of neo-liberal modes of governance (see also Callinicos 1999). Yet if the very techniques and procedures of responsibilization make claims to possess a 'deepened' and responsibilized self more available to heterosexuality, and indeed are constitutive of a hierarchy of sexualities, then a little more caution may need to be exercised than has so far been the case in answering questions such as 'why are increasing numbers of heterosexuals having HIV tests?' Indeed, if choosing subjects who make use of their own agency to govern and invent themselves are ideal subjects, then surely – as I hope to have underlined throughout this and other chapters in this book – a politics of 'the freeing of agents from structure' – a politics of reflexivity is in order. This politics of the social post social structure may be especially important if the technologies of this ideal constitute particular subjects in a way which makes claims of the possession of such capacities difficult. It may also be pressing if, as Beck and others have argued, social position is increasingly determined by the distribution of 'risks'. For if, as I have suggested here, reflexivity is closely aligned to such distributions, where, for example, those who are able to claim self-reflexivity are also able to claim their selves as 'low-risk', while those defined as unable to adequately take on technologies of the self are deemed to be 'at risk' and 'risky', then the ability to politicize and contest current definitions of risk may need to involve a politicization of the self-reflexive subject.

Such a politicization is however often deemed unnecessary because of the widely held assumption – highlighted throughout this book – that reflexivity simply flattens out and dissolves issues of power and difference. The problems associated with this assumption have also been highlighted by Vitellone (2000a) in an analysis of heterosexual culture 'post post AIDS'. Here, Vitellone draws attention to the widely held view that reflexivity towards sexual practices (and in particular safer heterosexual sexual practices) challenges and breaks down power relations in regard to both gender and heterosexuality. However, via an analysis of sexual safety, and in particular discourses of heterosexual sexual safety, Vitellone questions this assumption. She shows how on the one hand, the logic of safety in public health campaigns promoting safer heterosex practice have put in place a series of binaries (condom/no condom, safer/unsafe, good/bad heterosex) which attribute a reflexive, responsibilized attitude to heterosexuals who practise heterosexual sex with condoms, and how this is the case especially for heterosexual men. But on the other hand, this very logic (especially the conflation of condoms, safety, reflexivity, care and responsibility) is shown to rule out of court the ways in which heterosex with condoms may not be unproblematically experienced as a 'good', caring and responsible practice, especially for heterosexual women. In short this logic effaces the possibility that heterosex with condoms may be coercive. Vitellone shows how sociological analyses which assume that safer heterosex equals a good, responsible and caring practice reproduce this logic of safety, and as a consequence make coercive safer heterosex invisible, indeed a logical impossibility. This analysis therefore not only highlights the limits of assuming that reflexivity simply undoes 'the social', but also points to the ways in which reflexivity in regard to sexuality involves a reconfiguration and reworking of this terrain. In particular, Vitellone's analysis points to a new configuration of both consent and coercion in heterosexual culture 'post post AIDS'.

What such analyses and the analysis put forward in this chapter suggest is that for a politicization of the 'freeing of agents from structure' to take place, a number of moves are crucial. First, as pointed out at the start of this chapter via the analysis of Mitchell Dean, it seems important to recognize that the self-reflexive subject is closely aligned to neo-liberal modes of governance, indeed is the ideal and privileged subject of neo-liberalism. To do so it is crucial that reflexivity is not understood as a simple outcome of the social but to be reworking the very terrain of the social even as it ostensibly may seem to be a matter of its disappearance. Thus as I have argued, reflexivity should not be understood to be a simple outcome of social change (for example of an increasing mobility across fields or of a proliferation of ontologically prior 'risks'); rather it is crucial that reflexivity is understood to be constitutive of the social itself. Indeed, as I hope to have illustrated through discussions of cultural economy, the politics of knowledge and the regulation of sexuality post post AIDS, reflexivity is constitutive of new forms of classification, hierarchies, divisions, struggle and forms of contestation.

conclusion

This book has been concerned with the 'social' post social structure. More precisely it has examined gender and sexuality post social structure or post society. While there is a common assumption in sociological accounts that gender and sexuality are dispersed, undone or transgressed in this context, the overall argument of this book has been that to hold onto this assumption foregoes an analysis of the 'freeing of agents from structure' or of mobility post society. Such an analysis has been offered in this book in relation to cultural economy, the politics of knowledge, and the (neo-liberal) regulation of sexuality. In so doing it has been suggested that some of the key processes which have been understood to characterize the social after social structure or the social after society – including intensifying reflexivity, mobility and risk – should be understood to be central to new forms of classification, division and difference in relation to sexuality and gender. In short, I have suggested that reflexivity, mobility and risk are central to the reworking and reconfiguration of the 'social' (post social structure or post society) even as they appear to ostensibly undo it.

But this overall thesis needs to be supplemented with a number of caveats. In particular, and as has been stressed throughout previous chapters, in terms of sociological analysis – including sociological analyses of gender and sexuality – such an understanding is only viable if the 'social' (and especially the socio-structural and societal) is not allocated an a priori privileged status over other categories of analysis. This is so because to privilege the social in this way is to impose a number of limits to the analysis of gender and sexuality post social structure. The first of these is that such privileging and understanding leads to an assumption that reflexivity and mobility (as well as risk) are always and inevitably linked to various forms of detraditionalization. Thus to follow this assumption leads to the conclusion that the undoing of familiar patterns of socio-structural forms of determination (for example, the gender segmentation or segregation of labour markets) necessarily involves the dissolution of a social organized and regulated in terms of categories such as gender, sexuality and class, indeed will be 'liberatory' in regard to the latter.

Yet to pursue this line of reasoning is to assume that reflexivity, mobility and risk – including the take-up of a reflexive stance towards gender, the vision of a mobile relation to identity, or the cultivation of self-reflexivity in regard to sexuality post post AIDS – are themselves neutral in relation to sexuality and gender, an assumption which the chapters in this book has brought into doubt. In addition, it is also to assume that there are no other registers through which difference, classification and division take place other than via the socio-structural or 'society'. To pursue this logic is therefore to assume that matters defined to be outside of the socio-structural – which here would include reflexivity, mobility, and the various techniques and practices associated with risk rationalities – have little or no significance for sexuality and gender. It is, in other words, to take for granted that such issues are quite irrelevant to and separate from the constitution and ordering of gender and sexuality, and that this is especially so in comparison to the 'hard core' matters of the socio-structural and socio-historical. Indeed, and as I have made clear, reflexivity, mobility and risk are understood to be so disconnected from the constitution of gender and sexuality that they are widely assumed to disperse and flatten out differences and divisions and undo the bases of various forms of categorization and classification. And this latter is the case even when there are moves away from socio-structural or 'societal' understandings of the social (for example via the social theory of Bourdieu) and where it is suggested that reflexivity and mobility are by no means universal and their realization is uneven and contested. In short, to follow this line of argument is to fail to recognize that the 'social' – including gender and sexuality – may be organized via axes other than those associated with traditional definitions of the social and that reflexivity, mobility and risk may be less than neutral in regard to issues of difference, categorization, ordering and division.

Thus and as this book has also served to illustrate, there is a bizarre irony in the position of those who defend more traditional sociological understandings of sexuality and gender. Specifically, while such critics often accuse those who do not privilege the social (especially the socio-structural and institutional) of neglecting and indeed of sidestepping issues of power and inequality, division and difference, nonetheless the analyses presented in the previous chapters suggest that such a privileging of the 'social' is in fact itself likely to evade such issues. Such a position would, for example, fail to register that a take-up of a reflexive and mobile stance towards gender and sexuality relates to current articulations of difference. In particular, such a position would fail to register the ways in which the take-up of such a stance relates to the articulation of difference post social structure. Thus, and as Chapters 3 and 4 illustrated, differences post social structure are less an issue of social determinants and more one of positions of mobility and immanence vis-à-vis cultural styles. This I suggested is especially characteristic of gender post social structure, that is in contexts where gender has been detached from social forms of determination and has been made mobile, fluid and indeterminate. Moreover, the discussion in these chapters, and especially in Chapter 3, suggested that privileging the social (and in particular the socio-structural) makes invisible the ways in which the take-up of a reflexive stance may be converted into resources (including economic and cultural capital). Thus such a privileging bypasses those very issues – including uneven distributions of resources – that defenders of a more traditionally sociological position for the analysis of gender and sexuality claim to be at the heart of their territory, and hence to be able to illuminate. In short, such a position sidesteps and fails to register the ways in which the 'social' itself is being reworked and refashioned in terms of reflexivity, mobility and risk.

While this book has highlighted the assumption that many analyses of reflexivity, mobility and risk assume that the latter are neutral in regard to gender to sexuality, it has also suggested that there are two further related problems associated with many of the existing ways in which these issues have been understood vis-à-vis gender and sexuality. The first of these problems relates to the assumption that reflexivity, mobility and risk are best understood as the outcome or effect of social change. The second relates to the assumption (often closely associated with the privileging of the social – especially the socio-structural or societal – as a category of analysis) that the cultural has no effectivity for sexuality and gender – indeed is a field of free play and experimentation in relation to the latter (Lury 1995).

In regard to the first problem – viewing reflexivity, mobility and risk as outcomes or effects of specific forms of social change (for instance, as a consequence of the move from industrial to risk society, or the outcome of a feminization of social fields) – what this book has highlighted is that this understanding is once again to negate the effectivity of reflexivity, mobility and risk in terms of the refashioning of sexuality and gender post social structure. Thus seeing these issues as the outcome of, or flowing from, broader scale social changes is again to ascribe reflexivity, mobility and risk with a neutrality which denies their significance in reworkings of the social post social structure. For example, and as was illustrated in Chapter 5, to understand reflexivity as a simple outcome or effect of risk society, and in particular to view self-reflexivity towards sexuality in this way, is to negate the ways in which reflexivity and risk are central to contemporary forms of the categorization, regulation and hierarchicization of sexuality post post AIDS, indeed to the intelligibility of sexualities post post AIDS. Thus it is not that sexuality post post AIDS can be described as characterized by reflexivity or as being increasingly mediated by categories of risk. Rather the issue is that sexuality is being reworked and refigured in terms of risk and reflexivity.

Similarly in Chapter 3 it was suggested that to understand reflexivity enacted towards gender and in particular to understand a reflexive, mobile relation to gender as an outcome of the feminization of social fields is to sideline the ways in which the take-up of such a reflexive or mobile position is not 'liberatory' or indeed even 'critical' or dissonant in relation to gender norms but a privileged position in late modernity implicated in the politics of difference, division and hierarchy. Gender should therefore not simply be understood to be increasingly becoming an object of reflection, reflexivity or mobility post society or post structure. Rather the issue is that gender itself is being reworked in these terms. Thus, as illustrated in Chapter 3, in cultural economies, gender is being newly arranged in terms of positions of reflexivity or mobility and immanence. In short, to understand reflexivity, mobility and risk as outcomes or effects of social change and sexuality and gender as simply mediated by such societal processes is once again to forego an analysis of the 'freeing of agents from structure' or of mobilities post society. Thus reflexivity, mobility and risk should not be understood as simply the outcome of broad-scale social changes or even as increasingly mediating or characterizing the social. Rather they should be understood as central to the ways in which the social is currently being reworked.

The second problem, that is, assuming that the 'cultural' has little or no effectivity in regard to sexuality and gender, is found in the claim that it is the socio-structural, the socio-historical and the institutional that must be prioritized in the analysis of gender and sexuality, as well as in claims that social reflexivity is far more important and significant than, for example aesthetic reflexivity. What the analysis in this book however underlines is that such arguments often rely on the assumption that the cultural is a zone of freedom and free will – indeed is a field of experimentation. While not necessarily made explicit, this assumption is nonetheless found in claims that to consider, for example, the aesthetic aspects of reflexivity would somehow be to unproblematically accept a thesis of detraditionalization, or that to consider the discursive and linguistic in the constitution of gender and sexuality would be to forego an analysis of power, ordering, hierarchy and inequality. Thus in such claims there is an assumption that the cultural is detraditionalizing or transgressive of the ordering and regulation of gender and sexuality and that it does not concern issues of hierarchy and division.

Yet what the analyses offered in this book suggest is that such a line of reasoning – and in particular to assume that the cultural field is one of free play and to reject its significance in the analysis of gender and sexuality – is to seriously compromise an understanding of the constitution of gender and sexuality post social structure. So while many who prioritize the social over the cultural would, for example, reject a consideration of the aesthetic dimensions of reflexivity, the analyses of reflexivity and mobility offered here suggest that this is to make invisible the ways in which the aesthetic – and in particular aesthetic reflexivity – is tied into the very constitution of gender and sexuality post social structure. Thus and as my more substantive discussions have illustrated, the take-up of an aesthetic, reflexive stance in relation to gender should not be understood as denoting a critical conscious-ness of, and experimentation with, the norms and laws of sexuality and gender and hence to be disconnected from issues of difference, division and hierarchy. Rather, the techniques involved in such forms of experimentation are concerned with the articulation of gender post social structure. Thus as I have argued in relation to cultural economy and reflexive modes of knowing, adopting a mobile, reflexive position towards gender is a privileged position in late modernity, and moreover is itself tied into the articulation of gender post social structure. Experimentation should therefore not be understood as irrelevant in the analysis of sexuality and gender or as transgressive or 'liberatory'; rather it needs to be recognized as a technique central to the constitution of gender and sexuality post social structure or post society. As Ahmed (1998) has argued, experimentation reconstitutes differences differ-ently (see also Featherstone 1992; Lury 1996; Skeggs 2002).

While my analysis has suggested that to understand the aesthetic as a zone of free will which is irrelevant for the analysis of gender and sexuality and/or as detraditionalizing and transgressive is to overlook the significance of techniques such as reflexivity in the constitution and arrange-ments of gender and sexuality post social structure, nonetheless what I have also emphasized is that to consider the latter, it is also imperative to consider the relations between what are usually thought of as the cultural and the social. So for instance, in Chapter 2 I argued that while there is some considerable contestation in terms of whether or not reflexivity should be understood as social and/or cultural, and in Chapter 1 I showed there to be a similar contesta-tion concerning analyses of gender and sexuality, the analysis put forward in this book suggests that these issues are not as easily divided as such debates seem to suggest. For example, and as already mentioned, the take-up of a reflexive stance towards gender may be converted into resources, including forms of economic and cultural capital. As this suggests, and as indicated in Chapter 1, what is usually understood to be the social and the cultural need to be analysed when considering the configuration and constitution of gender and sexuality post social structure, indeed to separate them, appears to be anti-thetical to this task. To separate them may lead, for example, to problematic claims regarding a universal detraditionalizion of sexuality and gender.

But in considering the reflexive modernization thesis and socio-logy of mobilities in this book I have also argued that to consider gender and sexuality post social structure, it is vital that 'the social' is not attributed with an ontological status. This is because to understand the social, or society as existing prior to reflexivity, mobility and risk, and hence to understand the latter as a simple outcome of the social or society, is to fail to recognize that the latter are reworking the social, that is, are central to the constitution and ordering of the 'social' itself. Thus to consider gender and sexuality post social structure or post society I have argued that it is vital that this point is recognized and, linked to this, that this requires a recognition that ontological claims regarding the social work against such an understanding. So for example, I have argued that reflexivity should not be understood as simply reproductive of certain ontological properties of the social. Thus I have questioned the assumption found for example in the work of writers such as Hennessey that reflexivity simply reproduces pre-existing divisions and differences, for instance that an already existing urban middle class simply takes on reflexivity and mobility to shore up this position. Rather I have suggested, and I hope my substantive discussions have served to illustrate, that reflexivity reworks such differences, and indeed is a technique of categorization, classification, difference, division and hierarchy.

This leads me back to part of my discussion in Chapter 2 where I mentioned that Alexander questions Lash's analysis of hermeneutic reflexivity on the grounds that it cannot get at or account for increased capacities for reflexivity which Alexander sees as characterizing 'contemporary democratic, multicultural and civil societies' (1996: 13). Yet it is precisely this understanding of reflexivity – as simply being a characteristic of societies or as an outcome of specific forms of social change – which I am suggesting enacts this kind of ontological understanding of the social. Put simply, Alexander's understanding of reflexivity does not grasp or get at the ways in which reflexivity is central to the constitution and ordering of the 'social' itself. Indeed, while Alexander finds Lash's understanding of reflexivity problematic, I have argued that Lash's analysis does come to grips with the ways in which reflexivity is reworking the social *as well as* the cultural. Thus, and as I discussed in Chapter 2, he talks for example of the retrocession of social structures, but also of reflexivity winners and losers and of reflexivity being very masculinist in the post-traditional (de-differentiated) cultural field. Indeed while I suggested in Chapter 3 that Lash's analysis fails to register the ways in which reflexivity involves processes of 'ascription' – or as I have termed it immanence – nonetheless, his analysis of reflexivity has far more relevance and purchase for a consideration of gender and sexuality post social structure than many of the other analyses of reflexivity considered in this book. This is in part so because he is not working with an ontological understanding of the social or of the cultural. Indeed while I hope it is clear that universalizing and totalizing approaches to the social are not helpful in considering the 'social' post social structure, this is also the case for 'cultural'. Thus, on the analysis presented in this book it is clear that *both* the social and the cultural fields are being reworked in terms of reflexivity, mobility and risk and therefore that neither the social nor the cultural should be understood as fixed a priori. The implication of the analysis presented in this book is therefore that for considerations of the 'social' post social structure it is vital that neither the social nor the cultural are given ontological status, totalized or universalized. Rather than assuming in advance what the social and the cultural 'are' this should be a matter of exploration (Lury 1995).

The exploration of reflexivity, mobility and risk in the reconfiguration of gender and sexuality in late modernity in this book has generated a number of theses. As I have already stated, perhaps the most important of these are first, that reflexivity, mobility and risk are constitutive of the 'social' post social structure or the social post society, and second and more particularly, that reflexivity, mobility and risk are constitutive of gender and sexuality post social structure. But I have also offered a number of sub theses and points in making these arguments. These include the following.

1 For the analysis of sexuality and gender post social structure it is important to break with the assumption that reflexivity and mobility are unproblematically linked to forms of detraditionalization.

2 While not always made explicit, recent analyses of reflexivity link the constitution of reflexivity to the issue of mobility within and across fields of social action.

3 Post social structure, gender tends not to be articulated via social forms of determination. Thus I have highlighted how gender post social structure is articulated via positions of mobility and immanence in regard to cultural styles.

4 Aestheticization should not be understood as a process of feminization, for instance the making of a mobile femininity which may then become a universal source of innovation and experimentation. Rather aestheticization should be understood to concern such positions of mobility and immanence vis-à-vis cultural styles. Moreover mobility and reflexivity should be understood as privileged positions in late modernity.

5 Feminization – in particular the idea of the transposition of the feminine habitus into different fields of action – is therefore a bad trope for thinking about transformations of gender.

6 A reflexive and mobile relation to gender should not be understood as evading or as separate from the politics of subjectivity and identity, for example as being transgressive of identity, but that this relation to identity needs itself to be understood as a position from which there are a number of exclusions.

7 There are significant moves towards a desocialization of gender in relation to cultural economies, but this should not be understood as undoing gender (even though this may appear to pull against certain sociological instincts).

8 A reflexive social science inscribes a hierarchy of speaking positions even though it appears to undo them.

9 A reflexive social science does so since it enacts a vision of mobility on the side of the knower in relation to the known, a position from which I have also shown there to be a number of exclusions.

10 Sexualities post post AIDS are articulated and ordered via categories of risk and reflexivity, indeed are made intelligible via categories of risk and reflexivity. (Hence sexualities should not be thought of as increasingly characterized by risk and reflexivity as an outcome or effect of specific societal changes.)

11 The politics of reflexivity and risk in regard to sexuality should therefore not be understood to straightforwardly undo hierarchies and divisions in terms of sexuality since risk technologies and practices define heterosexuality as self-reflexive and self-managing and non-heterosexual sexualities as lacking in such capacities of self-management. Thus risk technologies and practices constitute a hierarchy of sexualities post post AIDS.

Taken together what these arguments suggest, and as argued in Chapter 3, is that the sociologies of reflexivity, mobility and risk are certainly of some significance for the analysis of gender and sexuality post social structure. This is especially so because reflexivity, mobility and risk are central to post structural forms of classification, difference, division and hierarchy, including those – as this book has served to illustrate – relating to gender and sexuality. But to repeat, the significance of the sociologies of reflexivity, mobility and risk for the analysis of gender and sexuality post social structure can only be realized if:

1 A sharp division is not enacted in terms of the social and the cultural.
2 In turn the social and the cultural are not understood in universal, totalizing and ontological terms.
3 Reflexivity, mobility and risk are understood not to be neutral in regard to gender and sexuality.
4 It is understood that there are other registers than those of the socio-structural or 'society' – through which classification, difference, division and hierarchy are articulated and constituted.
5 Reflexivity, mobility and risk are not understood as outcomes of social change or as the effects of a certain kind of society, but are understood to be reworking these very grounds, including the social and the cultural.
6 Techniques such as experimentation are not understood as unproblematically involving free play and free will and hence as 'liberatory' or detraditionalizing, but rather are understood as techniques which rework and are constitutive of differences.

Taking these points into account certainly puts into doubt the view found in the reflexive modernization thesis and indeed the view commonly articulated more broadly in the social sciences regarding reflexivity and sexuality and gender. Specifically, they question the view that reflexivity in regard to gender and sexuality concerns a kind of critical, cognitive reflection on the laws and norms which govern sexuality and gender, a reflection which is detraditionalizing of these laws and which is made possible via the retrocession of the socio-structural and contributes towards that very retrocession. Thus this book has underlined just how limited and problematic this understanding of reflexivity is for the analysis of gender and sexuality in late modernity. But it has also questioned some more nuanced accounts of the relations between reflexivity and mobility and sexuality and gender, including those such as McNay's which highlight the embodied and embedded aspects of gender and sexuality and which emphasize the universalizing assumptions of the reflexive modernization thesis in regard to sexuality and gender. Indeed the analyses presented in the chapters of this book have shown that such accounts accept the thesis that reflexivity or mobility vis-à-vis gender and sexuality amount to specific forms of detraditionalization. They therefore fail to recognize the ways in which reflexivity and mobility are significant in the constitution and ordering of gender and sexuality post social structure.

Yet while this book has highlighted this significance, and has hence underscored the importance of reflexivity, mobility and risk for the sociologies of gender and sexuality, including for feminist sociology, nonetheless it certainly questions the view discussed in Chapter 2 that reflexivity may form the basis for a feminist solidarity of difference. Indeed it suggests that rather than forming a solidarity of difference, such a strategy would involve the very inscription of differences. Thus, while as I mentioned in Chapter 2, Jodi Dean suggests that such reflexivity would turn differences such as those of race, class and sexuality into resources for connections among feminists (1997: 260), my analysis suggests that this is precisely the logic involved in the making of difference post social structure – in this case the making of a mobile (and privileged) speaking position in terms of race, class and sexuality. As I mentioned in Chapter 3 such 'in-the-world' reflexivity therefore appears to be only concerned with the making of a 'we' for some.

In closing I want to return to an issue raised in Chapter 5. Specifically I want to end with some of the comments made in Chapter 5 regarding the close alignment of subject which has been the focus of critical attention in this book (that is the reflexive subject with a mobile relation to identity who self-manages risk) with modes of governance. Specifically, I want to return to the suggestion made in the light of work by govermentalists that this subject may be the ideal subject of neo-liberalism. If this suggestion has any validity what it suggests is that there is both an idealization and normalization of this subject in recent social and cultural theory (and thus by implication an idealization and normalization of the relations of privilege and exclusion operating in regard to this position). Thus for example it is possible to see such a normalization and idealization in the reflexive modernization thesis as well as the sociology of mobilities. Specifically, it is possible to suggest that in their general failure to recognize this subject as being so closely aligned to neo-liberal modes of rule, such an idealization and normalization is taking place. In Chapter 2, I mentioned that McNay has argued that in universalizing reflexivity, the reflexive modernization thesis risks reinstating the masculinist subject of classical social thought. Yet the alignment of the reflexive subject with a mobile relation to identity and who is self-managing in issues of risk with neo-liberal modes of rule suggests that it may not exactly be a reinstatement or return to a previous model of privilege that is at issue here, but perhaps the normalization and indeed instatement of a rather more contemporary one.

notes

introduction

1 While this is a very common understanding of reflexivity implicit in many recent sociological discussions, here it is used as a very provisional definition. As I will go on to discuss in Chapters 1 and 2, there is some debate as to how reflexivity should be understood. For example, while for some reflexivity is an issue of self-conscious reflection, others have argued that reflexivity is better understood as unconscious and non-cognitive, that is, as grounded in categories of habit.

chapter one

1 This may be seen, for example, in the ways the notion of reflexivity is understood. As I noted in the introduction, for example, reflexivity is often literally understood as an issue of cognitive reflection, while for others reflexivity is understood to break with such objectivist ways of knowing. This latter understanding of reflexivity is, for example, at issue in relation to discussions of cultural economy (see e.g. Lash 1994) and methodology (see e.g. Denzin and Lincoln 1994) discussed in Chapters 3 and 4.

2 While Hennessy argues queer theory generally ignores the relation between sexuality and commodification, she also recognizes that this has not been the case for queer activism. However, in both queer theory and activism she suggests queer identities and visibility are fetishized, since the social relations on which they depend are concealed (Hennessy 1995: 146).

3 Hennessy argues that to ask how the achievement of lesbian and gay visibility by some rests on the invisible labour of others 'is to expose the unspeakable underside of queer critique' (1995: 175).

4 Lloyd argues one consequence is that 'it is easy to over-emphasize the discontinuities in gender performance; to present them as indicative of disruptive behaviour. What is occluded . . . is the space within which performance occurs, the others involved in or implicated by the production, and how they receive and interpret what they see (1999: 210). Thus while writers such as Nancy Fraser and Rosemary Hennessy argue for historicization, Lloyd argues for a contextualization of parodic performances for

an understanding of their political efficacy, and a recognition that 'only some performances in some contexts can compel categorial rethinking' (1999: 210).
5 This elision is an important point, for it is often unproblematically made. As Lloyd (1999) and others have pointed out Butler's analysis is often taken up with such a voluntarist inflection. Indeed, Butler (1998b: 285) herself notes, there has been a pervasive tendency to 'read "performativity" as a Goffmanesque project of putting on a mask or electing to play a role'. Lloyd however suggests this problem relates to the ambiguity in Butler's work regarding the relations between performativity and performance.
6 While this is a tendency in Hennessy's analysis of the connections between queer and lifestylization, in more recent work she appears to have revised this position. In particular, in a review of Nancy Fraser's *Justice Interruptus*, Hennessy (1999) discusses what she terms a political economy of sexual identity. Thus it appears that she no longer believes that it is only issues of class which pertain to questions of socio-economic conditions. As I will go on to discuss, in highlighting a political economy of sexuality, Hennessy's points of critique of *Justice Interruptus* share much in common with Butler's (1998a) points of contention with Nancy Fraser's analysis.
7 See also McRobbie (1999) for a discussion of similar moves in recent critiques of British cultural studies.

chapter two

1 At issue for Adam here is the reliance on a tradition/modern distinction which she says produces static, ahistorical and linear accounts, which decontextualize, disembody, fix and generalize processes and relationships which are 'specific, embodied and embedded' (1996: 141). For example, 'tradition' tends to be posited as a fixed, static state of the past. In short, with its roots in the tradition of objectivist thinking, Adam argues the reflexive modernization thesis is (ironically) deeply incompatible with its subject matter, that is 'with reflexivity, awareness of construction and personal responsibility' (1996: 146). As will become clear in this chapter these problems with the reflexive modernization thesis are pinpointed by a number of its critics.
2 As is well known, and as I will go on to discuss further in this chapter, in Bourdieu's social theory the social world is understood as organized into distinct (but overlapping) fields, for example, political, legal, intellectual and economic fields. Fields are conceived as a structured space of positions, are sites of struggle and conflict and as having their own logic. While not entirely locked together, the habitus operates within specific fields, indeed institutions (for instance, economic, academic) are only fully viable if they are durably embedded in the embodied and unconscious dispositions of agents operating with the field (Bourdieu 1977).
3 Here Alexander is raising a common objection to Bourdieu's social theory, namely that it does not include an account of social change.
4 Sydie for example comments on the consignment of women to 'the "natural", the "pre-social", or the "embryo of community"' (1987: 17) in classical sociological narratives on modernity which paradoxically make invisible the centrality of gender for such narratives (see also Woolf 1983; Pateman 1988; Barrett 1992; Felski 1995).
5 In particular, and as I hope I have made clear, Dean's reflective solidarity also makes explicit the kind of hermeneutic reflexivity which Lash suggests is at issue reflexive modernity. Dean's analysis therefore adds weight to Lash's claim that reflexivity does not simply concern individualization – 'I am I' – but new opportunities for forms of collective identity.
6 I use the term socio-cultural here because while on the one hand Lash's reflexivity concerns the cultural, McNay is concerned predominately with the social, a difference which, as I shall go on to discuss, marks a central point of contention between these analyses of reflexivity.

7 At times Bourdieu seems to reduce the field to the market and/or the economic. For example, in *Outline of a Theory of Practice*, he talks of how dispositions are 'in the last analysis' engendered by 'the economic bases of the social formation in question' (Bourdieu 1977: 83).

8 Lash is certainly aware of this issue (see Lash 1994: 161 as well as Lash 1990, 1993b) but he does not follow through on this in terms of his discussion of reflexivity losers.

9 We may then question Lash's separation of a reflexivity connected to mobility and a reflexivity of unthought categories and shared meanings, as it seems that hermeneutic reflexivity may well arise in the context of mobility in regard to fields.

10 On the relations between literature and science in the development of sociology see Lepenies (1988).

11 This connection is also explored by Lash (1990) in a discussion of the restabilization of bourgeois identities in the context of postmodern culture.

chapter three

1 In her discussion of the feminization of the labour force Bakker (1988) for instance documented the ways in which for the period 1950–84 in OECD countries women's participation rates rose steadily from 38.2 to 55.9 per cent while the participation rate for men declined from 97.2 to 83.8 per cent.

2 Some commentators, for example, questioned the way in which the term 'feminization' at times appeared to imply that a set of radically new processes was at play, and suggested instead that such processes had a much longer-term significance than the term feminization implied. Adkins and Lury (1992) for example suggested definitions of jobs in relation to caring, emotional and servicing skills were not as novel as some discussions of feminization seemed to assume. Other commentators took issue with the ways in which the notion of feminization took for granted certain assumptions regarding class and gender. Walby (1989), for example, looked at the problems attached to the ways the idea of the feminization relied upon the idea of a progressive deskilling of work and the proletarianization of workers. Others pointed to the ways in which the term 'feminization' was problematic in regard to questions of race, especially as it seemed only to have purchase for the situation of white women (see e.g. Haraway 1991).

3 For some this situation was interpreted as a case of job segregation in terms of gender, but most theorists of segregation assumed that jobs themselves were gender neutral.

4 See, for example, Beechey and Perkins 1987; Pringle 1988; Acker 1990; Cockburn 1991; Adkins 1995; Halford *et al.* 1997. Pringle (1988) for example looked at the ways in which the occupation of secretary has been defined almost exclusively in familial and sexual terms. She showed this sexual and familial constitution of the job to be central to understanding the organization of the secretarial occupation, for instance, how this gendering of the occupation allows bosses to establish a variety of forms sexual and familial power over secretaries.

5 See, for example, Pringle 1988; Cockburn 1991; Halford *et al.* 1997; McDowell 1997, although such moves have not entirely moved away from traditional assumptions. For instance in the case of writers who looked at sexuality at work there was often a continued assumption that the economic was a neutral domain and therefore had no effectivity in terms of sexuality and gender (see e.g. Adkins 1995; Adkins and Lury 1996 for a discussion of such assumptions).

6 Such processes of desegregation in relation to gender may be part of the breaking down of occupational distinctiveness as documented by Casey (1995), and the emergence of what she terms a postoccupational condition. Casey suggests that

such moves signal a decline of identifications in terms of class and status since occupational distinctiveness was historically central to their constitution. So although here I am focusing on desegregation in relation to gender, such moves may be linked to a more wide-ranging set of shifts relating to the breakdown of a range of socio-structural forms of classification.

7 Indeed, Crompton notes that one of the most rapidly growing occupations for men is 'care assistant'.

8 Although Halford, Savage and Witz provide extensive documentation of this shift they also stress that it should not be read unproblematically. For instance, they discuss new divisions between full-time and part-time workers, a clustering of women in senior jobs which they argue are removed from centres of organizational power, and the emergence of new forms of organizational masculinity based on macho competitiveness.

9 The idea that contemporary culture is a feminized culture is of course not a new one, for as Modleski has reminded us 'ways of thinking and feeling about mass culture are . . . intricately bound up with notions of the feminine' (1991: 22) and historically mass culture has often been condemned on such grounds. However, on more recent readings rather than condemned, contemporary culture is now often affirmed precisely on the grounds of its associations with the feminine.

10 For example, it has been argued Baudrillard's notion of simulation is a synonym for the Hegelian notion of feminine seduction (Modleski 1991).

11 Masculinity has been represented as culturally feminizing in other historical periods, and has been denigrated on these grounds (see e.g. Kimmel 1994 for an historical account of the feminization of American masculinity). However, like contemporary culture more generally, rather than condemned, contemporary masculinity is now often validated because of such associations with the feminine (see Vitellone 2000b for a critique of this view).

12 Felski, of course, is not the first feminist theorist to highlight gender hybridity in late capitalism. Haraway's 'Cyborg Manifesto', for example, drew attention to a range of boundary and dichotomy breakdowns – between human and animal, nature and culture, organism and machine – which challenge the dualisms 'which have been systemic to the logics of and practices of domination of women, people of color, nature, workers, animals' (1991: 177). Such breakdowns, Haraway suggested, mean that in the late twentieth century 'we find ourselves to be cyborgs, hybrids, mosaics, chimeras' (1991: 177). As is well known, Haraway's account of boundary breakdown, mobility and hybridity was concerned mostly with high-tech scientific culture. In this chapter while considering similar themes my concern is with these issues in relation to consumer culture and especially the 'culturalization' of the economic. Despite this significant difference however, while Haraway argues for a recognition of new forms of domination in a 'post-gender world' (1991: 150) I also suggest that at the same time as challenging and undoing traditional forms of domination, boundary and category breakdowns also concern new forms of power and new arrangements of gender.

13 See for example Bhabha (1990) and Hall (1990, 1997a) for discussions of hybridity, especially the ways in which hybridity involves the dual move of new positions and an effacement of the idea of 'origins'.

14 See Hall (1997a) on the distinction between hybridity and reversal.

15 In this study a number of theses are put forward, but here I focus on and pull out arguments made regarding feminization.

16 Illouz suggests that this new language of selfhood was articulated primarily via psychological expertise (see Rose 1990).

17 Although see Sedgwick's (1994) discussion of the phenomena of 'corporate drag'.

18 As Diawara notes his transtextuality/immanence scheme does not only accure to 'race' but to a range of positions (1998: 66).

19 This adds weight to Mariam Fraser's (1999) view discussed in Chapter 1 that a privileging of the visible is problematic for the contemporary politics of gender and sexuality. Moreover it underlines the point also made in Chapter 1 that issues of socio-economics and issues of identity and subjectivity cannot be easily divided.

20 I refer here to the debate between Butler (1998a) and Fraser (1998) discussed in Chapter 1 concerning the relations between questions of identity and questions of 'socioeconomics' and distribution.

21 Indeed this replacement of the masculine trope seems to reproduce the very binarism which the feminization of masculinity is assumed to undo.

22 Rouse has argued that the emergence of flexible worker subjectivities, that is, of workers with self-transformative capacities for 'moving fluidly back and forth between markedly different modes of experience and arenas of activity' (1995: 389) and for combining 'disparate aspects of personhood' (1995: 390), is linked to transnationalism, or what he sees as processes of capital accumulation organized along transnational lines (1995: 357). Moreover, Rouse suggests that the shift to transnationalism concerns a new set of class relations and a significant reconfiguration of the class structure 'manifest in occupational distinctions and income levels, from a broadly pyramidal structure to something that is shaped more like a *rocket*' (1995: 397, emphasis in original). It seems therefore that flexible worker subjectivities may be linked not just to refashionings of gender, but to a major refashioning of a range of differences along a number of axes.

chapter four

1 May recognizes that a set of diverse thinkers are classified under this term.

2 See also Lash (1994) who, as noted in Chapter 2, makes a similar point in regard to cognitive understandings of reflexivity in contemporary social theory.

3 The case studies looked at governance in tourist organizations including the regulation of employee behaviour and appearance and interactions with customers. This involved non-participant observation of employee and customer interactions and training sessions, semi-structured interviews with managers, supervisors and employees, and documentary research on the changing formal organizational policies regarding governance in these areas. The study of the occupation of public house management involved interviews with public house managers (husband and wife teams), interviews with company (brewery) personnel managers and documentary research regarding the shifting organization of this occupation. The latter primarily comprised an analysis of company records and policy documents.

4 See e.g. Kaufmann (1998) for an example of such a reading.

5 In so doing Williams disputes my account of the significance of heterosexuality as an organizing principle of service labour. This raises interesting – if complicated – issues regarding the politics of reflexivity in regard to sexuality which I address in the following chapter.

chapter five

1 The researchers used the term AIDS as piloting 'revealed that many people were unfamiliar with the term HIV' (Bray and Chapman 1991: 107).

2 The high levels of testing in Australia have been compared to those found in Sweden (see Lupton *et al.* 1995b) which 'has one of the highest rates of HIV testing per capita in Europe. By 1996, 9.5 million tests had been carried out among Sweden's population of 8.5 million' (Danziger 1998: 567).

3 For example, of 70,000 tests performed in Victoria in 1989 0.9 per cent of the specimens tested were reported seropositive, and in 1993 of the more than 120,000 tests performed 0.7 per cent of the specimens were reported seropositive (Thompson *et al.* 1996: 166).

4 Lupton (1995: 98–9) reports the findings of the study in the following terms,

> although the majority of respondents had not engaged in highest risk activities . . . many were using the test as a way of establishing body boundaries from invasion and re-establishing subjectivity and feelings of self-containment . . . For some interviewees, the test represented a disciplinary procedure, in which participants punished themselves for their lack of control over their bodies . . . The test was also used to punish others (one's unfaithful sexual partners) . . . or as a way of establishing purity, before launching into another relationship. For many participants . . . test[ing] . . . was a way of demonstrating their sense of responsibility and commitment to their partner. Others, particularly men, had the test only because they were under duress from their partner . . . while some seemed to see the HIV test as part of a general health care maintenance . . . The assumption was that a positive result . . . was very unlikely . . . the . . . test was symbolically acting as a preventative rather than a diagnostic measure.

5 This appears to give support to Waldby *et al.*'s (1993) thesis (see also Waldby 1996) that there is a privileging of (white) heterosexual men in AIDS policy.

references

Acker, Joan (1990) Hierarchies, jobs and bodies: a theory of gendered organizations. *Gender and Society*, 4(2): 139–58.

Adam, Barbara (1996) Detraditionalization and the certainty of uncertain futures, in P. Heelas, S. Lash and P. Morris (eds) *Detraditionalization: Critical Reflections on Authority and Identity*. Oxford: Blackwell.

Adkins, Lisa (1995) *Gendered Work: Sexuality, Family and the Labour Market*. Buckingham: Open University Press.

Adkins, Lisa (1999) Community and economy: a retraditionalization of gender. *Theory, Culture and Society*, 16(4): 119–39.

Adkins, Lisa (2000a) Mobile desire: aesthetics, sexuality and the 'lesbian' at work. *Sexualities*, 3(2): 201–18.

Adkins, Lisa (2000b) Objects of innovation: post-occupational reflexivity and re-traditionalizations of gender, in S. Ahmed, J. Kilby, C. Lury, M. McNeil and B. Skeggs (eds) *Transformations: Thinking Through Feminism*, New York: Routledge.

Adkins, Lisa and Lury, Celia (1992) Gender and the labour market: old theory for new? in H. Hinds, A. Phoenix and J. Stacey (eds) *Working Out: New Directions for Women's Studies*. London: Falmer Press.

Adkins, Lisa and Lury, Celia (1996) The cultural, the sexual and the gendering of the labour market, in L. Adkins and V. Merchant (eds) *Sexualizing the Social: Power and the Organization of Sexuality*. Basingstoke: Macmillan.

Adkins, Lisa and Lury, Celia (1999) The labour of identity: performing identities, performing economies. *Economy and Society*, 28(4): 598–614.

Ahmed, Sara (1998) *Differences That Matter: Feminist Theory and Postmodernism*. Cambridge: Cambridge University Press.

Ahmed, Sara (2000) *Strange Encounters: Embodied Others in Post-Coloniality*. New York: Routledge.

Alexander, Jeffrey C. (1996) Critical reflections on 'reflexive modernization'. *Theory, Culture and Society*, 13(4): 133–8.

Allen, Louise (1997) *The lesbian Idol: Martina, kd and the Consumption of Lesbian Masculinity*. London: Cassell.

Alvesson, Matts and Skoldberg, Kaj (2000) *Reflexive Methodology: New Vistas for Qualitative Research*. London: Sage.

Appadurai, Arjun (1993) Disjuncture and difference in the global cultural economy, in B. Robbins (ed.) *The Phantom Public Sphere*. Minneapolis, MN: University of Minnesota Press.

Armstrong, David (1995) The rise of surveillance medicine. *Sociology of Health and Illness*, 17(3): 393–404.

Bakker, Isabella (1988) Women's employment in comparative perspective, in J. Jenson, E. Hagen and C. Reddy (eds) *Feminization of the Labour Force: Paradoxes and Promises*. Cambridge: Polity.

Barnes, T., Horner, G., Murphy, A. *et al.* (2000) Capital culture: a review essay. *Environment and Planning D: Society and Space*, 18: 275–8.

Barrett, Michele (1990) Feminism's 'Turn to Culture'. *Women: A Cultural Review*, 1(1): 22–4.

Barrett, Michele (1992) Words and things: materialism and method in contemporary feminist analysis, in M. Barrett and A. Phillips (eds) *Destabilizing Theory: Contemporary Feminist Debates*. Cambridge: Polity.

Bartos, Michael (1996) The queer excess of public health policy. *Meanjin* 55(1): 122–31.

Baudrillard, Jean (1983) *In the Shadow of the Silent Majorities or the End of the Social and Other Essays*, trans. P. Foss, P. Patton and J. Johnston. New York: Semiotext(e).

Bauman, Zygmunt (1998) *Work, Consumerism and the New Poor*. Buckingham: Open University Press.

Bauman, Zygmunt (2000) *Liquid Modernity*. Cambridge: Polity.

Beck, Ulrich (1992) *Risk Society: Towards a New Modernity*, London: Sage.

Beck, Ulrich (1994) The reinvention of politics: towards a theory of reflexive modernization, in U. Beck, A. Giddens and S. Lash, *Reflexive Modernization: Politics, Tradition and Aesthetics in the Modern Social Order*. Cambridge: Polity.

Beck, Ulrich (1997) *The Reinvention of Politics*. Cambridge: Polity.

Beck, Ulrich (1999) *World Risk Society*. Cambridge: Polity.

Beck, Ulrich and Beck-Gernsheim, Elisabeth (1995) *The Normal Chaos of Love*. Cambridge: Polity.

Beck, Ulrich and Beck-Gernsheim, Elisabeth (1996) Individualization and 'precarious freedoms': perspectives and controversies of a subject-orientated sociology, in P. Heelas, S. Lash, and P. Morris (eds) *Detraditionalization: Critical Reflections on Authority and Identity*. Oxford: Blackwell.

Beck, Ulrich, Giddens, Anthony and Lash, Scott (1994) *Reflexive Modernization: Politics, Tradition and Aesthetics in the Modern Social Order*. Cambridge: Polity.

Beck-Gernsheim, Elisabeth (1998) On the way to a post-familial family: from a community of needs to elective affinities. *Theory, Culture and Society*, 15(3–4): 53–70.

Beechey, Veronica (1988) Rethinking the definition of work, in J. Jenson, E. Hagen and C. Reddy (eds) *Feminization of the Labour Force: Paradoxes and Promises*. Cambridge: Polity.

Beechey, Veronica and Perkins, Tessa (1987) *A Matter of Hours: Women, Part-Time Work and the Labour Market*. Cambridge: Polity.

Benjamin, Walter (1973) *Charles Baudelaire: A Lyric Poet in the Era of High Capitalism*. London: New Left Books.

Benjamin, Walter (1975) The work of art in the age of mechanical reproduction, in *Illuminations*. London: Fontana.

Bhabha, Homi (1990) The third space: interview with Homi Bhabha', in J. Rutherford (ed.) *Identity: Community, Culture, Difference*. London: Lawrence and Wishart.

Bourdieu, Pierre (1977) *Outline of a Theory of Practice*. Cambridge: Cambridge University Press.

Bourdieu, Pierre (1990) *In Other Words: Essays Towards a Reflexive Sociology*. Cambridge: Polity.
Bourdieu, Pierre and Wacquant, Loic J.D. (1992) *An Invitation to Reflexive Sociology*. Cambridge: Polity.
Bray, Fiona and Chapman, Simon (1991) Community knowledge, attitudes and media recall about AIDS, Sydney 1988 and 1989. *Australian Journal of Public Health*, 15(2): 107–13.
Bryant, Christopher (1995) *Practical Sociology: Post-empiricism and the Reconstruction of Theory and Application*. Cambridge: Polity.
Butler, Judith (1990) *Gender Trouble: Feminism and the Subversion of Identity*. New York: Routledge.
Butler, Judith (1993) *Bodies That Matter: On the Discursive Limits of 'Sex'*. New York: Routledge.
Butler, Judith (1997) *Excitable Speech: A Politics of the Performative*. New York: Routledge.
Butler, Judith (1998a) Merely cultural. *New Left Review*, 227: 33–44.
Butler, Judith (1998b) How bodies come to matter: an interview with Judith Butler. *Signs: Journal of Women in Culture and Society*, 23(2): 275–86.
Butler, Judith (1999) Performativity's social magic, in R. Shusterman (ed.) *Bourdieu: A Critical Reader*. Oxford: Blackwell.
Callinicos, Alex (1999) Social theory put to the test of politics: Pierre Bourdieu and Anthony Giddens. *New Left Review*, 23: 77–102.
Carter, Allison (1998) The image of the feminized male and its shadow in contemporary media theory. Paper presented at the British Sociological Association annual conference, Edinburgh, 6–9 April.
Casey, Catherine (1995) *Work, Self and Society: After Industrialism*. New York: Routledge.
Castells, Manuel (1998) *The Rise of Network Society*. Oxford: Blackwell.
Chippendale, Sarah, French, Patrick and Miller, David (1998) Reasons for HIV antibody testing: plus ca change? *International Journal of STD and AIDS*, 9: 219–22.
Clark, Anna (1991) Commodity lesbianism. *Camera Obscura*, 25–6: 180–201.
Clifford, James (1992) Travelling cultures, in L. Grossberg, C. Nelson and P. Treichler (eds) *Cultural Studies*. New York: Routledge.
Clifford, James (1997) *Routes: Travel and Translation in the Late Twentieth Century*. Cambridge, MA: Harvard University Press.
Coates, G. (1997) Organisation man – women and organisational culture. *Sociological Research Online*, 2(3): http://www.socresonline.org.uk/socresonline/2/3/7.html
Cockburn, Cynthia (1991) *In the Way of Women: Men's Resistance to Sex Equality in Organizations*. Basingstoke: Macmillan.
Craik, Jennifer (1997) The culture of tourism, in C. Rojek and J. Urry (eds) *Touring Cultures: Transformations of Travel and Theory*. New York: Routledge.
Crang, Philip (1997) Performing the tourist product, in C. Rojek and J. Urry (eds) *Touring Cultures: Transformations of Travel and Theory*. New York: Routledge.
Creith, Elaine (1996) *Undressing Lesbian Sex: Popular Images, Private Acts and Public Consequences*. London: Cassell.
Crompton, Rosemary (1997) *Women and Work in Modern Britain*. Oxford: Oxford University Press.
Cronin, Ann (1999) Seeing through transparency: performativity, vision and intent. *Cultural Values*, 3(1): 54–72.
Cronin, Ann (2000a) *Advertising and Consumer Citizenship: Gender, Images and Rights*. New York: Routledge.
Cronin, Ann (2000b) Consumerism and 'compulsory individuality': women, will and potential, in S. Ahmed, J. Kilby, C. Lury, M. McNeil and B. Skeggs (eds) *Transformations: Thinking Through Feminism*. New York: Routledge.

Crossley, Nick (2001) The phenomenological habitus and its construction. *Theory and Society*, 30: 81–120.

Danziger, R. (1998) HIV testing for HIV prevention: a comparative analysis of policies in Britain, Hungary and Sweden. *AIDS Care*, 10(5): 563–70.

Dean, Jodi (1996) *Solidarity of Strangers: Feminism After Identity Politics*. Berkeley, CA: University of California Press.

Dean, Jodi (1997) The reflective solidarity of democratic feminism, in J. Dean (ed.) *Feminism and the New Democracy*. London: Sage.

Dean, Mitchell (1998) Risk, calculable and incalculable. *Soziale Welt*, 49: 25–42.

Dean, Mitchell (1999) Risk, calculable and incalculable, in D. Lupton (ed.) *Risk and Sociocultural Theory: New Directions and Perspectives*, Cambridge: Cambridge University Press.

Denzin, Norma and Lincoln, Yvonne (1994) Entering the field of qualitative research, in N. Denzin and Y. Lincoln (eds) *Handbook of Qualitative Research*. London: Sage.

Diawara, Manthia (1998) Homeboy cosmopolitan: Manthia Diawara interviewed by Silivia Kolbowski. *October*, 83: 51–70.

Du Gay, Paul (1993) 'Numbers and souls': retailing and the de-differentiation of economy and culture. *British Journal of Sociology*, 44(4): 563–87.

Du Gay, Paul (1996) *Consumption and Identity at Work*. London: Sage.

Du Gay, Paul (1997) (ed.) *Production of Culture/Cultures of Production*. London: Sage.

Edwards, Tim (1998) Queer fears: against the cultural turn. *Sexualities*, 1(4): 471–84.

Ewald, Francois (1991) Insurance and risk, in G. Burchell, C. Gordon and P. Miller (eds) *The Foucault Effect: Studies in Governmentality*. Harvester: Hemel Hempstead.

Featherstone, Mike (1991) The body in consumer culture, in M. Featherstone, M. Hepworth and B. Turner (eds) *The Body: Social Process and Cultural Theory*. London: Sage.

Featherstone, Mike (1992) Postmodernism and the aestheticization of everyday life, in S. Lash and J. Freidman (eds) *Modernity and Identity*. Oxford: Blackwell.

Featherstone, Mike (1995) *Undoing Culture: Globalization, Postmodernism and Identity*. London: Sage.

Felski, Rita (1995) *The Gender of Modernity*. Cambridge, MA: Harvard University Press.

Felski, Rita (1997) Judith Krantz, author of 'the cultural logics of late capitalism'. *Women: a Cultural Review*, 8(2): 129–42.

Ferguson, Kathy (1993) *The Man Question*. Berkeley, CA: University of California Press.

Finch, Janet (1989) *Family Obligations and Social Change*. Cambridge: Polity Press.

Foucault, Michel (1978) *The History of Sexuality: An Introduction*. Harmondsworth: Penguin.

Foucault, Michel (1985) *The Uses of Pleasure*. Harmondsworth: Penguin.

Frankin, Sarah, Lury, Celia and Stacey, Jackie (2000) *Global Nature, Global Culture*. London: Sage.

Fraser, Mariam (1999) Classing queer: politics in competition. *Theory, Culture and Society*, 16(2): 107–31.

Fraser, Nancy (1997) *Justice Interruptus: Critical Reflections on the 'Postsocialist' Condition*. New York: Routledge.

Fraser, Nancy (1998) Heterosexism, misrecognition and capitalism: a response to Judith Butler. *New Left Review*, 228: 140–9.

Frisby, David (1985) *Fragments of Modernity: Theories of Modernity in the Work of Simmel, Kracauer and Benjamin*. Cambridge: Polity.

Frisby, David (1992) *Sociological Impressionism: A Reassessment of Georg Simmel's Social Theory*, 2nd edn. New York: Routledge.

Game, Ann (1991) *Undoing the social: towards a deconstructive sociology*. Toronto: University of Toronto Press.

Gergen, K. and Gergen, M. (1991) From theory to reflexivity in research practice, in F. Steier (ed.) *Research and Reflexivity*. London: Sage.

Gibbs, Liz (1994) *Daring the Dissent: Lesbian Culture from the Margin to the Mainstream*. London: Cassell.

Giddens, Anthony (1991) *Modernity and Self-Identity: Self and Society in the Late Modern Age*. Cambridge: Polity.

Giddens, Anthony (1992) *The Transformation of Intimacy: Sexuality, Love and Eroticism in Modern Societies*. Cambridge: Polity.

Giddens, Anthony (1994) Risk, trust, reflexivity, in U. Beck, A. Giddens and S. Lash, *Reflexive Modernization: Politics, Tradition and Aesthetics in the Modern Social Order*. Cambridge: Polity.

Gilroy, Paul (1993) *The Black Atlantic: Modernity and Double Consciousness*. London: Verso.

Grace, Helen (1991) Business, pleasure, narrative: the folktale in our times, in R. Diprose and R. Ferrell (eds) *Cartographies: Poststructuralism and the Mapping of Bodies and Spaces*. St Leonards: Allen & Unwin.

Griggers, Camilla (1997) *Becoming-Woman*. Minneapolis, MN: University of Minnesota Press.

Gullette, Margaret Morganroth (1994) All together now: the new sexual politics of midlife bodies, in L. Goldstein (ed.) *The Male Body: Features, Destinies, Exposures*. Ann Arbor, MI: University of Michigan Press.

Hagen, Elisabeth and Jenson, Jane (1988) Paradoxes and promises: work and politics in the postwar years, in J. Jenson, E. Hagen and C. Reddy (eds) *Feminization of the Labour Force: Paradoxes and Promises*. Cambridge: Polity.

Halberstam, Judith (1998) *Female Masculinity*. Durham, NC: Duke University Press.

Halford, Susan, Savage, Mike and Witz, Anne (1997) *Gender, Careers and Organisations: Current Developments in Banking, Nursing and Local Government*. Basingstoke: Macmillan.

Hall, Stuart (1990) Cultural identity and diaspora, in J. Rutherford (ed.) *Identity: Community, Culture, Difference*. London: Lawrence and Wishart.

Hall, Stuart (1997a) Culture and power. *Radical Philosophy*, 86: 24–41.

Hall, Stuart (1997b) The centrality of culture: notes on the cultural revolutions of our time, in K. Thompson (ed.) *Media and Cultural Regulation*. London: Sage/The Open University.

Haraway, Donna (1991) *Simians, Cyborgs and Women: The Reinvention of Nature*. New York: Routledge.

Haraway, Donna (1997a) The virtual speculum in the new world order. *Feminist Review*, 55: 22–72.

Haraway, Donna (1997b) *Modest_Witness@Second_Millennium.FemaleMan_Meets_OncoMouse: Feminism and Technoscience*. New York: Routledge.

Harvey, David (1989) *The Condition of Postmodernity*. Oxford: Blackwell.

Hawkes, Gail (1996) *A Sociology of Sex and Sexuality*. Buckingham: Open University Press.

Heaphy, Brian (1996) Medicalisation and identity formation: identity and strategy in the context of AIDS and HIV, in J. Weeks and J. Holland (eds) *Sexual Cultures: Communities, Values and Intimacy*. Basingstoke: Macmillan.

Heaphy, Brian, Donovan, Catherine and Weeks, Jeffrey (1998) That's like my life: researching stories of non-heterosexual relationships. *Sexualities*, 1(4): 453–70.

Heelas, Paul (1996) Detraditionalization and its rivals, in P. Heelas, S. Lash, P. Morris (eds) *Detraditionalization: Critical Reflections on Authority and Identity*, Oxford: Blackwell.

Heelas, Paul, Lash, Scott and Morris, Paul (eds) (1996) *Detraditionalization: Critical Reflections on Authority and Identity*. Oxford: Blackwell.

Hennessy, Rosemary (1995) Queer visibility in commodity culture, in L. Nicholson and
    S. Seidman (eds) *Social Postmodernism: Beyond Identity Politics.* Cambridge:
    Cambridge University Press.
Hennessy, Rosemary (1999) Review of Nancy Fraser's justice interruptus: critical reflec-
    tions on the 'postsocialist' condition. *Hypatia,* 14(1): 126–32.
Higgs, Paul (1998) Risk, governmentality and the reconceptualization of citizenship, in
    G. Scambler and P. Higgs (eds) *Modernity, Medicine and Health: Medical
    Sociology Towards 2000.* New York: Routledge.
Hochschild, Arlie R. (1983) *The Managed Heart: The Commercialization of Human Feeling.*
    Berkeley, CA: University of California Press.
Hunter, Nan D. (1997) Censorship and identity in the age of AIDS, in M. Levine,
    P. Nardi and J. Gagnon (eds) *In Changing Times: Gay Men and Lesbians
    Encounter HIV/AIDS.* Chicago, IL: University of Chicago Press.
Illouz, Eva (1997) Who will care for the caretaker's daughter? Toward a sociology of
    happiness in the era of reflexive modernity. *Theory, Culture and Society,*
    14(4): 31–66.
Jackson, Stevi (1998) Theorizing gender and sexuality, in S. Jackson and J. Jones (eds)
    Contemporary Feminist Theories. Edinburgh: Edinburgh University Press.
Jackson, Stevi and Scott, Sue (1997) Gut reactions to matters of the heart: reflections on
    rationality, irrationality and sexuality. *Sociological Review,* 15(4): 551–74.
Jamieson, Lynn (1998) *Intimacy: Personal Relationships in Modern Societies.* Cambridge:
    Polity.
Jenson, Jane, Hagen, Elisabeth and Reddy, Ceallaigh (1988) (eds) *Feminization of the
    Labour Force: Paradoxes and Promises.* Cambridge: Polity.
Jones, Gill and Wallace, Claire (1992) *Youth, Family and Citizenship.* Buckingham:
    Open University Press.
Joseph, Miranda (1998) The performance of production and consumption. *Social Text,*
    16(1): 25–61.
Kaufmann, Linda (1998) *Bad Girls and Sick Boys: Fantasies in Contemporary Art and
    Culture.* Berkeley, CA: University of California Press.
Kimmel, Michael (1994) Consuming manhood: the feminization of American culture
    and the recreation of the male body, 1832–1920, in L. Goldstein (ed.) *The
    Male Body: Features, Destinies, Exposures.* Ann Arbor, MI: University of
    Michigan Press.
Lamont, Leonie (1998) The condom generation conquers campus, *Sydney Morning
    Herald,* 14 November.
Lamos, Colleen (1994) The postmodern lesbian position: on our backs, in L. Doan
    (ed.) *The Lesbian Postmodern.* New York: Columbia University Press.
Lash, Scott (1988) Discourse or figure: postmodernism as a regime of signification.
    Theory, Culture and Society, 5(2–3): 311–36.
Lash, Scott (1990) *Sociology of Postmodernism.* New York: Routledge.
Lash, Scott (1993a) Reflexive modernization: the aesthetic dimension. *Theory, Culture
    and Society,* 10(1): 1–23.
Lash, Scott (1993b) Pierre Bourdieu: cultural economy and social change, in C. Calhoun,
    E. LiPuma and M. Postone (eds) *Bourdieu: Critical Perspectives,* Chicago, IL:
    University of Chicago Press.
Lash, Scott (1994) Reflexivity and its doubles: structure, aesthetics, community' in
    U. Beck, A. Giddens and S. Lash, *Reflexive Modernization: Politics, Tradition
    and Aesthetics in the Modern Social Order.* Cambridge: Polity.
Lash, Scott (1999) *Another Modernity: A Different Rationality.* Oxford: Blackwell.
Lash, Scott and Urry, John (1994) *Economies of Signs and Space.* London: Sage.
Latour, Bruno (1991) The politics of explanation: an alternative, in S. Woolgar (ed.)
    Knowledge and Reflexivity: New Frontiers in the Sociology of Knowledge. London:
    Sage.

Lawler, Stephanie (1999) 'Getting out and getting away': women's narratives of class mobility. *Feminist Review*, 63(1): 3–24.

Lawler, Stephanie (2000) *Mothering the Self: Mothers, Daughters, Subjects*. New York: Routledge.

Lepenies, Wolf (1988) *Between Literature and Science: The Rise of Sociology*. Cambridge: Cambridge University Press.

Lewis, Reina and Rolley, Katrina (1997) (Ad)dressing the dyke: lesbian looks and lesbians looking, in M. Nava, A. Blake, I. MacRury and B. Richards (eds) *Buy This Book: Studies in Advertising and Consumption*. New York: Routledge.

Lichtblau, Klaus (1999) Differentiations of modernity. *Theory, Culture and Society*, 16(3): 1–30.

Lloyd, Moya (1999) Performativity, parody, politics. *Theory, Culture and Society*, 16(2): 195–213.

Lovell, Terry (2000) Thinking feminism with and against Bourdieu. *Feminist Theory*, 1(1): 11–32.

Lupton, Deborah (1993) AIDS risk and heterosexuality in the Australian press. *Discourse and Society*, 4(3): 307–28.

Lupton, Deborah (1995) *The Imperative of Health: Public Health and the Regulated Body*. London: Sage.

Lupton, Deborah (1999) Introduction: risk and sociocultural theory, in D. Lupton (ed.) *Risk and Sociocultural Theory: New Directions and Perspectives*. Cambridge: Cambridge University Press.

Lupton, Deborah, McCarthy, Sophie and Chapman, Simon (1995a) 'Doing the Right Thing': the symbolic meanings and experiences of having an HIV antibody test. *Social Science and Medicine*, 41(2): 173–80.

Lupton, Deborah, McCarthy, Sophie and Chapman, Simon (1995b) 'Panic Bodies': discourses on risk and HIV antibody testing. *Sociology of Health and Illness*, 17(1): 89–108.

Lupton, Deborah and John Tulloch (1998) The adolescent 'unfinished body': reflexivity and HIV/AIDS risk. *Body and Society*, 4(2): 19–34.

Lury, Celia (1995) The rights and wrongs of culture, in B. Skeggs (ed.) *Feminist Cultural Theory: Process and Production*. Manchester: Manchester University Press.

Lury, Celia (1996) *Consumer Culture*. New York: Routledge.

Lury, Celia (1997) The objects of travel, in C. Rojek and J. Urry (eds) *Touring Cultures: Transformations of Travel and Theory*. New York: Routledge.

McCrombie, S.C. (1986) The cultural impact of the 'AIDS' test: the American experience. *Social Science and Medicine*, 23(5): 455–9.

McDowell, Linda (1991) Life without father and Ford: the new gender order of post-Fordism. *Transactions, Institute of British Geographers*, 16(4): 400–19.

McDowell, Linda (1997) *Capital Culture: Gender at Work in the City*. Oxford: Blackwell.

McDowell, Linda and Court, Gill (1994a) Missing subjects: gender, power, and sexuality in merchant banking. *Economic Geography*, 70(3): 229–51.

McDowell, Linda and Court, Gill (1994b) Performing work: bodily representations in merchant banks. *Environment and Planning D: Society and Space*, 12: 727–50.

MacInnes, John (1998) *The End of Masculinity*. Buckingham: Open University Press.

McNay, Lois (1999a) Gender, habitus and the field: Pierre Bourdieu and the limits of reflexivity. *Theory, Culture and Society*, 16(1): 95–117.

McNay, Lois (1999b) Subject, psyche and agency: the work of Judith Butler. *Theory, Culture and Society*, 16(2): 175–93.

McRobbie, Angela (1999) *In the Culture Society: Art, Fashion and Popular Music*. New York: Routledge.

Maffesoli, Michel (1996) *The Time of The Tribes*. London: Sage.

Marshall, Barbara (1994) *Engendering Modernity: Feminism, Social Theory and Social Change*. Cambridge: Polity.

Martin, Bill (1998) Knowledge, identity and the middle class: from collective to indi-
  vidualized class formation? *Sociological Review*, 46(4): 653–86.
Martin, Emily (1994) *Flexible Bodies: Tracking Immunity in American Culture – From the
  Days of Polio to the Age of AIDS*. Boston, MA: Beacon.
Martin, Emily (1997) The end of the body? in R.N. Lancaster and M. di Leonardo (eds)
  The Gender/Sexuality Reader: Culture, History, Political Economy. New York:
  Routledge.
Martin, Emily (2000) Flexible survivors. *Cultural Values*, 4(4): 512–17.
Massey, Doreen (1984) *Spatial Divisions of Labour: Social Structures and the Geography of
  Production*. Basingstoke: Macmillan.
May, Tim (1998) Reflexivity in the age of reconstructive social science. *International
  Journal of Social Research Methodology*, 1(1): 7–24.
Melucci, Alberto (1996) *The Playing Self: Person and Meaning in the Planetary Society*.
  Cambridge: Cambridge University Press.
Meyrick, Jane, Lawrence, A.G., Barton, S.E. and Boag, F.C. (1997) To test or not to test,
  could you repeat the question? *International Journal of STD and AIDS*, 8:
  36–9.
Modleski, Tania (1991) *Feminism Without Women: Culture and Criticism in a 'Postfeminist'
  Age*, New York: Routledge.
Morlet, Andrew, Guinan, James, Diefenthaler, Irwin and Gold, Julian (1988) The impact
  of the 'Grim Reaper' national AIDS educational campaign on the Albion
  Street (AIDS) Centre and AIDS hotline. *The Medical Journal of Australia*,
  148: 282–6.
Morley, David and Robins, Kevin (1995) *Spaces of Identity: Global Media, Electronic
  Landscapes and Cultural Boundaries*. New York: Routledge.
Nettleton, Sarah (1997) Governing the risky self: how to become healthy, wealthy and
  wise, in A. Peterson and R. Brunton (eds) *Foucault, Health and Medicine*.
  New York: Routledge.
Nicholson, Linda and Seidman, Steven (1995) Introduction, in L. Nicholson and S.
  Seidman (eds) *Social Postmodernism: Beyond Identity Politics*. Cambridge:
  Cambridge University Press.
Nixon, Sean (1996) *Hard Looks: Masculinities, Spectatorship and Contemporary Consumption*.
  UCL Press: London.
Ong, Aihwa (1999) *Flexible Citizenship: The Cultural Logics of Transnationality*. Durham,
  NC: Duke University Press.
Pateman, Carol (1988) *The Sexual Contract*. Cambridge: Polity.
Patton, Cindy (1990a) What science knows: formations of AIDS knowledges, in
  P. Aggelton, P. Davies and G. Hart (eds) *AIDS: Individual, Cultural and
  Policy Dimensions*. London: Falmer.
Patton, Cindy (1990b) *Inventing AIDS*. New York: Routledge.
Patton, Cindy (1993) Tremble, hetero swine, in M. Warner (ed.) *Fear of a Queer Planet*.
  Minneapolis, MN: University of Minnesota Press.
Pellizzoni, Luigi (1999) Reflexive modernization and beyond: knowledge and value in
  the politics of environment and technology. *Theory, Culture and Society*,
  16(4): 99–125.
Perry, Nick (1998) *Hyperreality and Global Culture*. New York: Routledge.
Peterson, Alan (1997) Risk, governance and the new public health, in A. Peterson and
  R. Brunton (eds) *Foucault, Health and Medicine*. New York: Routledge.
Peterson, Alan and Lupton, Deborah (1996) *The New Public Health: Health and Self in
  the Age of Risk*. St Leonards: Allen & Unwin.
Postone, Moishe, Lipuma, Edward and Calhoun, Craig (1993) Introduction: Bourdieu
  and social theory, in C. Calhoun, E. LiPuma and M. Postone (eds) *Bourdieu:
  Critical Perspectives*. Chicago, IL: University of Chicago Press.
Pringle, Rosemary (1988) *Secretaries Talk: Sexuality, Power and Work*. London: Verso.

Pringle, Rosemary (1998) *Sex and Medicine: Gender, Power and Authority in the Medical Profession.* Cambridge: Cambridge University Press.

Probyn, Elspeth (1993) *Sexing the Self: Gendered Positions in Cultural Studies.* New York: Routledge.

Roper, Michael (1994) *Masculinity and the British Organization Man since 1945.* Oxford: Oxford University Press.

Rose, Nikolas (1990) *Governing the Soul: The Shaping of the Private Self.* New York: Routledge.

Rouse, Roger (1995) Thinking through transnationalism: notes on the cultural politics of class relations in the contemporary United States. *Public Culture,* 7: 353–402.

Saso, Mary (1990) *Women in the Japanese Workplace.* London: Shipman.

Schiller, Nina, Crystal, Stephen and Lewellen, Denver (1994) Risky business: the cultural construction of risk groups. *Social Science and Medicine,* 38(10): 1337–46.

Sedgwick, Eve (1994) *Tendencies.* New York: Routledge.

Segal, Lynne (1990) *Slow Motion: Changing Masculinities, Changing Men.* New Brunswick, NJ: Rutgers University Press.

Seidman, Steven (1995) Deconstructing queer theory or the under-theorization of the social and the ethical, in L. Nicholson and S. Seidman (eds) *Social Postmodernism: Beyond Identity Politics.* Cambridge: Cambridge University Press.

Seidman, Steven (1997) *Difference Troubles: Queering Social Theory and Sexual Politics.* Cambridge: Cambridge University Press.

Simmel, Georg (1950) The metropolis and mental life, in K.H. Wolff (ed.) *The Sociology of Georg Simmel.* New York: Free Press.

Simpson, Mark (1996) *It's a Queer World.* London: Vintage.

Skeggs, Beverley (1995) Introduction, in B. Skeggs (ed.) *Feminist Cultural Theory: Process and Production.* Manchester: Manchester University Press.

Skeggs, Beverley (1997) *Formations of Class and Gender: Becoming Respectable.* London: Sage.

Skeggs, Beverley (2002) Mobile selves?: authority, reflexivity and positioning, in T. May (ed.) *Qualitative Research: Issues in International Practice.* London: Sage.

Smith, Anna Marie (1997) The good homosexual and the dangerous queer: resisting the new homophobia, in L. Segal (ed.) *New Sexual Agendas,* Basingstoke: Macmillan.

Steier, Frederick (ed.) (1991) *Research and Reflexivity.* London: Sage.

Stern, Katherine (1997) What is femme? the phenomenology of the powder room. *Women: a Cultural Review,* 8(2): 183–96.

Sydie, R.A. (1987) *Natural Women, Cultured Men: A Feminist Perspective on Sociological Theory.* Milton Keynes: Open University Press.

Tasker, Yvonne (1998) *Working Girls: Gender and Sexuality in Popular Cinema.* New York: Routledge.

Thompson, Sandra, Stevenson, Elaine and Crofts, Nick (1996) A profile of HIV testing in Victoria to the end of 1993. *Australian and New Zealand Journal of Public Health,* 20: 165–71.

Treichler, Paula (1988) AIDS, gender and biomedical discourse: current contests for meaning, in E. Fee and D. Fox (eds) *AIDS. The Burdens of History.* Berkeley, CA: University of California Press.

Trinh, T. Minh-ha (1990) Not you/like you: postcolonial women and the interlocking questions of identity and difference, in G. Anzaldua (ed.) *Making Face, Making Soul.* San Francisco, CA: Aunt Lute Foundation Books.

Tulloch, John and Lupton, Deborah (1997) *Television, AIDS and Risk: A Cultural Studies Approach to Health Communication.* St Leonards: Allen & Unwin.

Turner, Bryan (1997) From governmentality to risk: some reflections on Foucault's contribution to medical sociology, in A. Peterson and R. Bunton (eds) *Foucault, Health and Medicine.* New York: Routledge.

Urry, John (2000) *Sociology Beyond Societies: Mobilities for the Twenty-First Century.* New York: Routledge.

Van de Ven, Paul, Kippax, Susan, Crawford, June and French, Judy (1997) HIV testing among heterosexual tertiary students. *Venereology,* 10(1): 26–9.

Vitellone, Nicole (2000a) AIDS culture: condoms and the making of heterosexuality. Unpublished PhD thesis, Department of Sociology, Monash University.

Vitellone, Nicole (2000b) Condoms and the making of testosterone man: a cultural analysis of the male sex drive in AIDS research on safer heterosex. *Men and Masculinities,* 3(2): 152–67.

Wacquant, Loic J.D. (1992) Toward a praxeology: the structure and logic of Bourdieu's sociology, in Pierre Bourdieu and Loic J.D. Wacquant (1992) *An Invitation to Reflexive Sociology.* Cambridge: Polity.

Walby, Sylvia (1986) *Patriarchy at Work: Patriarchal and Capitalist Relations in Employment.* Cambridge: Polity Press.

Walby, Sylvia (1989) Flexibility and the changing sexual division of labour, in S. Wood (ed.) *The Transformation of Work?* London: Unwin Hyman.

Walby, Sylvia (1990) *Theorizing Patriarchy.* Oxford: Blackwell.

Waldby, Catherine (1996) *AIDS and the Body Politic: Biomedicine and Sexual Difference.* New York: Routledge.

Waldby, Catherine, Kippax, Susan and Crawford, June (1993) Cordon sanitaire: 'clean' and 'unclean' women in the AIDS discourse of young heterosexual men, in P. Aggleton, P. Davies and G. Hart (eds) *AIDS: Facing the Second Decade.* London: Falmer Press.

Weeks, Jeffrey (1995) *Invented Moralities: Sexual Values in An Age of Uncertainty,* Cambridge: Polity.

Weeks, Jeffrey (1998) The sexual citizen. *Theory, Culture and Society,* 15(3–4): 35–52.

Williams, L. (1997) Review essay. *Journal of Contemporary Ethnography,* 25(4): 516–20.

Williams, Simon (1995) Theorising class, health and lifestyles: can Bourdieu help us? *Sociology of Health and Illness,* 17(5): 577–604.

Willis, Evan (1992) The social relations of HIV testing, in S. Scott, G. Williams, S. Platt and H. Thomas (eds) *Private Risks and Public Dangers.* Aldershot: Avebury.

Woolf, Janet (1983) The invisible flaneuse: women and the literature of modernity. *Theory, Culture and Society,* 2: 37–48.

Woolgar, Steve (ed.) (1991a) *Knowledge and Reflexivity: New Frontiers in the Sociology of Knowledge.* London: Sage.

Woolgar, Steve (1991b) Reflexivity is the ethnographer of the text, in S. Woolgar (ed.) *Knowledge and Reflexivity: New Frontiers in the Sociology of Knowledge.* London: Sage.

Woolgar, Steve and Ashmore, Malcolm (1991) The next step: an introduction to the reflexive project, in S. Woolgar (ed.) *Knowledge and Reflexivity: New Frontiers in the Sociology of Knowledge.* London: Sage.

index